Physical Electronics
and Circuit Models
of Transistors

Semiconductor Electronics Education Committee Books

Vol. 1 Introduction to Semiconductor Physics
R. B. Adler, A. C. Smith, and R. L. Longini

Vol. 2 Physical Electronics and Circuit Models of Transistors
P. E. Gray, D. DeWitt, A. R. Boothroyd, and J. F. Gibbons

Vol. 3 Elementary Circuit Properties of Transistors
C. L. Searle, A. R. Boothroyd, E. J. Angelo, Jr., P. E. Gray, and D. O. Pederson

Vol. 4 Characteristics and Limitations of Transistors
R. D. Thornton, D. DeWitt, E. R. Chenette, and P. E. Gray

Vol. 5 Multistage Transistor Circuits
R. D. Thornton, D. O. Pederson, C. L. Searle, E. J. Angelo, Jr., and J. Willis

Vol. 6 Digital Transistor Circuits
J. N. Harris

Vol. 7 Handbook of Basic Transistor Circuits and Measurements
R. D. Thornton, J. G. Linvill, E. R. Chenette, H. L. Ablin, J. N. Harris, and A. R. Boothroyd

Physical Electronics and Circuit Models of Transistors

Semiconductor Electronics Education Committee, Volume 2

Paul E. Gray
Massachusetts Institute of Technology

David DeWitt
International Business Machines Corp., Poughkeepsie, N. Y.

A. R. Boothroyd
The Queen's University of Belfast
formerly at Imperial College, London

James F. Gibbons
Stanford University

John Wiley & Sons, Inc., New York · London · Sydney

Foreword

The importance of transistors and other semiconductor devices is now well established. The subsequent development of microminiaturized electronic circuits has blurred the dividing line between the "device" and the "circuit," and thus has made it increasingly important for us to understand deeply the relationship between the internal physics and structure of a device, and its potentialities for circuit performance. Furthermore, the small size and efficient operation of semiconductor devices make possible for the first time a much closer integration between the theoretical and laboratory aspects of the educational process.

To prepare new educational material which would reflect these developments, there was formed in the Fall of 1960 a group known as the Semiconductor Electronics Education Committee (SEEC). This committee is comprised of university and industrial members, brought together by several of the faculty of the Electrical Engineering Department at the Massachusetts Institute of Technology, with Professor C. L. Searle acting as Chairman and Professor R. B. Adler acting as Technical Director. The committee undertook the production of a multipurpose course in semiconductor electronics, designed primarily for use in universities at the third or fourth year undergraduate level.

The success of the high-school physics course developed by the Physical Science Study Committee (PSSC) lead the SEEC to believe that the same kind of combination used there—text, laboratory experiments, and films, in a complementary format— would be the most practical way of providing uniformly high-quality instruction over the wide range of material involved. It was hoped that this arrangement would lead to broad applicability of the course in the academic world, and also in some professional training activities of industry and government. This book is one in the SEEC series, all volumes of which are listed here:*

Vol. 1 (ISP)   *Introduction to Semiconductor Physics*, R. B. Adler, A. C. Smith, and R. L. Longini

Vol. 2 (PEM)   *Physical Electronics and Circuit Models of Transistors*, P. E. Gray, D. DeWitt, A. R. Boothroyd, and J. F. Gibbons

Vol. 3 (ECP)   *Elementary Circuit Properties of Transistors*, C. L. Searle, A. R. Boothroyd, E. J. Angelo, Jr., P. E. Gray, and D. O. Pederson

Vol. 4 (CLT)   *Characteristics and Limitations of Transistors*, R. D. Thornton, D. DeWitt, E. R. Chenette, and P. E. Gray

Vol. 5 (MTC)   *Multistage Transistor Circuits*, R. D. Thornton, D. O. Pederson, C. L. Searle, E. J. Angelo, Jr., and J. Willis

Vol. 6 (DTC)   *Digital Transistor Circuits*, J. N. Harris

Vol. 7 (TCM)   *Handbook of Basic Transistor Circuits and Measurements*, R. D. Thornton, J. G. Linvill, E. R. Chenette, H. L. Ablin, J. N. Harris, and A. R. Boothroyd

These books have all gone through at least one "preliminary edition," many through two or more. The preliminary editions were used in teaching trials at some of the participating colleges and industrial training activities, and the results have been used as a basis for revision.

* Minor changes in title or authorship may take place in some of the volumes, which are still in preparation at the time of this writing.

It is almost impossible to enumerate all those people who have contributed some of their effort to the SEEC. Certain ones, however, have either been active with the Committee steadily since its inception, or have made very major contributions since then. These may be thought of as "charter members," deserving special mention.

From Universities

California, Berkeley: D. O. Pederson
Imperial College, London: A. R. Boothroyd△
Iowa State: H. L. Ablin*
M.I.T.: R. B. Adler, P. E. Gray, A. L. McWhorter, C. L. Searle, A. C. Smith, R. D. Thornton, J. R. Zacharias, H. J. Zimmermann (Research Laboratory of Electronics), J. N. Harris (Lincoln Laboratory)
Minnesota: E. R. Chenette
New Mexico: W. W. Grannemann
Polytechnic Institute of Brooklyn: E. J. Angelo, Jr.
Stanford: J. F. Gibbons, J. G. Linvill
U.C.L.A.: J. Willis

From Industries

Bell Telephone Laboratories: J. M. Early, A. N. Holden, V. R. Saari
Fairchild Semiconductor: V. R. Grinich
IBM: D. DeWitt
RCA: J. Hilibrand, E. O. Johnson, J. I. Pankove
Transitron: B. Dale,† H. G. Rudenberg‡
Westinghouse Research Laboratories: A. I. Bennett, H. C. Lin, R. L. Longini§

General management of the SEEC operations is in the hands of Educational Services, Inc. (abbreviated ESI), Watertown, Mass.,

△ Now at Queen's University, Belfast.
* Now at the University of Nebraska, Department of Electrical Engineering.
† Now at Sylvania Corp.
‡ Now at A. D. Little, Inc.
§ Now at Carnegie Institute of Technology, Department of Electrical Engineering.

a nonprofit corporation that grew out of the PSSC activities and is presently engaged in a number of educational projects at various levels. In addition to providing general management, ESI has supplied all the facilities necessary for preparing the SEEC films. These are 16-mm sound films, 20 to 40 minutes in length, designed to supplement the subject matter and laboratory experiments presented in the various text books. Two of the films are already available:

"Gap Energy and Recombination Light in Germanium"—
J. I. Pankove and R. B. Adler
"Minority Carriers in Semiconductors"—J. R. Haynes and
W. Shockley

At this writing two more films are still in the early stages of preparation: one deals with the *pn* junction, and the other with the relationship between physical structure, fabrication processes, and circuit performance of transistors. Pending arrangements for commercial distribution, completed films are available (purchase or rental) directly from Educational Services, Inc., 47 Galen Street, Watertown, Mass.

The committee has also endeavored to develop laboratory materials for use with the books and films. This material is referred to in the books and further information about it can be obtained from ESI.

The preparation of the entire SEEC program, including all the books, was supported at first under a general grant made to the Massachusetts Institute of Technology by the Ford Foundation, for the purpose of aiding in the improvement of engineering education, and subsequently by specific grants made to ESI by the National Science Foundation. This support is gratefully acknowledged.

Campbell L. Searle
Chairman, SEEC
Richard B. Adler
Technical Director, SEEC

Preface

This textbook has been written on the premise that both developers and users of semiconductor junction devices need to understand the important relationships between the structure and internal behavior of the device, and its circuit characteristics and capabilities. Because of the advantages of smaller size, better performance, and lower cost, electronic circuit packaging is moving in the direction of much greater circuit integration, with all or part of the *circuit* fabricated in the same process which produces the *active semiconductor device*. In this emerging art, the designers of circuit, device, and process work as a team. Clearly, it is desirable for each member of the team to be aware of the opportunities and limitations facing his teammates.

This book has four objectives:

(1) To develop a sound understanding of the internal physical behavior of junction diodes and transistors.
(2) To obtain approximate circuit models which characterize the device under appropriately limited operating conditions.
(3) To develop an understanding of both the limitations inherent in the various circuit models and the relationships between different models.

(4) To show how the parameters of a circuit model depend on the physical structure of the device, its electrical operating point, and its temperature.

Although we believe this book will stand on its own, we must point out that it was conceived as one of a series covering transistor electronics from the physical background through circuit-design considerations. The series is intended to provide a fairly complete experience with *one* device of unquestioned technological importance—the transistor. Inasmuch as this objective does not normally characterize a first course in electronics, use of the entire series of books is envisioned by the authors primarily as a "second contact" with electronics. However, by providing several separate books, such as this one, we hope to have achieved enough flexibility to permit very wide use of the material, in whole or in part, from the junior year in the university through the early graduate and professional level.

This book, like the others in the SEEC series, is limited to junction diodes and transistors. Our principal justification for the exclusion of other semiconductor devices is the growing need we find for a work which treats *one device* in sufficient detail so that students will be familiar enough with its internal physics, structure, and characteristics to begin to apply it in the design sense with some sophistication. In addition, it has so far proved to be true that a good understanding of transistors makes easier the comprehension of all other semiconductor junction devices.

Because of our belief that second-order physical effects are best understood after a preliminary treatment of circuit properties, the present book is focused on the *first-order* physical electronics and circuit models of diodes and transistors. Another book in this series, namely, (CLT) *Characteristics and Limitations of Transistors,* by R. D. Thornton, D. DeWitt, E. R. Chenette, and P. E. Gray, presents in detail the important second-order effects which often determine the ultimate limitations on device performance.

For the usual traditional reasons, a number of problems have been included at the end of most chapters. Some of these problems illustrate analytical developments which would otherwise have been presented in the text. Others are exercises which will contribute to the students' confidence in their ability to *use* the techniques described in the text.

Readers of this book are assumed to have studied elementary electronic circuits, including linear two-port theory and use of dependent generators. Also, readers are assumed to understand the mechanisms of electrical conduction in semiconductors, including:

(a) The possibility of two distinct modes of electrical conduction associated with electron motion in a solid, leading to the concepts of *holes* and *conduction electrons* as current carriers.

(b) The metallurgical and environmental means of varying the numbers of each kind of carrier present in a semiconductor.

(c) The dynamical properties of the carriers, namely, the processes of *drift* in an electric field, *diffusion* in a concentration gradient, and *generation* and *recombination* of hole-electron pairs.

These fundamental matters are treated appropriately in another volume of this series, namely, (ISP) *Introduction to Semiconductor Physics*, by R. B. Adler, A. C. Smith, and R. L. Longini.

The authors listed below are indebted to the entire SEEC membership for their encouragement, guidance, and criticism. Their assistance in the preparation of the outlines, formulation of technical arguments, and critical review and correction of the preliminary editions has been of major importance in shaping the objectives and content of this book. We are also indebted to Lawrence Castro, John Kassakian, and Alton Tripp, who, as M.I.T. students working with us at the SEEC summer workshops, did most of the measurement work, oscilloscope photography, and calculations used in this book.

Paul E. Gray
David DeWitt
A. R. Boothroyd
James F. Gibbons

Cambridge, Massachusetts
May 1964

Contents

1 Semiconductor Junction Devices, 1

1.0 Introduction, 1
1.1 Junction Diodes, 1
1.2 Junction Transistors, 3

2 Physical Operation of pn-Junction Diodes, 8

2.0 The Abrupt pn-Junction Diode, 8
2.1 The pn Junction in Equilibrium, 9
2.2 The Effect of a Bias Voltage on
the pn Junction, 14
2.3 Analysis of the Space-Charge Layer, 18
2.4 Graded pn Junctions, 27

3 The dc Behavior of pn-Junction Diodes, 32

3.0 The Idealized pn-Junction Diode, 32
3.1 Charge Distribution and Flow
in the Idealized Diode, 33

3.2 Minority-Carrier Distribution
and Flow, 38
3.3 The Idealized *pn*-Junction Diode
Equation, 42
3.4 Majority-Carrier Distributions
and Currents, 50

4 Other Effects in pn-Junction Diodes, 57

4.0 Limitations of the Idealized Model, 57
4.1 Voltage Drops in the Neutral Regions, 58
4.2 Carrier Generation and Recombination
in the Space-Charge Layer, 59
4.3 Deviations from Reverse-Current
Saturation, 61
4.4 Junction Breakdown, 63
4.5 Ohmic Contacts, 69
4.6 Surface Recombination and the
Thin-Base Diode, 72

5 Dynamic Behavior of pn-Junction Diodes, 77

5.0 Dynamic Effects in Diodes, 77
5.1 The Dynamics of Excess Minority
Carriers, 78
5.2 Junction Diode Switching Transients, 81
5.3 Small-Signal Sinusoidal Behavior of
the Junction Diode, 90
5.4 Dynamic Changes in the Charge Stored
in the Space-Charge Layer, 93

6 Lumped Models for Junction Diodes, 99

6.0 Introduction, 99
6.1 A Lumped Model for a Junction Diode, 100
6.2 Use of the Lumped Model, 114

7 **Structure and Operation of Transistors, *121***

    7.0 Introduction, 121
    7.1 Transistor Operation in the
        Active Mode, 125
    7.2 The Transistor as an Amplifier, 132
    7.3 Current-Actuated Circuit Models, 136
    7.4 A Small-Signal Dynamic Circuit Model, 138

8 **Small-Signal Transistor Models, *148***

    8.0 Introduction, 148
    8.1 Collector Signal Voltage and Base-Width
        Modulation, 148
    8.2 Base Resistance—dc Large Signal, 155
    8.3 Small-Signal Base-Resistance Effects, 162
    8.4 Small-Signal Models which Include
        Space-Charge Capacitance, 168

9 **The Ebers-Moll Model for Transistor
Volt-Ampere Characteristics, *174***

    9.0 Nonlinear Transistor Operation, 174
    9.1 Internal dc Behavior of the
        Idealized Transistor, 175
    9.2 dc Volt-Ampere Characteristics, 183
    9.3 Regions of Operation, 187
    9.4 The Effects of a Graded Base on
        Large-Signal Behavior, 192

10 **Transistor Models for Dynamic Switching, *200***

    10.0 Introduction, 200
    10.1 Basic Ideas: Charge Definition of
         Device Properties and Charge Control, 201
    10.2 The Two-Lump Model of the Transistor, 209
    10.3 Conditions of Validity of the Two-Lump
         Model and Charge-Control Equations, 214

10.4 Example of Use of the Lumped Model
      for Transient Calculations, 223
10.5 Representation of Charge Storage in
      Space-Charge Layers, 230
10.6 Charge Storage in the Collector and
      Remote Regions of Base, 235

APPENDIX A   *A Closer Look at the pn-Junction
               Space-Charge Layer, 245*

              A.0 Introduction, 245
              A.1 The Space-Charge Layer in Equilibrium,
                   245
              A.2 Changes Produced by a Bias Voltage, 251

APPENDIX B   *The Electric Field in the Neutral Regions
               of a pn Junction, 254*

              B.1 The Electric Field, 254
              B.2 The Space Charge, 257

INDEX, 259

List of Symbols

A	junction area
C_j	incremental junction space-charge-layer capacitance
C_{jc}	incremental capacitance of the collector junction
C_{je}	incremental capacitance of the emitter junction
C_V	nonlinear junction space-charge-layer charge store
C_{VC}	nonlinear charge store of the collector junction
C_{VE}	nonlinear charge store of the emitter junction
D	charge-carrier diffusion constant—see Note 1
E_g	ionization energy required to produce a hole-electron pair, i.e., the width of the energy gap
E_{go}	width of the energy gap extrapolated to absolute zero
$\mathcal{E}$	electric field
$\mathcal{E}_o$	electric field at the metallurgical boundary of a pn junction
f_τ	the frequency at which the incremental component of base current required to charge the base excess carrier store equals the incremental collector current
g	incremental conductance of a junction diode
g_m	incremental transconductance of a junction transistor
H_c, H_C	the combinance parameter used in lumped models
H_D	the diffusance parameter used in lumped models
I, i	electric current—see Note 2
I_{co}	the collector-junction saturation current of a transistor with the emitter open

I_{CS}	the collector-junction saturation current of a transistor with the emitter shorted to the base
I_{ES}	the emitter-junction saturation current of a transistor with the collector shorted to the base
I_f	forward current of a junction diode
I_r	reverse current of a junction diode
I_s	saturation current of an idealized junction diode
J	electric current density. Subscripts h and e denote hole and electron current densities.
k	Boltzmann's constant
L	charge carrier diffusion length—see Note 1
$\mathcal{L}$	characteristic length of the exponential impurity distribution in a graded-base transistor
L_D	extrinsic Debye length
L_i	intrinsic Debye length
l	total width of the depletion layer at a junction
l_n	width of the portion of the depletion layer lying in the n-type material
l_p	width of the portion of the space charge layer lying in the p-type material
M	avalanche multiplication ratio
M_j	space-charge-layer capacitance multiplier used in large-signal calculations
N	net impurity concentration, i.e., excess of donor concentration over acceptor concentration
N_a	acceptor impurity concentration
N_A	acceptor concentration on the p-type side of an abrupt pn junction
N_d	donor impurity concentration
N_D	donor concentration on the n-type side of an abrupt pn junction
n	electron concentration—see Note 3
n'	excess electron concentration—see Note 3
$n_i, n_i(T)$	intrinsic carrier concentration
p	hole concentration—see Note 3
p'	excess hole concentration—see Note 3
P	complex amplitude of the excess hole concentration
q	magnitude of the electronic charge
q_b, q_B	total excess minority-carrier charge stored in the base of a transistor
q_e	total excess stored electron charge
q_F	forward component of excess minority-carrier charge stored in the base
q_h	total excess stored hole charge
q_j	charge in either half of the dipole layer of the space-charge region at a junction
q_R	reverse component of excess minority-carrier charge stored in the base

q_S	saturation charge stored in the base of a transistor
q_{VE}	emitter junction space-charge-layer charge measured with respect to the charge for $V_{EB} = 0$
q_{VC}	collector junction space-charge-layer charge measured with respect to the charge for $V_{CB} = 0$
R_B	dc large-signal base resistance
r_b	incremental low-frequency base resistance
S	the storance parameter used in lumped models
S_r	surface recombination velocity
s	complex frequency variable
T	absolute temperature
t_s	storage delay time of a junction diode
V,v	terminal-pair voltage—see Note 2
V_a	avalanche breakdown voltage
W	width of the neutral base region in a transistor or thin-region diode
x,x',x''	longitudinal position coordinate in the one-dimensional diode or transistor model
$\mathcal{Y}$	incremental differential operator
y	tranverse position coordinate in the active base region of a transistor; incremental admittance parameter
y_f	incremental common-emitter forward or mutual admittance of a transistor
y_i	incremental common-emitter input admittance of a transistor
y_o	incremental common-emitter output admittance of a transistor
y_r	incremental common-emitter reverse admittance of a transistor
z_b	incremental base impedance
α	incremental common-base short-circuit current gain
α_F	large-signal forward-injection common-base short-circuit current gain
α_R	large-signal reverse-injection common-base short-circuit current gain
β	incremental common-emitter short-circuit current gain
β_F	large-signal forward-injection common-emitter short-circuit current gain
β_R	large-signal reverse-injection common-emitter short-circuit current gain
γ	hole injection efficiency of a pn junction
Δ	designates a small change when used in front of a variable
δ	transistor base-recombination and emitter-efficiency defect
δ_b	transistor base-recombination defect
ϵ	absolute dielectric permittivity
η	base width modulation factor
Λ	complex diffusion length—see Note 1
μ	charge carrier mobility—see Note 1
ρ	space charge concentration
τ	lifetime of excess charge carriers—see Note 1

τ_{BF}	effective base-region lifetime with forward injection
τ_{BR}	effective base-region lifetime with reverse injection
τ_F	forward injection charge-control parameter
τ_R	reverse injection charge-control parameter
τ_S	saturation region charge-control parameter
ψ	electrostatic potential
ψ_0	thermal equilibrium electrostatic potential barrier at a pn junction (contact potential)
ω	angular frequency
ω_τ	angular frequency at which the incremental component of base current required to charge the base excess carrier store equals the incremental collector current

Note 1

In designating diffusion constants, mobilities, lifetimes, and diffusion lengths, the subscripts e and h are used *with reference to diodes* to indicate that the parameters describe the dynamical properties of minority carrier electrons or holes, respectively. *With reference to transistors*, the subscripts e, b, and c are used to indicate that the parameter applies to the minority carriers in the emitter, base, and collector regions. In those few cases where majority carrier diffusion constants or mobilities are used, double subscripts are employed if there is possibility of confusion.

Note 2

Currents and voltages at the terminals of diodes and transistors are designated in the following manner:

For diodes:
    dc or operating-point variables—upper case symbols
    total instantaneous variables—lower case symbols
    incremental variables—Δ in front of upper case symbol

For transistors: subscripts indicate the terminal at which the current flows or the terminal pair at which a voltage appears.
    dc or operating-point variables—upper case symbols with upper case subscripts
    total instantaneous variables—lower case symbols with upper case subscripts
    incremental instantaneous variables—lower case symbols with lower case subscripts
    complex amplitudes of incremental components—upper case symbols with lower case subscripts

Note 3

In designating carrier concentrations, the semiconductor region is indicated by a subscript n or p for a diode or e, b, and c for a transistor. The use of a second subscript o denotes the thermal equilibrium value of the corresponding concentration.

1

Semiconductor Junction Devices

1.0 INTRODUCTION

This book deals with the relationships between the internal physical behavior of junction diodes and transistors and their properties as electric circuit components. However, before beginning our detailed study of the physical electronics of these devices, we describe qualitatively the general principles of operation and the major electrical features of junction diodes and transistors.

1.1 JUNCTION DIODES

A *pn*-junction diode consists of a semiconductor having a region of *p*-type material and a region of *n*-type material separated by a relatively thin region of transition from one conductivity type to the other. This transition region may be of the order of 10^{-6} to 10^{-4} cm in thickness, depending on the method of construction. A representative diode structure is shown in Fig. 1.1. The *p*-type region has many more holes than conduction electrons, whereas in the *n*-type region the electrons are the dominant or majority carrier. This circumstance leads to a marked difference in the amount of current that flows across the junction when the polarity of the applied voltage is reversed, and is consequently responsible for the rectifying characteristics of the structure.

1

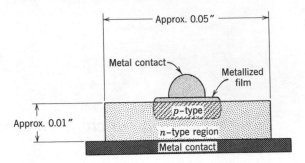

Fig. 1.1. Physical structure of a diffused *pn*-junction diode. The diode is manufactured by diffusing a *p*-type impurity into the *n*-type starting material. Consequently, a portion of the semiconductor is converted to *p*-type. Electrical connections are made through metals which are soldered, vapor deposited, or compression-bonded to the semiconductor.

If the applied voltage makes the *p*-type region positive with respect to the *n*-type region, both holes and electrons are encouraged to converge inward upon the junction. They flow from regions of copious supply, where they are majority carriers, across the junction into regions where they are ordinarily in short supply as minority carriers. The current is large for small applied voltage; and, because of the Boltzmann distribution of carrier energies, it tends to increase exponentially with applied voltage. This polarity, with the *p*-type region positive with respect to the *n*-type region, is known as *forward bias*.

A very important corollary of the forward-bias situation is the penetration of holes across the junction and on into the *n*-type material, and the similar penetration of electrons into the *p*-type material. This penetration extends over the distances which the excess minority carriers can travel before they vanish by recombination with the majority carriers present. Over these distances, usually of the order of 10^{-3} to 10^{-1} cm, there is said to occur significant *minority-carrier injection* on either side of the junction.

The situation is quite different if the applied voltage makes the *p*-type region *negative* with respect to the *n*-type region. Holes and electrons are then being required to *diverge* away from the junction. There can be no steady current of this type across the junction, unless there is a supply of holes from the *n*-type side and/or of electrons from the *p*-type side. Thus carriers are being

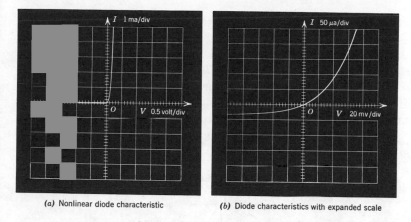

(a) Nonlinear diode characteristic

(b) Diode characteristics with expanded scale

Fig. 1.2. Current-voltage characteristics of a junction diode.

sought from regions of short supply, where they are in the *minority*, and the current is very small. This is the *reverse-bias* condition of operation. Inasmuch as the supply of minority carriers is limited by the rate at which bonds are broken thermally, the reverse current is virtually independent of the reverse voltage over a large range. It is, however, extremely sensitive to the temperature because the minority-carrier population, from which the reverse current is drawn, depends directly upon the temperature [through $n_i^2(T)$].

Typical volt-ampere characteristics of a germanium pn-junction diode are shown in Fig. 1.2. The gross difference between forward bias and reverse bias is shown in Fig. 1.2a, which has a voltage scale of 0.5 volt per division. Figure 1.2b, with expanded scales, shows the behavior of the diode near zero bias more clearly. Note the strong increase of current with forward bias and the nearly constant reverse current.

1.2 JUNCTION TRANSISTORS

A junction transistor has the physical configuration of two pn junctions back-to-back with a thin p-type or n-type region between them. The structures of two typical junction transistors are shown in Fig. 1.3. These are called pnp transistors in accordance with the ordering of the layers. The thin n-type region between the junctions, called the *active base region,* is the most significant feature of these physical arrangements.

A transistor used as an amplifier is normally operated with one *pn* junction, referred to as the *emitter,* forward-biased, and with the other junction referred to as the *collector,* reverse-biased, as indicated in Fig. 1.4*a*. Under these conditions the collector current is much larger than the reverse bias current of an isolated *pn* junc-

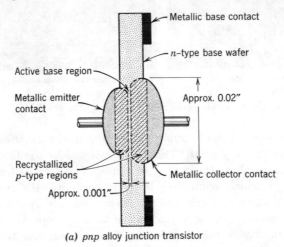

(*a*) *pnp* alloy junction transistor

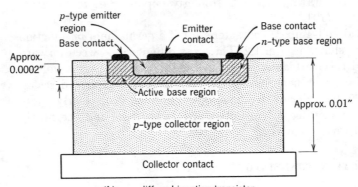

(*b*) *pnp* diffused junction transistor

Fig. 1.3. Physical structures of junction transistors. The alloy unit is made by alloying a metal containing large amounts of *p*-type impurity into the *n*-type semiconductor wafer. When the wafer cools the semiconductor recrystallizes with a preponderance of *p*-type impurities in the recrystallized regions. The diffused unit is made by diffusing *n*-type and *p*-type impurities into the *p*-type collector region. Other sketches of these structures are shown in Fig. 7.1.

tion. In fact, the collector current is only slightly less than the emitter current, which is large and strongly dependent on the emitter-base voltage, because the emitter junction is forward-biased. Figure 1.4*b* shows the strong dependence of the emitter and collector currents on the emitter-base voltage. The base current, which is simply the difference between the emitter current and the collector current, cannot be deduced from these curves because those currents are so nearly equal. Therefore, the base current is shown separately on a current scale expanded by a factor of 100. Although these curves were obtained for a fixed reverse bias on the collector junction, the results are substantially independent of the magnitude of the reverse bias on the collector junction.

In the simplest possible terms, the collector current is almost equal to the emitter current and is under direct control of the emitter-base voltage. This situation results, first, because the emitter and base doping levels are adjusted so that the emitter current consists almost entirely of holes injected into the base (rather than of electrons injected into the emitter) by the forward-biased emitter junction, and, second, because almost all of these injected holes traverse the thin base region without recombination and are swept into the collector junction where they contribute to the collector current. That is, the physical structure of the transistor permits control of the reverse-bias current of one *pn* junction by the forward bias applied to a second *pn* junction. *The transistor is thus a valve whereby the collector current is controlled by the emitter-base voltage.*

This control is accomplished with very little current at the base terminal. The base current, which is typically 1/10 to 1/200 the collector current, results from the injection of electrons from the base to the emitter and also from recombination in the base of a small fraction of the holes injected into the base by the emitter. The principal components of the terminal currents of a transistor are illustrated schematically in Fig. 1.4*c*.

That the transistor valve has power gain should be clear from the previous description of its operation. The power expended at the emitter-base terminals is small because the forward-biased emitter-base junction requires relatively small changes in voltage to produce large changes in collector current (see Fig. 1.4*b*), and because there is very little base current. The power which can be

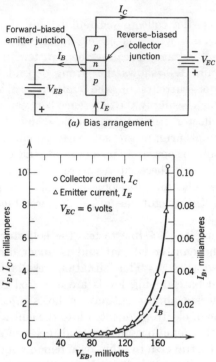

(a) Bias arrangement

(b) Dependence of collector current and emitter current on emitter-base voltage

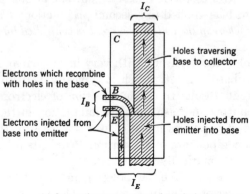

(c) Schematic representation of terminal currents

Fig. 1.4. The *pnp*-junction transistor. Note that in (b) the base current scale is expanded by a factor of 100.

developed in a load at the collector is potentially large because the collector current is substantially independent of the collector junction voltage as long as the collector junction is reverse-biased. Therefore, the load resistance connected in series with the collector can be quite large, permitting large swings of collector-base voltage. For example, when the transistor whose characteristics are shown in Fig. 1.4b is used in the circuit of Fig. 1.5, the ratio of the ac power dissipated in the load to the ac power supplied at the transistor input is about 10^4. Values of this ratio up to about 5×10^4 are attainable in a single-stage transistor amplifier.

The symbol used to represent the transistor in Fig. 1.5 is standard notation for a *pnp* transistor. The identification of the three terminals shown on the sketch is the same for all *pnp* and *npn* transistors. However, to represent *npn* units, the arrow on the emitter points away from the base rather than toward the base. In either type, the direction of the arrow is the *same* as the direction of the emitter current in the *normal mode* of operation (forward-biased emitter, reverse-biased collector).

The analysis of transistor behavior and the development of circuit models which characterize the device depend on a good understanding of the basic internal mechanisms. Since transistor action is an extension of *pn* junction diode behavior, and requires a good background in the physical electronics of diodes, we shall proceed directly with our study of junction diodes and defer further treatment of transistors until Chapter 7.

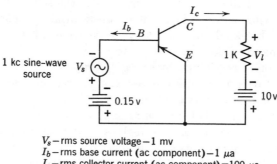

V_s — rms source voltage — 1 mv
I_b — rms base current (ac component) — 1 μa
I_c — rms collector current (ac component) — 100 μa
V_l — rms load voltage (ac component) — 0.1 v

$$\frac{\text{ac load power}}{\text{ac input power}} = \frac{I_c \times V_l}{I_b \times V_s} = 10^4$$

Fig. 1.5. A basic transistor amplifier.

2

Physical Operation
of pn-Junction Diodes

2.0 THE ABRUPT *pn*-JUNCTION DIODE

Although there are several different basic processes for fabricating junction diodes, the internal physical behavior and the electrical properties of diodes made by all the various methods are remarkably similar. We shall find that the differences in detail which do occur are related to the distribution of donor and acceptor impurities near the junction. To emphasize the salient features of diode behavior, without introducing unessential and complicated details, we shall study first an *abrupt pn junction*. This is a junction in which the transition from *p*-type to *n*-type semiconductor occurs over a region of negligible thickness, "abruptly." Junctions fabricated by alloying techniques have transition regions less than 10^{-6} cm thick and thus qualify as abrupt junctions.

We also assume that the *metallurgical junction* or boundary between the *n*-type and *p*-type regions is a plane, that all carrier distributions and currents are uniform on planes parallel to the boundary plane, and that all currents are directed perpendicularly to the boundary plane, as shown in Fig. 2.1. This *one-dimensional* model is reasonable for the representative structures shown in Figs. 1.1 and 1.3, and is justifiable for most *pn* junctions.

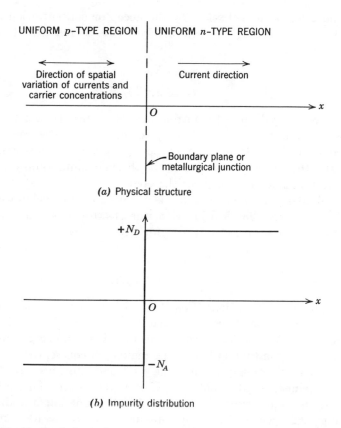

(a) Physical structure

(b) Impurity distribution

Fig. 2.1. The idealized physical arrangement and impurity distribution of an abrupt *pn* junction.

2.1 THE *pn* JUNCTION IN EQUILIBRIUM

A *pn* junction is said to be *in equilibrium* when it is at a uniform temperature and when no external disturbances, such as light or a bias voltage, are acting on it. Under equilibrium conditions the hole current and the electron current must *each* vanish at every point in the semiconductor.

2.1.1 *The Equilibrium Potential Barrier*

In the homogeneous *p*-type material well away from the metallurgical junction, the hole and electron concentrations are uniform and are determined solely by the acceptor concentration N_A and the temperature.* For reasonably extrinsic material $(N_A \gg n_i)$ we have:

$$p_{po} \cong N_A$$
$$n_{po} \cong n_i^2(T)/N_A \qquad (2.1a,b)$$

where $n_i(T)$ denotes the intrinsic carrier concentration.† The subscript p on the symbols n and p for conduction electron and hole concentrations denotes the p-type region, and the subscript o indicates that the concentration has its thermal equilibrium value. This notation is used throughout the book.

Similarly, in the homogeneous extrinsic n-type region well away from the metallurgical junction, the electron and hole concentrations are uniform and are given, for $N_D \gg n_i$, by:

$$n_{no} \cong N_D$$
$$p_{no} \cong n_i^2(T)/N_D \qquad (2.2a,b)$$

These four equations (Eqs. 2.1 and 2.2) show that the hole concentration is much greater in the p-type region than in the n-type region, and that the electron concentration is much greater in the n-type region than in the p-type region. Of course, the np product is equal to n_i^2 everywhere in the semiconductor, because the junction is in thermal equilibrium. Clearly, concentration gradients of both holes and electrons must exist at the junction, as indicated in Fig. 2.2 (which has been prepared for $N_A = 10^{16}$ cm^{-3} and $N_D = 2 \times 10^{16}$ cm^{-3}). The concentration gradients near the metallurgical junction are normally very large because the equilibrium minority-carrier concentrations are usually *at least* three orders of magnitude below the corresponding majority-carrier concentrations. Because of these large concentration gradients, holes tend to diffuse across the junction from the p-type region to the n-type region while electrons tend to diffuse in the opposite direction.

---

* The symbols N_A and N_D are reserved for the constant acceptor and donor concentrations on the two sides of an *abrupt* pn junction, while N_a and N_d refer to acceptor and donor concentrations in general.

† See for example: R. B. Adler, A. C. Smith, and R. L. Longini, *Introduction to Semiconductor Physics* (hereafter referred to as ISP), Sec. 3.5.3, John Wiley and Sons, 1964.

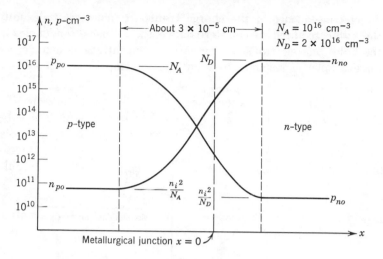

Fig. 2.2. Approximate distributions of carriers near the boundary plane of a germanium *pn* junction in equilibrium at room temperature.

Inasmuch as the hole and electron currents crossing the junction are zero in equilibrium, there must be an electric field near the junction. This electric field must oppose the diffusive tendencies of both the holes and the electrons, and must therefore be directed from the *n*-type region to the *p*-type region.

The origin of the electric field at the junction can be understood by imagining what would happen if it were absent. Without an electric field, holes and electrons would diffuse across the junction because of the large concentration gradients. Since the holes leave behind negatively charged acceptor ions while the electrons leave behind positively charged donor ions, the net result of their diffusive flows would be to charge the *n*-type region positive with respect to the *p*-type region. Therefore, a dipole layer of charge would be established at the junction and the electrostatic potential of the *n*-type region would become positive with respect to the *p*-type region. These diffusive flows could not continue, however, because the charge imbalance which they establish would produce an electric field which itself would *oppose* the diffusive tendencies and produce a stable equilibrium state.

In other words, any flow of charge across the junction is a self-limiting process because the electric field at the junction, which is a direct consequence of the charge transport, increases to exactly the value required to counterbalance the diffusive tendencies of the holes and electrons. If the carrier concentrations change, as, for example, in response to a change in temperature, there is a

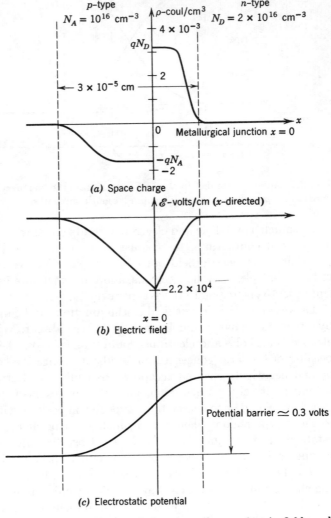

Fig. 2.3. Approximate distributions of the space charge, electric field, and electrostatic potential at a germanium *pn* junction in equilibrium at room temperature.

transient flow of charge across the junction which produces compensating changes in the dipole layer of space charge, the electric field, and the potential distribution. The general forms of the space charge, electric field, and electrostatic potential in the space-charge layer are shown in Fig. 2.3.

The "built-in" potential barrier at the junction is the *contact potential* characteristic of the *p*-type and *n*-type semiconductors comprising the junction. No *terminal voltage* results from the contact potential, because such contact potentials exist at *every* junction of dissimilar materials. If we connect any conductor to the two sides of the *pn* junction, contact potentials will exist at the two new junctions thereby created, and the sum of the contact potentials around the closed loop will be precisely zero. If this were not so, a current would exist and self-heating would occur in violation of the second law of thermodynamics. It follows that the contact potential of a *pn* junction in thermal equilibrium *cannot* be measured by any voltmeter requiring a steady current, however small.

2.1.2 *The Space Charge Layer and the Neutral Regions*

In most *pn* junctions the contact potential is a few tenths of a volt. The region over which the electrostatic potential changes is usually of the order of 10^{-5} cm. Consequently, the electric field near the metallurgical junction is usually very large (the order of 10^4 volts per cm) and the associated space charge is large. Inspection of Figs. 2.2 and 2.3 shows that, near the metallurgical junction, the space-charge density is approximately equal to the density of charge associated with the impurity atoms.

The region straddling the metallurgical junction, which contains the electric field and the space charge, and across which is developed the contact potential, is usually referred to as the *space-charge layer*. In Figs. 2.2 and 2.3 the space-charge layer is the region between the dashed lines. This layer is sandwiched between two regions in which the electrostatic potential is constant, and the electric field and charge density are zero. These outer layers are called the *neutral regions* because they are free of electric charge. This resolution of the *pn* junction into a space-charge layer located between a *p*-type neutral region and an *n*-type neutral region is the basis for our analysis of the electrical behavior of the junction. We shall find that the same type of resolution is meaningful when the equilibrium situation is disturbed by applying a bias voltage to the junction.*

2.2 THE EFFECT OF A BIAS VOLTAGE ON THE *pn* JUNCTION

To examine the consequences of a bias voltage, it is necessary to specify how electrical contact is made to the semiconductor. We assume that the homogeneous *p*-type and *n*-type regions are provided with metal contacts, placed so that at the *pn* junction the one-dimensional assumption (see Fig. 2.1*a*) is not violated, and applied so that the electrostatic potential drop between the metal contact and the adjacent semiconductor is sensibly independent of the magnitude and direction of the current. A metal-semiconductor contact of this type, for which the contact potential does not change much when there is current, is referred to as an *ohmic contact*. Although it is certainly not obvious that such a low-resistance ohmic contact between a metal and a semiconductor is possible, techniques have been developed for making contacts of this type. Indeed, the very understanding of *pn*-junction behavior, in which we are now engaged, is essential background for subsequent study of metal-semiconductor contacts. Therefore, at this point in our study we shall assume that a contact which introduces negligible voltage drop in the presence of current is provided, and shall consider the subject of metal-semiconductor contacts further in Sec. 4.5.

A schematic representation of the junction diode with metal contacts is shown in Fig. 2.4. Few practical diodes are made with this particularly simple physical arrangement. Nevertheless, the results of our analysis will be applicable to many practical devices because the two key assumptions of one-dimensionality and of negligible contact-voltage drop are satisfied.

When a voltage is applied to the terminals of the junction diode, a current appears because the applied voltage disturbs the equilibrium which exists for zero bias. Because of this current, we expect voltage drops in the neutral regions outside the space-charge layer, as these regions have a nonzero electrical resistivity (which is in fact much larger than the resistivity of good metallic conductors).

---

* The properties of *pn* junctions are examined experimentally in an SEEC film now in preparation. Upon completion, this film will be distributed as described in the Foreword.

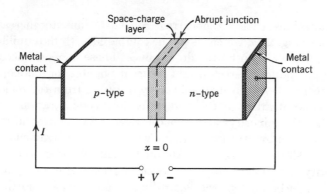

Fig. 2.4. Schematic representation of a *pn*-junction diode.

For the present, however, we assume that the voltage drops in the neutral regions are negligible compared with the applied voltage V (see Fig. 2.4). In Sec. 4.1 we examine the consequences of removing this restriction.

2.2.1 *Changes in the Space-Charge Layer*

Inasmuch as the voltage drops in the neutral regions and the *changes* in the potential barriers at the contacts are neglected in our present model, the entire applied voltage appears as a *change* in the height of the potential barrier in the space-charge layer. If the applied voltage V has the polarity shown in Fig. 2.4, the height of the potential barrier changes from the contact potential ψ_0 to $(\psi_0 - V)$. Of course the electric field and the space-charge distribution must change accordingly. A *forward bias* which makes the *p*-type contact positive with respect to the *n*-type contact $(V > 0)$ reduces the height of the potential barrier, decreases the electric field, and decreases the space charge in both halves of the dipole layer. This decrease in space charge occurs principally as a shrinkage in the width of the space-charge layer. A *reverse bias* $(V < 0)$ increases the height of the potential barrier, increases the electric field, and increases the space charge in both halves of the dipole layer.

2.2.2 *Changes in the Neutral Regions*

The changes in the potential barrier produced by a bias voltage cause important changes in the concentrations of the holes and electrons in the neutral regions as well as in the space-charge layer.

Forward bias causes the carrier concentrations to increase as shown in Fig. 2.5a, which should be compared with the equilibrium distributions shown by the dotted lines. These increases occur because the reduced barrier height makes it possible for more carriers to traverse the space-charge layer by diffusing from the regions of high concentration to the regions of low concentration. Consequently, the minority-carrier concentrations in the neutral regions are increased greatly (more than two orders of magnitude in the example shown in Fig. 2.5). Although small changes occur in the majority-carrier concentrations in the neutral regions, they are not perceptible because of the logarithmic scale used in plotting the carrier concentrations.

The augmented minority-carrier concentrations outside the space-charge layer decrease toward equilibrium at distances the order of 10^{-3} cm to 10^{-1} cm away from the edges of the space-charge layer. Because the space-charge layer itself is about 10^{-5} cm in width these decreases are not perceptible in Fig. 2.5a, but are shown on a greatly reduced distance scale in Fig. 2.5b.

Although the minority-carrier concentrations in the neutral regions are disturbed greatly by the bias voltage, there is very little space charge produced in these regions outside the space-charge layer. The augmented minority-carrier populations produced by the bias voltage are almost exactly balanced by increases in the majority-carrier populations, so that there is very little net charge. Inasmuch as the equilibrium majority-carrier concentrations are several orders of magnitude greater than the equilibrium minority-carrier concentrations, very small fractional changes in majority-carrier concentration can balance the space charge produced by the oppositely charged minority carriers, which undergo major fractional changes in concentration. Consequently, our resolution of the *pn* junction into a space-charge layer sandwiched between two neutral regions, which was postulated for equilibrium, remains valid when the equilibrium is disturbed by a bias voltage.

2.2.3 *A Method of Attack*

We base our analysis of the physical and electrical behavior of *pn* junctions upon the resolution into a space-charge layer and neutral regions which has been discussed in the preceding section. This resolution is particularly useful because electrical conditions in the

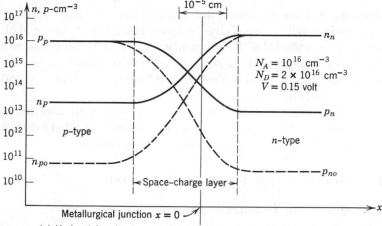

(a) Horizontal scale chosen to display concentrations in the space–charge layer

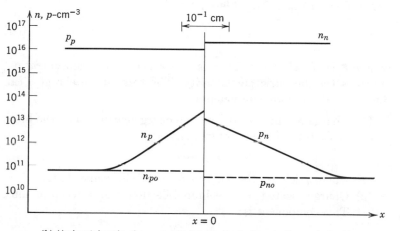

(b) Horizontal scale chosen to display concentrations in the neutral regions

Fig. 2.5. Approximate carrier distributions near a germanium pn junction under forward-bias conditions at room temperature.

space-charge layer differ tremendously from electrical conditions in the neutral regions. More precisely, the space-charge layer is characterized by large concentration gradients, large space-charge density, and very large electric fields. The neutral regions, on the other hand, have concentration gradients two to five orders of magnitude smaller, essentially no space charge, and, as we shall see, small electric fields. Consequently, it is reasonable to use one set of approximations in analysis of charge transport within the space-charge layer, and a distinctly different set in the neutral regions outside the space-charge layer.*

The remainder of this chapter is concerned with analysis of phenomena in the space-charge layer, whereas the behavior of carriers in the neutral regions is considered in Chapter 3.

2.3 ANALYSIS OF THE SPACE-CHARGE LAYER

2.3.1 *Quantitative Description of the Space-Charge Layer*

The fundamental physical principle governing the electrical behavior of the space-charge layer is Gauss' law which relates the electric field to the space-charge concentration. For our one-dimensional model, Gauss' law is:

$$\frac{d\mathcal{E}}{dx} = \frac{\rho}{\epsilon} \tag{2.3}$$

where $\mathcal{E}$ is the electric field, ρ is the space-charge concentration, and ϵ is the dielectric permittivity. The total space charge ρ can be resolved into two components:

(1) Charge residing on the mobile charge carriers, i.e., the holes and electrons. This component is:

$$q(p - n)$$

where q denotes the *magnitude* of the electronic charge.

(2) Charge located on the immobile donor and acceptor ions. This component is:

$$q(N_d - N_a)$$

* Note that the methods discussed in Section 4.3 of ISP cannot be used in the space-charge layer because they are based upon approximate electrical neutrality and upon the concepts of drift mobility and diffusion constant. The electric field and concentration gradients in the space-charge layer are so large that these flow parameters are not meaningful. We shall see that it is never necessary to calculate the current of either holes or electrons in the space-charge layer on the basis of drift and diffusion components. On the other hand, the methods of ISP, Section 4.3, are applicable in the neutral regions, and form the basis for our analysis of the distribution and flow of carriers in those regions.

For an abrupt junction, $(N_d - N_a)$ is equal to N_D in the n-type material and to $-N_A$ in the p-type material, as shown in Fig. 2.1b.

Consequently, Gauss's law can be written as:

$$\frac{d\mathcal{E}}{dx} = \frac{q}{\epsilon}(p - n + N_d - N_a) \qquad (2.4)$$

Near the center of the space-charge layer $p - n$ is much less than either N_a or N_d (see Fig. 2.2), so that the immobile impurity charge dominates the charge concentration. Therefore, the distribution of the space charge in this central region is the same as the impurity-charge distribution, as shown in Fig. 2.3. On the other hand, near the edges of the space-charge layer the mobile carriers make important contributions to the space charge and restore neutrality as the neutral regions are approached. The majority carriers are, of course, much more effective than the minority carriers in this respect because of their greater numbers.

The contact potential or *equilibrium* potential barrier height can be computed easily because the equilibrium carrier concentrations at any plane are related to the electrostatic potential at that plane through the Boltzmann factor:*

$$p = n_i e^{-q\psi/kT}$$
$$n = n_i e^{+q\psi/kT} \qquad (2.5a,b)$$

where $\psi = 0$ corresponds to intrinsic material.† Throughout the p-type neutral region the sum of the mobile and immobile charge concentrations must be zero:

$$q(p - n) + q(-N_A) = 0$$

Inasmuch as the p-type region is assumed to be reasonably extrinsic $(N_A \gg n_i)$, n is much less than p, and the potential ψ_p in the p-type neutral region is given approximately by

$$n_i e^{-q\psi_p/kT} = N_A$$

or

$$\psi_p = -\frac{kT}{q}\ln\left(\frac{N_A}{n_i}\right) \qquad (2.6)$$

* ISP, Sec. 3.5.3.

† This choice of the potential reference is arbitrary and is made for algebraic convenience only.

Similarly, the potential ψ_n in the n-type neutral region is approximately

$$\psi_n = +\frac{kT}{q}\ln\left(\frac{N_D}{n_i}\right) \tag{2.7}$$

where we have assumed that the n-type region is reasonably extrinsic $(N_D \gg n_i)$ so that $n \gg p$.

The contact potential is simply $\psi_0 = \psi_n - \psi_p$, or:

$$\psi_0 = \frac{kT}{q}\ln\left(\frac{N_A N_D}{n_i^2}\right) \tag{2.8}$$

The contact potential lies in the range 0.2 volt to 1 volt for typical *pn*-junction diodes.

2.3.2 *The Depletion Approximation*

We now consider an extremely important approximate method of obtaining solutions for the charge, the electric field, and the electrostatic potential in the space-charge layer. This method has two significant advantages:

(1) It gives results which agree well with the experimental facts when the junction is reverse-biased.

(2) It yields results in closed form and does not require numerical calculation.

This approximation is based on the assumption that the *entire* space-charge layer is void or *depleted* of mobile charge carriers, i.e., holes and electrons. In other words, we assume that those portions of the space-charge layer which are not fully depleted of mobile charge are of negligible thickness. The entire space-charge layer may then be treated as a *depletion layer*, i.e., a region in which the space charge is determined solely by the impurity distribution, as shown in Fig. 2.6.

Inasmuch as the form of the space-charge distribution is *assumed* at the outset (although l_p and l_n are not known) the electric field can be determined by applying Gauss' law to the space-charge distribution. With reference to Fig. 2.7a, the electric field must be zero at $x = -l_p$ and at $x = +l_n$, because these planes define the limits of the depletion layer. Consequently, the field at x_1 must be

$$\mathcal{E}_1 = \frac{1}{\epsilon}(-qN_A\Delta x) \tag{2.9}$$

because the charge per unit area to the left of x_1 is $-qN_A\Delta x$, as shown by the shaded area in Fig. 2.7a. The field thus increases linearly with Δx up to $x = 0$ where it has the value

$$\mathcal{E}_0 = -\frac{q}{\epsilon}N_A l_p \tag{2.10}$$

For $x > 0$, the electric field must decrease linearly to zero at $x = l_n$. This condition can be met because the negative charge in the left half of the depletion layer is exactly equal to the positive charge in the right half of the layer. That is:

$$N_A l_p = N_D l_n \tag{2.11}$$

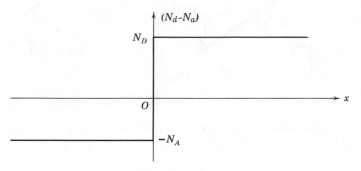

(a) Impurity distribution

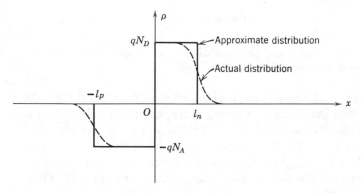

(b) Space–charge distribution

Fig. 2.6. The depletion approximation.

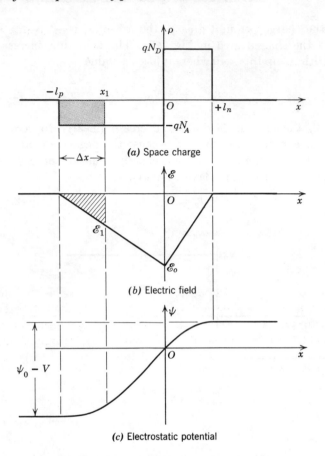

(a) Space charge

(b) Electric field

(c) Electrostatic potential

Fig. 2.7. Charge, field, and potential as determined by assuming that the entire space-charge region is a depletion layer.

The potential distribution is obtained simply by integrating the electric field distribution. Consequently, the potential ψ_1 at x_1 is greater than the potential at $-l_p$ by the area of the crosshatched triangle in Fig. 2.7b. The complete potential distribution is shown in Fig. 2.7c. The height of the potential barrier ($\psi_0 - V$) is equal to the negative of the area under the large triangle in Fig. 2.7b. Thus:

$$(\psi_0 - V) = -\tfrac{1}{2}\,\mathscr{E}_0(l_n + l_p) = -\tfrac{1}{2}\,\mathscr{E}_0 l \qquad (2.12)$$

where l is the total width of the space-charge layer.

Equations 2.10, 2.11, and 2.12 can be solved simultaneously to yield:

$$l = \left[\frac{2\epsilon}{q}(\psi_0 - V)\left(\frac{1}{N_A} + \frac{1}{N_D}\right)\right]^{\frac{1}{2}}$$

$$\mathcal{E}_0 = -\left[\frac{2q}{\epsilon}(\psi_0 - V)\left(\frac{1}{1/N_A + 1/N_D}\right)\right]^{\frac{1}{2}} \qquad (2.13a,b)$$

The widths of the p-type and n-type portions of the depletion layer are:

$$l_p = l\frac{N_D}{N_A + N_D}$$

$$l_n = l\frac{N_A}{N_A + N_D} \qquad (2.14a,b)$$

The results of this approximate calculation agree with our qualitative arguments that reverse bias $(V < 0)$ increases the width of the space-charge layer, and increases the magnitude of the electric field. The space-charge layer width l and the maximum field $\mathcal{E}_0$ vary as $(\psi_0 - V)^{\frac{1}{2}}$. These results also show that the penetration of the space-charge layer is greatest on the side of the junction which has the least impurity concentration.

These approximate calculations are inaccurate in their description of behavior at the edges of the space-charge layer. The actual change from full depletion to space-charge neutrality is smeared out, as suggested by Fig. 2.6. The electrostatic potential difference developed across either "tail" of the charge distribution is of the order of $5(kT/q)$ because the carrier concentrations vary as $e^{\pm q\psi/kT}$, and because the "tail" of the charge distribution ends when the corresponding majority-carrier concentration is reduced to a negligible fraction (e.g., e^{-5}) of its value in the neutral region. Consequently, the total potential difference across the two "tails" is about $10\ kT/q$ or about 0.25 volt at room temperature.* The remainder of the potential difference is developed over the depleted region. This suggests that the "tails" should indeed be negligible in width compared with the depleted region if the total potential

* $kT/q \cong 25$ mv for $T = 290°$K.

barrier height ($\psi_0 - V$) is large compared with 0.25 volt. This condition is certainly met with at least one or two volts of *reverse* bias. For some very heavily doped silicon *pn* junctions, the depletion approximation may yield useful results even at small forward biases because the contact potential alone approaches 1 volt.

The limitations of the depletion approximation are examined in more detail in Appendix A.

2.3.3 Carrier Concentrations at the Edges of the Space-Charge Layer

Application of a voltage to a *pn* junction changes the height of the potential barrier and thus disturbs the concentrations of holes and electrons in the neutral regions outside the space-charge layer. We shall find in Chapter 3 that the carrier distributions throughout the neutral regions, and thus the corresponding current distributions, can be determined if the carrier concentrations at the edges of the space-charge layer can be specified in terms of the bias voltage. We therefore seek to determine these edge concentrations.

For equilibrium conditions, the distributions of both holes and electrons in the space-charge layer are determined by the requirement that the drift tendencies caused by the electric field balance the diffusive tendencies caused by the concentration gradients. This equilibrium situation may be regarded as a balance between these oppositely directed components of both hole and electron current. Because the concentration gradients and the electric field in the space-charge layer are very large, there is copious two-way flow of carriers in the space-charge layer. When a bias voltage is applied carriers flow into the neutral regions. Nevertheless, the two-way flow of either the holes or the electrons in the space-charge layer will not be unbalanced significantly if the *net* flows of the carriers into the neutral regions are small. For this case, it is reasonable to regard both the hole distribution and the electron distribution as approximately equal to corresponding *equilibrium* distributions which conform to the new potential barrier height ($\psi_0 - V$). In other words, we assume that in the space-charge layer the holes and electrons are separately very nearly in equilibrium, with distributions governed by the height of the potential barrier in the presence of the bias voltage (see also pp. 26–27).

Consequently, the ratio of the hole concentration p_n at the *edge* of the space-charge layer on the n-type side to hole concentration p_p at the *edge* of the space-charge layer on the p-type side is

$$\frac{p_n}{p_p} = e^{-q(\psi_0 - V)/kT} \tag{2.15a}$$

where $\psi_0 - V$ is the barrier height. The corresponding relationship for the electrons is:

$$\frac{n_p}{n_n} = e^{-q(\psi_0 - V)/kT} \tag{2.15b}$$

These relationships can be simplified somewhat by recognizing that, in equilibrium ($V = 0$), the carrier concentration ratios are given by:

$$\frac{p_{no}}{p_{po}} = e^{-q\psi_0/kT}$$

$$\frac{n_{po}}{n_{no}} = e^{-q\psi_0/kT} \tag{2.16a,b}$$

Consequently, Eqs. 2.15 may be written:

$$\frac{p_n}{p_p} = \frac{p_{no}}{p_{po}} e^{qV/kT}$$

$$\frac{n_p}{n_n} = \frac{n_{po}}{n_{no}} e^{qV/kT} \tag{2.17a,b}$$

Most of the diode and transistor analysis in the following chapters is limited to *low-level injection* conditions.* Thus, we assume that the concentration of injected excess carriers is small enough so that the *majority* carrier concentrations are not substantially affected by the bias voltage applied to a junction. For this important special case we have:

$$p_p \cong p_{po}$$

$$n_n \cong n_{no} \tag{2.18a,b}$$

so that Eqs. 2.17 become:

$$p_n \cong p_{no} e^{qV/kT}$$

$$n_p \cong n_{po} e^{qV/kT} \tag{2.19a,b}$$

* ISP, Sec. 4.3.1.

These equations, relating the *minority*-carrier concentrations at the *edges* of the space-charge layer to the change in the height of the potential barrier at the junction, are valid for low-level injection situations provided that the junction current is limited by transport processes in the neutral regions and *not* by the rate at which the space-charge layer can supply carriers.

These boundary conditions on the *minority*-carrier concentrations effectively determine the *majority*-carrier concentrations at the edges of the space-charge layer as well, because electrical neutrality exists at these points, even in the presence of injection. Consequently, the *change* in the majority-carrier concentration must equal the *change* in the corresponding minority-carrier concentration, if the semiconductor is to remain neutral. That is:

$$(n_n - n_{no}) = (p_n - p_{no})$$
$$(p_p - p_{po}) = (n_p - n_{po})$$

(2.20a,b)

These equations show clearly that the low-level injection condition is satisfied if

$$p_n{}' = p_n - p_{no} \ll n_{no}$$
$$n_p{}' = n_p - n_{po} \ll p_{po}$$

(2.21a,b)

that is, if the *excess* minority-carrier concentration remains small compared with the *equilibrium* majority-carrier concentration.

Before terminating this discussion, we should consider the evidence which supports our assumption that the holes and electrons are separately very nearly in thermodynamic equilibrium throughout the space-charge layer. On purely theoretical grounds it is possible to make two separate arguments, differing only in the method of resolution of the currents, which support this assumption.

The first of these arguments* is based upon a resolution of the net hole or electron current into random one-way component currents across the junction. This resolution is feasible only if the space-charge layer is so narrow that the probability of a carrier making a scattering collision in the space-charge layer is very low. In the limit of an infinitesimally thin space-charge layer, the random currents of either holes or electrons in both directions may be calculated by statistical averaging methods. Except for large

* This approach was suggested by Dr. R. L. Longini. See P2.8.

reverse bias, each of these one-way currents is much larger than the net current of the corresponding carrier that can be supported by the transport mechanism in the neutral regions. Consequently, the random one-way currents must be approximately equal, even when V is not zero and when junction current exists. Equating them yields Eqs. 2.15. Although this calculation verifies our postulate, most practical *pn* junctions have wide enough space-charge layers to cause some scattering of carriers therein, thus casting doubt on the essential requirement.

The second argument is based upon a resolution of the net hole or electron current into drift and diffusion component currents in the space-charge layer. This resolution and the subsequent use of the concepts of drift mobility and diffusion constant are reasonable only if the space-charge layer is so wide that carriers traversing it make many scattering collisions within the layer. In the limit of many collisions within the layer, the drift and diffusion components of either the hole or electron current are related to the electric field and the concentration gradient through the drift mobility and diffusion constant, respectively. Furthermore, each of these component currents is large with respect to the net current which can be supported by the neutral regions except for large reverse bias. Consequently, the drift and diffusion component currents must be nearly equal, and equating them yields Eqs. 2.15. Unfortunately, as in the first case, this calculation is not completely valid for most practical *pn* junctions because the space-charge layers are not wide enough to validate our requirement that carriers are strongly scattered in that region. However, the "thin-region" and "wide-region" calculations yield the same result, and thereby give support to our postulate (see P2.9).

Perhaps the best argument in support of Eqs. 2.15 is the excellent agreement between results based on them and the expermiental facts for germanium and silicon *pn* junctions, as we shall see in Chapter 4.

2.4 GRADED *pn* JUNCTIONS

The depletion approximation and our qualitative conclusions regarding the space-charge layer can be applied to junctions having more gradual regions of transition from *p*-type to *n*-type material.

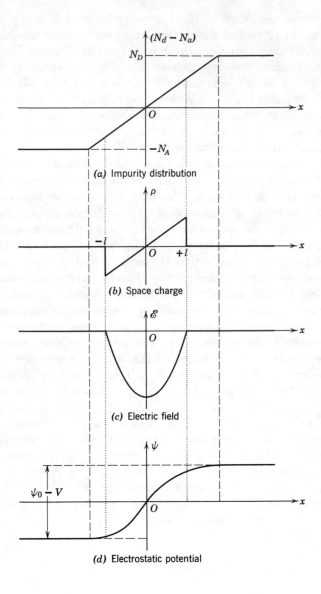

Fig. 2.8. Impurity distribution, space charge, field, and electrostatic potential for a linearly graded junction (based on the depletion assumption).

We assume that the impurity gradient is large enough so that a *pn* junction having an identifiable space-charge layer is formed, rather than simply an inhomogeneous semiconductor without a junction.*

As an example of a graded junction, we consider a diode in which the impurity distribution changes linearly with position, as shown in Fig. 2.8a. The depletion assumption yields the results shown in Fig. 2.8b,c, and d. The analysis is completely analogous to that outlined in Sec. 2.3.2, with one complication. Because in this example the impurity grading extends beyond the depleted region into the neutral regions, some of the contact-potential portion of the potential barrier appears in the neutral regions. Therefore, the portion of the total contact potential which appears across the depletion layer depends on the bias voltage. Even though the potential has a gradient in part of the neutral regions, space-charge neutrality is maintained approximately, in the sense that the net space-charge concentration is negligible compared with both the mobile charge density and the immobile impurity charge density. Although Gauss's law requires some space charge in these regions, which are more correctly referred to as *quasi-neutral*, the space charge is quantitatively negligible compared with either of its components. For a sufficiently greater value of impurity concentration gradient, or a larger potential barrier produced by increased reverse bias, the depletion layer would extend into the uniformly doped regions.

PROBLEMS

P2.1 Verify Eqs. 2.13 and 2.14 which describe the depletion layer in an abrupt *pn* junction.

P2.2 An abrupt germanium *pn* junction has the following impurity concentrations:

$$N_A = 5 \times 10^{14}\,\text{cm}^{-3}$$
$$N_D = 10^{16}\,\text{cm}^{-3}$$

(a) Calculate the contact potential ψ_0 at $T = 300°\text{K}$ ($n_i^2 = 6 \times 10^{26}\,\text{cm}^{-6}$).
(b) Calculate the peak electric field in the space-charge layer and the width of the layer for $V = 0$ and $V = -20$ volts. Assume full depletion of the space-charge layer.
(c) Would you expect the concepts of drift mobility and diffusion constant to be applicable in this space-charge layer?

* ISP, Sec. 3.5.1.

P2.3 Use the depletion approximation to determine the distribution of space charge at an asymmetrically doped *pn* junction having $N_A \gg N_D$. Show that essentially all of the depletion layer lies on one side of the metallurgical junction, and derive an expression for the width of the depletion layer in terms of qN_D, ϵ, and $(\psi_0 - V)$.

P2.4 Use the depletion approximation to determine the distributions of space charge, electric field, and electrostatic potential in a *linearly graded pn* junction at which the barrier height is $(\psi_0 - V)$, as shown in Fig. 2.8. Assume that the depletion layer is entirely confined to the linearly graded region and that the impurity concentration in the graded region can be written

$$N_d - N_a = ax$$

Neglect the portion of the contact potential that appears outside the depletion layer.

P2.5 Consider an asymmetrically doped *pn* junction with $N_A \gg N_D$. Solve Eqs. 2.17 for p_n, the hole concentration on the lightly doped side, and for n_p, the electron concentration on the heavily doped side, by assuming that the heavily doped side remains in low-level injection $(p_p \cong p_{po})$ but that the lightly doped side may exceed the low-level injection condition. Assume space-charge neutrality: $(p_n - p_{no}) = (n_n - n_{no})$.

P2.6 Using your results for P2.5, estimate the bias voltage at which the excess minority-carrier concentration on the *n*-type side equals the equilibrium majority-carrier concentration if $N_D = 10^{16}$ cm^{-3} and $n_i{}^2 = 6 \times 10^{26}$ cm^{-6}. This voltage may be regarded as defining the boundary between low-level and high-level injection on the *n*-type side.

P2.7 Prove that under low-level injection conditions the np product at both edges of the space-charge layer is increased above the corresponding equilibrium value by $e^{qV/kT}$.

P2.8 This problem is concerned with the carrier concentration ratios at the edges of a *pn* junction space-charge layer. We assume that the layer is much thinner than a mean free path for either holes or electrons. Consequently, essentially all the carriers entering the space-charge layer traverse it without being scattered. To be specific, we consider holes, although exactly analogous calculations apply to the electrons. The average flux of holes per unit of time per unit of area from the *n*-type region down the barrier to the *p*-type region is shown by an average over the energy distribution to be (see ISP, P3.3):

$$F_{n \to p} = p_n v / 4$$

where v, the mean thermal speed, is approximately 10^7 cm/sec for holes or electrons at 300°K. The average flux of holes from the *p*-type region having enough energy to climb the potential barrier of height $(\psi_0 - V)$ is

$$F_{p \to n} = \frac{p_p v}{4} \exp - \frac{q(\psi_0 - V)}{kT}$$

(a) Consider an abrupt junction having $N_A = 10^{16} \, \text{cm}^{-3}$ and $N_D = 10^{15}$ cm^{-3}; $n_i{}^2 = 6 \times 10^{26} \, \text{cm}^{-6}$ at $300°\text{K}$. Use the above equations to calculate the contact potential by considering conditions for thermal equilibrium ($V = 0$).

(b) Calculate the fluxes $F_{n \rightarrow p}$ and $F_{p \rightarrow n}$ at zero bias. Express your results in holes per second per square centimeter.

(c) Show that, if the net hole flux is small compared with either random flux $F_{n \rightarrow p}$ or $F_{p \rightarrow n}$, the carrier concentration ratio p_n/p_p is given by Eq. 2.15a.

P2.9 This problem is concerned with the carrier concentration ratios at the edges of a pn-junction space-charge layer. We *assume* that the layer is much wider than a mean free path for either holes or electrons. Consequently, carriers make many collisions in traversing the space-charge layer. We consider holes, although exactly analogous calculations can be made for the electrons.

(a) Using the equilibrium distributions of carrier concentration and electric field shown in Figs. 2.2 and 2.3, *estimate* the equilibrium values of the drift and diffusion "components" of hole current crossing the junction.

(b) Show that Eq. 2.15a (with $V = 0$) follows from equality of the magnitudes of these components at every point in the space-charge layer.

3

The dc Behavior of
pn-Junction Diodes

3.0 THE IDEALIZED pn-JUNCTION DIODE

In this chapter we continue our analysis of the pn-junction diode by studying the behavior of holes and electrons in the neutral regions of the diode. Initially we focus attention on static or dc conditions so that the carrier distributions do not change with time. Consequently, our analysis does not include components of terminal current which result from either changing charge distributions in the space-charge layer, or changing carrier distributions in the neutral regions. The current components which are the consequence of changing carrier and charge distributions are considered in Chapter 5.

Our analysis is based on the simple one-dimensional model introduced in Sec. 2.0. This model is characterized by an abrupt junction between homogeneous p-type and n-type regions. We assume that voltage applied to the diode appears across the space-charge layer as a change in the height of the potential barrier. This model is used not because it provides a particularly faithful characterization of actual diodes, but because it emphasizes, without excessive complexity, the fundamental mechanisms which occur in junction devices. As is true of any model for a physical device, our present diode model, referred to as the *idealized pn-junction diode*, represents a conscious compromise between accuracy of representation and ease of analysis.

3.1 CHARGE DISTRIBUTION AND FLOW
IN THE IDEALIZED DIODE

When a bias voltage is applied to the simple diode structure illustrated in Fig. 2.4, the height of the potential barrier at the junction changes, and current appears. Because of the enormous asymmetry of the hole and electron concentrations on the two sides of the junction, the magnitude of the current is much greater if the barrier is reduced in height $(V > 0)$ than if it is increased in height $(V < 0)$. We first consider qualitatively the consequences of a reduction in barrier height caused by a forward bias.

A decrease in the potential barrier permits holes to flow from the p-type region to the n-type region, and electrons to flow in the opposite direction. These processes are described as *minority-carrier injection* because the holes and electrons that traverse the junction augment the *minority*-carrier concentrations in the regions into which they are injected. As a consequence of the increased minority-carrier concentration at each edge of the space-charge layer, minority-carrier holes flow (by diffusion) away from the junction in the n-type region and minority-carrier electrons flow away from the junction in the p-type region. The injected minority-carrier concentrations and the resulting minority-carrier currents decrease at greater distances from the space-charge region because the excess minority carriers disappear by recombination with the majority carriers. Consequently, at some distance from the space-charge layer edges, the minority carrier concentrations have decayed to their thermal equilibrium values.

Figure 3.1 shows the general form of the minority-carrier concentrations and the associated minority-carrier currents. In constructing these sketches we have used the convention (defined in Fig. 2.1) that positive current consists of the flow of positive charges to the right. Also, we have used electric current densities and not particle fluxes. We must remember that the electric current carried by electrons is opposite to the flux of particles, because the

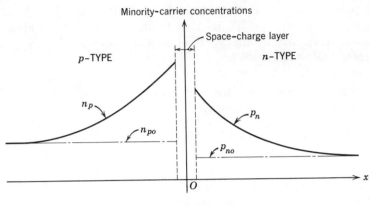

Minority-carrier concentrations

(a) Minority-carrier concentrations

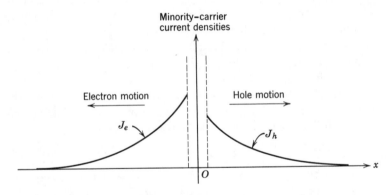

(b) Minority-carrier electric current densities

Fig. 3.1. Minority-carrier concentrations and currents in the neutral regions near a *pn* junction with forward bias.

electrons carry negative charge. Consequently, in the *p*-type region the *x*-directed electron particle flux is negative because electrons are moving away from the junction in this region, while the *x*-directed electric-current density resulting from electron motion is positive, as shown in Fig. 3.1*b*. The space-charge layer width is greatly exaggerated in Fig. 3.1 inasmuch as the space-charge layer is usually two or three orders of magnitude thinner than the portions of the neutral regions that contain the injected carriers.

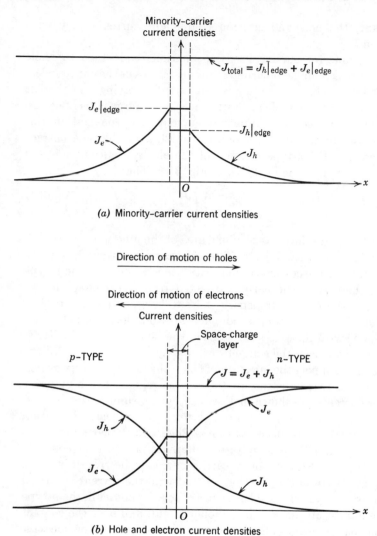

(a) Minority-carrier current densities

(b) Hole and electron current densities

Fig. 3.2. Hole and electron current densities in the forward-biased idealized *pn*-junction diode.

The total diode current is comprised of the flow of both holes and electrons, and under steady-state conditions is the same at every plane cut through the diode. Although the total current is constant, the hole and electron component currents vary with position.

We assume for our idealized *pn*-junction diode that the hole and electron component currents are constant over the entire space-charge layer. This assumption is equivalent to saying that there is no net recombination of carriers in the space-charge layer. Because the hole and electron component currents are constant in this region, the total current is simply the sum of the hole current injected into the *n*-type region and the electron current injected into the *p*-type region as shown in Fig. 3.2*a*. That is:

$$I = A\left(J_h + J_e\right)\Big|_{\text{in the scl}} = A\left(J_h\Big|_{\substack{n\text{-type}\\ \text{edge of}\\ \text{scl}}} + J_e\Big|_{\substack{p\text{-type}\\ \text{edge of}\\ \text{scl}}}\right) \quad (3.1)$$

where A denotes the cross-sectional area of the junction.

In addition to the injected minority carrier currents shown in Fig. 3.1, there are currents of majority carriers. Thus, in the *p*-type region there is a hole current directed from the contact to the junction. This current transports holes to the junction, where they are injected into the *n*-type side, and also provides the holes that recombine with the excess electrons in the *p*-type region. Similarly, electrons flow from the contact on the *n*-type material toward the junction to support the injection of electrons into the *p*-type region and to feed recombination in the *n*-type region. These majority carrier currents are shown in Fig. 3.2*b*, which summarizes the distributions of the hole and electron currents in the idealized junction diode under forward-bias conditions. The majority-carrier currents shown in Fig. 3.2*b* are simply the difference between the constant *total current* and the minority carrier currents shown in Fig. 3.2*a*. At points far from the junction, virtually all the current is carried by the majority carriers. That is, near the end contact in the *p*-type region almost all the current is hole current, and near the contact in the *n*-type region almost all the current is electron current. Although the current is everywhere directed from the *p*-type region to the *n*-type region in forward bias, the holes and electrons are moving toward each other from the contacts toward the junction, near which they recombine.*

---

* The distributions of excess carriers near a forward-biased *pn* junction are investigated experimentally in the SEEC film entitled *Gap Energy and Recombination Light in Germanium*, by J. I. Pankove and R. B. Adler. Arrangements for the distribution of SEEC films are described in the Foreword.

If the applied voltage V is negative rather than positive, the height of the potential barrier at the junction increases, and the flow of holes into the n-type region and the flow of electrons into the p-type region are decreased. However, the minority-carrier *holes* in the *n-type region* near the junction readily fall down the potential barrier toward the p-type side. Likewise, electrons traverse the junction from the p-type side to the n-type side. These flows of holes and electrons cause a reverse current.

As a consequence of the extraction of holes and electrons from the regions where they are minority carriers, the minority-carrier concentrations are depressed below their equilibrium values at

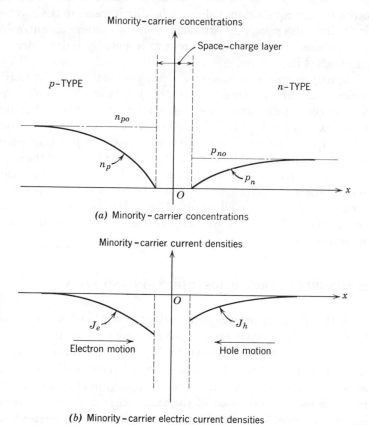

(a) Minority – carrier concentrations

(b) Minority – carrier electric current densities

Fig. 3.3. Minority-carrier concentrations and currents in the neutral regions near a pn junction with reverse bias.

the space-charge layer edges. Thus minority carriers flow in the neutral regions toward the junction in an effort to supply the extraction of carriers at the space-charge layer edges. The minority carriers comprising these currents are thermally generated in the regions near the junction where the concentrations are depressed (inasmuch as the excess concentrations are negative in these regions, there is net generation of carriers). Figure 3.3 shows the general form of the minority carrier concentration and current distributions near the junction with reverse bias.

We shall see subsequently that a very small reverse-bias voltage reduces the minority-carrier concentrations at the edges of the space-charge layer to values that are small compared with the corresponding equilibrium values. A further increase in the reverse-bias voltage has relatively little effect on the carrier concentration distributions, so the reverse current is essentially independent of the reverse-bias voltage.

Majority-carrier currents must flow to remove the majority carriers that are generated near the junctions. The hole- and electron-current distributions are shown for reverse bias in Fig. 3.4. In contrast to the forward-bias situation shown in Fig. 3.2, holes and electrons flow *away from* the region near the junction where they are generated, and *toward* the contacts at the ends of the semiconductor. Furthermore, the reverse currents shown in Fig. 3.4 are several orders of magnitude less than the forward currents shown in Fig. 3.2. At points well-removed from the junction, nearly all the current is the flow of majority carriers, as was the case with forward bias.

3.2 MINORITY-CARRIER DISTRIBUTION AND FLOW

For the idealized *pn*-junction diode, the total current is simply the sum of the injected minority-carrier currents at the edges of the space-charge layer, as shown by Eq. 3.1. We shall now investigate the factors which determine the behavior of the minority carriers on each side of the junction, thereby providing a quantitative basis for determination of the static current-voltage relationship of the diode. We focus attention on the minority carrier holes in the *n*-type region of the diode, recognizing that similar considerations apply to the electrons in the *p*-type side.

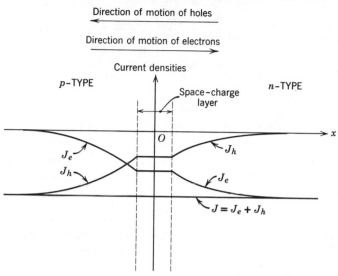

Direction of motion of holes

Direction of motion of electrons

Fig. 3.4. Hole and electron currents in the reverse-biased idealized *pn*-junction diode.

3.2.1 *The Minority-Carrier Diffusion Equation*

The distribution and flow of the holes in the *n*-type neutral region is governed by a continuity equation which states that the net rate of influx of holes into a differential volume of semi-conductor must equal the sum of the recombination rate and the rate of increase of stored holes. We are concerned with minority-carrier flow in homogeneous material having no "built-in" electric field and a reasonably large conductivity. If we consider *low-level injection* conditions (for which the excess carrier concentration is small compared with the equilibrium majority-carrier concentration) and limit ourselves to situations in which the minority-carrier current is a significant fraction of the total current, the minority carriers flow almost entirely by diffusion. This dominance of minority-carrier flow by diffusion occurs because the majority carriers, which are much more numerous than the minority carriers, shield or screen the minority carriers from the small electric field which accompanies the injection of excess carriers. In this important case, the continuity relationship, which is usually referred to as the *minority-carrier diffusion equation*, is:*

* For a thorough discussion of the factors influencing the distribution and flow of minority carriers, see ISP, Chapter 4.

$$D_h \frac{\partial^2 p_n}{\partial x^2} = \frac{\partial p_n}{\partial t} + \frac{p_n - p_{no}}{\tau_h} \qquad (3.2)$$

where we have assumed that the recombination process for excess carriers is such that the recombination rate is proportional to the excess carrier concentration, and have used τ_h, the lifetime for excess holes, to characterize this recombination process.

For our purposes it is convenient to work in terms of the excess hole concentration $p_n{}'$ rather than the total hole concentration p_n. The excess concentration is defined as the difference between the total concentration and the corresponding equilibrium concentration. That is:

$$p_n{}' = p_n - p_{no} \qquad (3.3)$$

Inasmuch as p_{no} is *not* dependent on time or position in homogeneous material, the diffusion equation for holes becomes:

$$D_h \frac{\partial^2 p_n{}'}{\partial x^2} = \frac{\partial p_n{}'}{\partial t} + \frac{p_n{}'}{\tau_h} \qquad (3.4)$$

The corresponding diffusion equation for the minority-carrier electrons in the p-type region is:

$$D_e \frac{\partial^2 n_p{}'}{\partial x^2} = \frac{\partial n_p{}'}{\partial t} + \frac{n_p{}'}{\tau_e} \qquad (3.5)$$

where the excess electron concentration $n_p{}'$ is:

$$n_p{}' = n_p - n_{po} \qquad (3.6)$$

3.2.2 *Solution of the Diffusion Equation*

In solving Eq. 3.4 to determine the hole distribution, we shall locate the origin of our position coordinate x *at the n-type edge of the space-charge layer*.* Under dc or static conditions, the excess hole distribution must satisfy Eq. 3.4 with $\partial p_n{}'/\partial t = 0$.

$$D_h \frac{\partial^2 p_n{}'}{\partial x^2} = \frac{p_n{}'}{\tau_h} \qquad (3.7)$$

---

* Our use of origins in describing minority-carrier flow in the neutral regions different from the origin used in describing electrical behavior in the space-charge layer is simply a matter of convenience. In our description of the neutral p-type region we measure from the edge of the space-charge layer on the p-type side.

The general solution of this linear differential equation is:

$$p_n'(x) = C_1 e^{-x/L_h} + C_2 e^{+x/L_h} \tag{3.8}$$

where C_1 and C_2 are constants of integration and L_h, defined by

$$L_h = \sqrt{D_h \tau_h} \tag{3.9}$$

is known as the *diffusion length* for minority-carrier holes. It is typically in the range 10^{-3} cm to 10^{-1} cm.

One boundary condition which must be satisfied by this solution is given by the carrier concentration ratios at the edges of the space-charge layer. These ratios, which are the result of the quasi-equilibrium that exists in the space-charge layer even with a bias applied, are expressed for low-level injection situations by Eqs. 2.19. If we designate the hole concentration at the edge of the space-charge layer ($x = 0$) as $p_n(0)$, Eq. 2.19a requires:

$$p_n(0) = p_{no} e^{qV/kT} \tag{3.10}$$

which can be written in terms of the excess concentration as:

$$p_n'(0) = p_n(0) - p_{no} = p_{no}(e^{qV/kT} - 1) \tag{3.11}$$

The second boundary condition is that far away* from the junction in the n-type region, the excess hole concentration must vanish because recombination tends to restore equilibrium.

$$\lim_{x \to \infty} p_n'(x) = 0 \tag{3.12}$$

This boundary condition for large x requires $C_2 = 0$, and the boundary condition at the edge of the space-charge layer requires

$$C_1 = p_{no}(e^{qV/kT} - 1) \tag{3.13}$$

Therefore, the excess hole concentration in the n-type region decays exponentially with distance away from the space-charge layer:

$$p_n'(x) = p_{no}(e^{qV/kT} - 1)e^{-x/L_h} \tag{3.14}$$

In a distance L_h from the edge of the neutral region, the injected concentration decays to $1/e$ of its value at the edge. The distributions shown in Fig. 3.1a and in Fig. 3.3a are thus exponentials. It follows from this exponential behavior that the mean distance traveled by a hole before recombining is a diffusion length.

---

* "Far away" implies several diffusion lengths.

Inasmuch as the hole current in the n-type region is substantially all due to diffusion and has no appreciable drift component, the hole current is

$$J_h(x) = -qD_h \frac{\partial p_n'}{\partial x} = q \frac{D_h p_{no}}{L_h} (e^{qV/kT} - 1)e^{-x/L_h} \qquad (3.15)$$

which also varies exponentially with distance. The injected hole current at the edge of the space-charge layer is:

$$J_h(0) = q \frac{D_h p_{no}}{L_h} (e^{qV/kT} - 1) = q \frac{D_h}{L_h} p_n'(0) \qquad (3.16)$$

The second form of the equation emphasizes that the injected current is *linearly dependent* on the excess concentration, which is a consequence of the linearity of the diffusion equation. The exponential nonlinearity comes from the excess concentration-junction voltage relationship imposed by the space-charge layer.

A similar analysis of excess electron behavior on the p-type side yields a distribution which decreases exponentially with distance away from the space-charge layer. The diffusion length L_e for minority-carrier electrons in the p-type region is given by:

$$L_e = \sqrt{D_e \tau_e} \qquad (3.17)$$

The injected electron current also decreases exponentially with distance, and has a value at the edge of the p-type neutral region of

$$J_e(0) = q \frac{D_e n_{po}}{L_e} (e^{qV/kT} - 1) \qquad (3.18)$$

3.3 THE IDEALIZED pn-JUNCTION DIODE EQUATION

The total current I of the idealized pn-junction diode is the sum of the injected hole current at the n-type edge of the space-charge layer and the injected electron current at the p-type edge, as indicated by Eq. 3.1:

$$I = A[J_e(0) + J_h(0)] = Aq \left(\frac{D_h p_{no}}{L_h} + \frac{D_e n_{po}}{L_e} \right) (e^{qV/kT} - 1) \qquad (3.19)$$

With forward bias $(V > 0)$, the diode current is strongly dependent on the voltage because the concentrations of injected carriers increase strongly with increasing voltage. On the other hand, with reverse bias $(V < 0)$, the minority-carrier concentrations at the edges of the space-charge layer decrease with increased reverse bias. Reverse bias a few kT/q ($kT/q = 25$ mv at room temperature) in magnitude causes the minority-carrier concentrations at the edges to become negligible compared with the corresponding equilibrium concentrations, thereby causing the gradients to approach fixed values, which are *independent* of the reverse bias, as shown in Fig. 3.5. Because of this, the reverse current is independent of bias voltage for reverse bias in excess of a few kT/q.

3.3.1 Saturation Current

The idealized diode current-voltage relationship of Eq. 3.19 may be written as:

$$I = I_s(e^{qV/kT} - 1) \tag{3.20}$$

where

$$I_s = Aq \left(\frac{D_h p_{no}}{L_h} + \frac{D_e n_{po}}{L_e}\right) \tag{3.21}$$

If the voltage is made large and negative, the current approaches $-I_s$, which is usually referred to as the *saturation current* of the diode. The term "saturation" indicates that I approaches an asymptote and becomes independent of the voltage V.

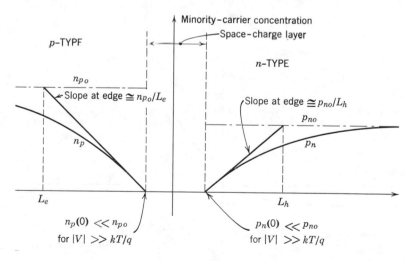

Fig. 3.5. Junction diode minority-carrier concentrations for reverse bias.

The saturation current, given by Eq. 3.21, can be written in a different form which permits a simple physical interpretation. We use Eqs. 3.9 and 3.17 to express the diffusion constants in terms of the diffusion lengths and lifetimes and obtain:

$$I_s = Aq \left(\frac{p_{no}L_h}{\tau_h} + \frac{n_{po}L_e}{\tau_e} \right) \tag{3.22}$$

The rate at which carriers are thermally generated in an n-type region in which the hole concentration is depressed well below the corresponding equilibrium concentration is simply p_{no}/τ_h, inasmuch as the net rate at which excess carriers recombine is assumed to be $(p_n - p_{no})/\tau_h$ (see Eq. 3.2). Therefore, the first term in Eq. 3.22 is the current which is thermally generated in the region of area A and width L_h which lies next to the space-charge layer. A similar interpretation holds for the second term. In other words, the saturation current of the idealized junction diode can be thought of as resulting from the thermal generation of minority carriers in the neutral regions within a diffusion length of the space-charge layer.

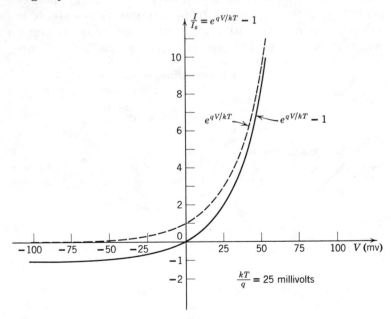

Fig. 3.6. Diode characteristics at low levels.

3.3.2 *Graphical Diode Characteristics*

Figure 3.6 is a graphical study of $I/I_s = (e^{qV/kT} - 1)$ in the region near $V = 0$. It is made for a temperature of 17°C or 290°K at which $kT/q = 25$ millivolts. Reverse saturation is reached at approximately -75 millivolts, or at about $-3kT/q$. For forward bias in excess of $+100$ millivolts, the -1 in the diode equation is negligible compared with $e^{qV/kT}$. For comparison, Fig. 3.7a shows the measured current-voltage characteristic of a germanium *pn*-junction diode.

The saturation current of many junction diodes is 3 to 12 orders of magnitude smaller than the rated forward current. Consequently, the factor $e^{qV/kT}$ must be in the range 10^3 to 10^{12} to produce rated forward current. Because of this, a linear plot on which the current scale is chosen to display rated forward current has the form shown in Fig. 3.7b, which was measured for the same germanium diode used in Fig. 3.7a. If we examine the forward current over a range of only 10:1, the device appears to have a voltage threshold, and to be approximately voltage saturated, because large increases in current result from small increases in voltage.

3.3.3 *Small-Signal Conductance of the Forward-Biased Diode*

In some applications, a forward-biased diode is subjected to a small slowly applied change of voltage. We are interested in the corresponding small change of current, which is proportional to the

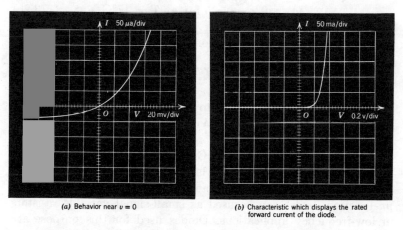

(a) Behavior near $v = 0$

(b) Characteristic which displays the rated forward current of the diode.

Fig. 3.7. Measured germanium-junction diode characteristics.

change in voltage, if the voltage change is small enough. This linear relationship can be used to define a *small-signal conductance g*.

$$\Delta I = g\Delta V \tag{3.23}$$

Inasmuch as the conductance is a dc or low-frequency concept, it can be evaluated by using the large-signal dc current-voltage relationship of Eq. 3.20.

If we consider the diode voltage V as comprised of an operating-point voltage V_o and a small-signal component ΔV,

$$V = V_o + \Delta V \tag{3.24}$$

we may expand the current-voltage relationship of Eq. 3.20 in a Taylor series about V_o:

$$I = I_s(e^{qV_o/kT} - 1) + I_s e^{qV_o/kT}\left[\frac{q\Delta V}{kT} + \frac{1}{2!}\left(\frac{q\Delta V}{kT}\right)^2 + \ldots\right] \tag{3.25}$$

The first term on the right side of this equation is the operating-point current I_o. The second term is ΔI, the small-signal component of the current, which is approximately linearly related to ΔV if:

$$\frac{1}{2!}\left(\frac{q\Delta V}{kT}\right)^2 \ll \frac{q\Delta V}{kT}$$

If we demand that the error introduced by the small-signal approximation be less than 10%,

$$\Delta V < 0.2\,\frac{kT}{q} = 5 \text{ mv at } T = 17°\text{C} \tag{3.26}$$

Consequently, the small-signal conductance is:

$$g = \frac{\Delta I}{\Delta V} = \frac{q}{kT}I_s e^{qV_o/kT} = \frac{q}{kT}(I_o + I_s) \tag{3.27}$$

Figure 3.8 shows that g is equal to the *slope* of the static characteristic at the operating point. With moderate reverse bias, the current I_o is negative and approaches the saturation current, so that the conductance g is zero. On the other hand, for moderate forward bias, the current is much larger than the saturation current, and the conductance is approximately proportional to I_o. Therefore, *pn*-junction diodes can be used as small-signal variable resistors in low-frequency applications. Diodes used for this purpose are known as *varistors* and are frequently used in variable attenuators.

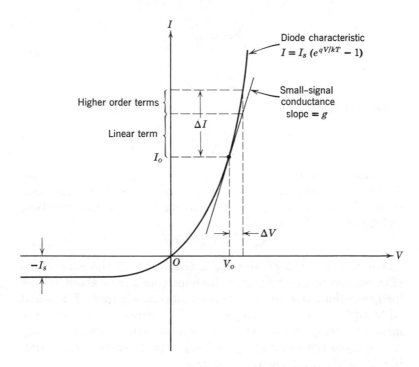

Fig. 3.8. Relationship between diode static V-I characteristics and the small-signal conductance.

3.3.4 *Temperature Dependence of the Idealized Diode Characteristics*

In many applications of junction diodes (and of transistors) the temperature dependence of the idealized diode characteristic is important. Although the diode equation contains the absolute temperature explicitly in the exponent qV/kT, the principal temperature dependence of the characteristic results from the extremely strong implicit temperature dependence of the saturation current I_s.

The saturation current contains six parameters which depend on temperature. However, the temperature dependence of I_s is dominated by the strong dependence of the equilibrium minority-carrier concentrations on temperature. These equilibrium concentrations are related to the intrinsic carrier concentration and to the doping by*

* ISP, Sec.. 3.5.3.

$$p_{no} \cong \frac{n_i^2}{N_D}$$

$$n_{po} \cong \frac{n_i^2}{N_A}$$

(3.28a,b)

Consequently the saturation current is approximately:

$$I_s = A q n_i^2 \left(\frac{D_h}{N_D L_h} + \frac{D_e}{N_A L_e} \right)$$

(3.29)

The factor in parentheses is not strongly temperature-dependent. Therefore, the *principal* temperature dependence of the saturation current is that of the square of the intrinsic carrier concentration, which is:[*]

$$n_i^2 = K T^3 e^{-E_{go}/kT}$$

(3.30)

where K is a constant and E_{go} is the width of the energy gap extrapolated to absolute zero. Inasmuch as E_{go} is about 0.8 ev for germanium and about 1.2 ev for silicon, whereas kT is about 25×10^{-3} ev at room temperature, n_i^2 increases strongly with increasing temperature. The temperature dependence of n_i^2 may be displayed conveniently by plotting $\ln (n_i^2)$ versus $1/T$. According to Eq. 3.30, the logarithm of n_i^2 is:

$$\ln (n_i^2) = \ln (K T^3) - \left(\frac{E_{go}}{k} \right) \frac{1}{T}$$

(3.31)

In the operating range of semiconductor devices, the temperature dependence of n_i^2 is dominated by the second term in Eq. 3.31. Therefore, a plot of $\ln (n_i^2)$ versus $1/T$ is approximately linear with a slope of $-E_{go}/k$, as shown in Fig. 3.9.

The fractional change in I_s per unit change in temperature is approximately equal to the fractional change in n_i^2 per unit change in temperature, which is given by:

$$\frac{1}{n_i^2} \frac{d}{dT} (n_i^2) = \frac{3}{T} + \frac{E_{go}}{kT^2}$$

(3.32)

Near room temperature, the first term is approximately 1% per °K whereas the second term is about 10% per °K for germanium and 16% per °K for silicon. In other words, I_s approximately doubles

[*] ISP, Sec 3.4.3.

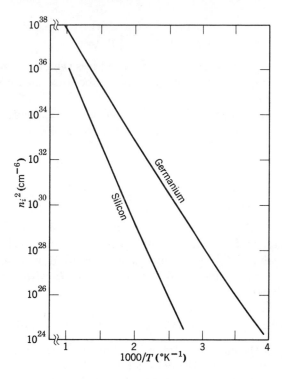

Fig. 3.9. Intrinsic carrier concentration as a function of reciprocal temperature.

every 10°C in germanium or every 6°C in silicon. These very large temperature coefficients lead to enormous changes in diode characteristics for moderate changes in temperature. For example, if the operating temperature of a germanium diode increases from 25° to 75°C, the saturation current and, therefore, to a good approximation the diode current at any fixed voltage will increase by a factor of about 30. The temperature coefficient of the diode current for fixed forward bias is obtained by evaluating $(\partial I/\partial T)_V$ from Eq. 3.20. If $e^{qV/kT} \gg 1$, we have:

$$\frac{\partial I}{\partial T}\bigg|_V = \frac{\partial}{\partial T}\,(I_s e^{qV/kT}) = I\left(\frac{1}{I_s}\frac{dI_s}{dT} - \frac{qV}{kT^2}\right) \qquad (3.33)$$

Therefore, the fractional change in current per unit change in temperature at fixed bias voltage is:

$$\frac{1}{I}\frac{\partial I}{\partial T}\bigg|_V \cong \frac{E_{go} - qV}{kT^2} \qquad (3.34)$$

This temperature coefficient is somewhat less than the coefficient of the saturation current given by Eq. 3.32, because the forward bias subtracts from E_{go}.

In certain transistor-biasing situations, the temperature coefficient of the forward voltage at fixed current is important. This coefficient is obtained by solving the idealized diode equation for V and evaluating the partial derivative with respect to T. For $I \gg I_s$:

$$\frac{\partial V}{\partial T}\bigg|_I = \frac{V}{T} - \frac{kT}{q}\frac{1}{I_s}\frac{dI_s}{dT} = -\frac{E_{go}/q - V}{T} \qquad (3.35)$$

This coefficient usually lies in the range -1 to $-3 \ \mathrm{mv}/°\mathrm{K}$.

In summary, the current of an idealized junction diode *increases nearly exponentially* with temperature for fixed voltage. On the other hand, the voltage *decreases nearly linearly* with temperature for fixed current.

3.4 MAJORITY CARRIER DISTRIBUTIONS AND CURRENTS

Although the current-voltage relationship of the diode has been obtained without considering in detail the behavior of the majority carriers, we shall now consider their distribution and flow to augment our understanding of the physical electronics of the idealized *pn*-junction diode.

Fortunately, it is very easy to determine the majority-carrier distributions as well as the corresponding currents, because the neutrality of the regions outside the space-charge layer can be satisfied only when the *excess* majority-carrier concentration is nearly equal to the *excess* minority-carrier concentration, and because the *total* current must be the same at every plane cut through the diode. The majority carrier distributions for forward bias are shown in Fig. 3.10. Although the *deviations* from equilibrium are nearly the same for both minority and majority carriers, the *fractional* change in the majority-carrier concentration is very small for low-level injection.

The majority-carrier currents are found by subtracting the minority-carrier currents from the total current, as shown in Figs. 3.2 and 3.4. Inasmuch as the excess majority carriers have

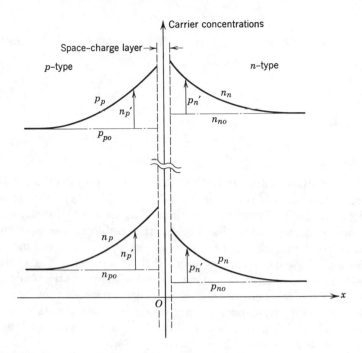

Fig. 3.10. Excess carrier concentrations in a forward-biased *pn*-junction diode. Note that the linear vertical scale is broken because the majority-carrier concentrations are much larger than the minority-carrier concentrations.

the same spatial distribution as the excess minority carriers, the diffusion component of majority-carrier current has the same distribution as the minority-carrier current (which is *all* diffusion component), but is oppositely directed because of the difference in the sign of the charge on the two carrier types, and differs in magnitude by the ratio of the diffusion constants. That is, for the *n*-type side:

$$(J_e)_{\text{diff.}} = - \left(\frac{D_e}{D_h}\right) J_h \tag{3.36}$$

Because we know the *total* electron current from consideration of the continuity of the total (hole plus electron) current, the electron drift-component current must be such that when it is added to the electron diffusion-component current, the required total majority carrier current is obtained:

$$J_e = (J_e)_{\text{drift}} + (J_e)_{\text{diff.}}$$ (3.37)

Inasmuch as $J_e = J - J_h$, where J is the *total* current density, Eq. 3.37 may be written:

$$(J_e)_{\text{drift}} = J - J_h \left(1 - \frac{D_e}{D_h}\right)$$ (3.38)

That is:

$$\varepsilon \cong \frac{(J_e)_{\text{drift}}}{q\mu_e n_{no}} = \frac{J - J_h(1 - D_e/D_h)}{q\mu_e n_{no}}$$ (3.39)

This resolution of the majority-carrier current into drift and diffusion components is shown in Fig. 3.11 for the n-type side of our idealized diode. These curves show that near the junction the majority carrier current has both drift and diffusion components, but several minority-carrier diffusion lengths from the junction, the majority-carrier current is all drift component. The electric field in the neutral region must show the same spatial variation as the drift component of the majority-carrier current because the total majority-carrier concentration is nearly constant under low-level injection conditions. Therefore, some space charge in the "neutral" regions is required by Gauss's law. The distributions of electric field and space charge are examined quantitatively in Appendix B with the conclusions that the minority carrier current has negligible drift component and that the deviations from space-charge neutrality are exceedingly small.

It should be clear at this point that our decision to study first the distribution and flow of the minority carriers has resulted in major simplifications because the electric field has negligible effect on the minority carriers under low-level injection conditions. Analogous simplifications result even if inhomogeneous material having built-in fields is considered. In this case, the minority-carrier distribution and flow can be determined by ignoring *per-turbations* to the field caused by injection, and by using the equilibrium built-in field alone.

Our analysis of the idealized pn-junction diode is based on the assumption (made in Sec. 2.3.3) that the distributions of the holes and electrons in the space-charge layer are given by equilibrium statistics which conform to the modified potential-barrier height. The exponential character of the idealized diode equation is a

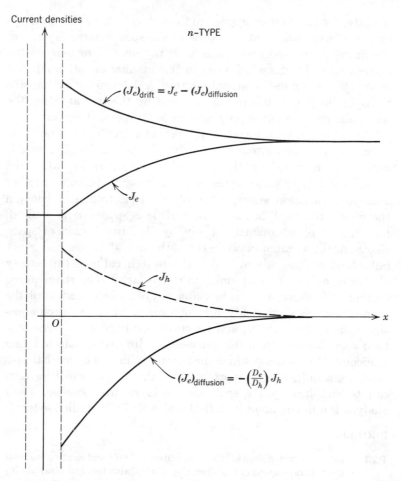

Fig. 3.11. Resolution of majority-carrier current into drift and diffusion components.

direct consequence of this assumption. This assumption is certainly invalid if the currents injected into, or extracted from, the neutral regions are large enough to interfere with the free two-way traffic of carriers in the space-charge layer, which is essential for a near-equilibrium state. Silicon and germanium *pn*-junction diodes have neutral region currents which are small enough so that the equilibrium in the space-charge layer is not disturbed appreciably. Consequently, the bias voltage applied to these devices fixes the minority-carrier concentrations at the edges of the space-charge layer, and the diffusive transport mechanisms in the neutral regions set the current level. Diodes which work in this manner are often referred to as *diffusion-limited* because the current is determined by diffusive transport in the neutral regions and not by the rate at which the space-charge layer can supply carriers to the neutral regions.

This situation is analogous to the rate at which water flows from a small hole in the bottom of a nearly full bucket. The flow rate is determined by the size of the hole and not by the rate at which the bucket can supply water to the neighborhood of the hole. Another analogous situation arises in the physical electronics of vacuum thermionic diodes. When a vacuum diode is space-charge limited, the current is determined entirely by the distribution of space charge in the vacuum between the cathode and anode, and is not influenced by the rate at which the heated cathode can supply electrons, as long as that emission rate is larger than the required current. Of course, the diode voltage can be increased until the current reaches a limiting value determined by the electron emission rate at the cathode, and its current-voltage characteristic is then very different from the space-charge limited situation. Other semiconductor diodes in which the current is limited by mechanisms other than diffusive transport, such as the rate at which carriers can be supplied by the space-charge layer, are possible. Their analysis is quite different from that which we have studied so far.

PROBLEMS

P3.1 Construct a sketch showing the distributions of hole and electron currents in the neutral regions of a pn-junction diode (with forward bias) having significant recombination in the space-charge layer. *Assume* that:

(a) The injected hole current is twice the injected electron current.

(b) The net rate at which pairs recombine in the space-charge layer is equal to half of the net rate at which electrons recombine in the p-type region.

Demonstrate that the total diode current is given by adding a term which describes the space-charge layer recombination current to Eq. 3.1.

P3.2 Use Eqs. 3.14 and 3.16 to prove that the injected hole current $J_h(0)$ is proportional to the excess hole charge in the n-type region, and determine the constant of proportionality.

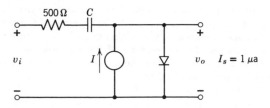

Fig. 3.12.

P3.3 In the circuit shown in Fig. 3.12, a diode is used as a variable resistor in an attenuator. The diode is biased by the dc current source I and signals are coupled in through the capacitor C whose reactance is negligible compared with the 500-ohm resistor. Compute and sketch the attenuation in decibels ($20 \log_{10} v_o/v_i$) as a function of I for $10 \ \mu a < 1 < 10$ ma. Assume that v_i is small enough so that the diode is linear for small signals.

P3.4 Explain the following statement: Under dc conditions all the current of a forward-biased pn-junction diode is accounted for by the recombination of excess carriers.

P3.5 The current crossing the space-charge layer of a pn-junction diode consists in part of holes injected into the n-type region and in part of electrons injected into the p-type region.
(a) Show that the ratio of the hole current to the total current can be controlled by varying the relative doping of the p-type and n-type regions.
(b) We shall later have need for the ratio of the hole current to the total current, usually called hole injection efficiency γ. Find γ as a function of N_A/N_D.

P3.6 An idealized long-base one-dimensional abrupt-junction diode, having no net recombination or generation in the space-charge layer, has the following parameters:

$$\text{on the } p\text{-type side} \begin{cases} \text{acceptor concentration}: N_A = 6.25 \times 10^{16} \ \text{cm}^{-3} \\ \text{diffusion constant for electrons}: D_e = 50 \ \text{cm}^2/\text{sec} \\ \text{lifetime}: \tau_e = 2 \ \mu\text{sec} \end{cases}$$

$$\text{on the } n\text{-type side} \begin{cases} \text{donor concentration}: N_D = 6.25 \times 10^{15} \ \text{cm}^{-3} \\ \text{diffusion constant for holes}: D_h = 50 \ \text{cm}^2/\text{sec} \\ \text{lifetime}: \tau_h = 2 \ \mu\text{sec} \end{cases}$$

Intrinsic carrier concentration: $n_i = 2.5 \times 10^{13} \ \text{cm}^{-3}$
(a) Approximately what fraction of the current crossing the space-charge layer is electron current?
(b) What is the saturation current of this diode if the cross-sectional area is $10^{-2} \ \text{cm}^2$?

P3.7 In Problem P2.8 we determined the carrier concentration ratios at the edges of the space-charge layer by assuming that the net flux of carriers was negligible compared with either one-way flux. Inasmuch as we have now computed the net current of holes across the space-charge layer ($J_h(0)$ in Eq. 3.16), we can check this assumption for self-consistency. Using the notation of P2.8:

(a) Express $F_{n \to p}$ in terms of V.

(b) Determine the ratio $F_h/F_{n \to p}$ in terms of V, where $F_h = J_h(0)/q$.

(c) Assume that $v = 10^7$ cm/sec, $D_h = 50$ cm^2/sec, $L_h = 2 \times 10^{-2}$ cm, and sketch $F_h/F_{n \to p}$ versus V. Show that our approximation that $F_{n \to p} \cong F_{p \to n}$ is valid for zero bias and forward bias, but breaks down for moderate reverse bias.

(d) Discuss the effect of the invalidity of Eq. 2.19a for moderate and large reverse bias on our result for $J_h(0)$, given by Eq. 3.16.

4

Other Effects in
pn-Junction Diodes

4.0 LIMITATIONS OF THE IDEALIZED MODEL

Although most junction diodes have static characteristics which agree in general with the dc behavior of the idealized pn-junction diode, there are significant differences in detail. Several of the mechanisms which cause the performance of actual diodes to differ from the predictions of the idealized model are important to our understanding of the physical electronics of transistors. Therefore, in this chapter we explore the consequences of several of these effects, including:

(a) Voltage drops associated with the electric field in the neutral regions.

(b) Carrier generation and recombination in the space-charge layer.

(c) Currents resulting from leakage across the surface of the junction.

(d) Internal breakdown associated with large reverse voltage.

In addition, we consider the electrical behavior of the metal-semiconductor contacts, and investigate the consequences of locating the contacts within a diffusion length of the junction.

Although each of these deviations from the idealized model has consequences which can be observed in the electrical behavior of one or another actual diode, we are not attempting to describe in detail the performance of any particular class of diode, such as power rectifiers or high-speed switching diodes. Such a goal would require far more diversion from our central purpose than can be undertaken at this point. Rather, we limit our investigation to those matters which are essential to an understanding of the physical electronics of transistors.

4.1 VOLTAGE DROPS IN THE NEUTRAL REGIONS

As we found in Sec. 3.4, the injection or extraction of excess minority carriers across the space-charge layer is invariably accompanied by an electric field in the neutral regions. For low-level injection conditions this electric field is proportional to the total diode current, as shown by Eq. 3.39. Consequently, the voltage drops in the neutral regions which are associated with this electric field are linearly dependent on the total current. These voltage drops can be evaluated by integrating the electric field over the neutral regions. Inasmuch as these voltage drops cause the change in the height of the potential barrier V_B to be less than the applied voltage V, we can write

$$V = V_B + \int_{\substack{\text{neutral} \\ \text{regions}}} (-\mathcal{E})\, dx \qquad (4.1)$$

Because V_B is related to the total current I by Eq. 3.20, which is the result of our idealized model, Eq. 4.1 may be written as:

$$V = \frac{kT}{q} \ln\left(1 + I/I_s\right) + IR_s \qquad (4.2)$$

where the *series resistance* R_s is:

$$R_s = \frac{1}{I} \int_{\substack{\text{neutral} \\ \text{regions}}} (-\mathcal{E})\, dx \qquad (4.3)$$

Equation 4.2 suggests that for small forward currents the total diode voltage V should vary logarithmically with I, in accordance with our idealized model, while for large forward current the voltage should increase linearly with I because IR_s increases faster than $(kT/q) \ln (1 + I/I_s)$, and thus dominates V. Most modern junction diodes have very thin neutral regions so that R_s is quite small. Therefore, the transition from logarithmic to linear behavior may not occur before the limit of low-level injection is exceeded, so that no region of linearity may be observed in the V-I characteristics. Although the voltage drops across the neutral regions may be of major importance under high-level injection conditions, their evaluation is quite complicated because the minority-carrier flow is influenced by nonlinear effects, and because the excess injected carriers modulate the conductivity of the neutral regions. For these reasons the potential drops are not linearly related to the total current, and the effect cannot be described by a linear series resistance.

Even though the effects of voltage drops in the neutral regions may not be represented by a constant series resistance, the V-I characteristic of a diode can frequently be approximated, for high forward current, by an equivalent forward resistance, offset by a constant voltage. For example, the forward V-I characteristic of the diode of Fig. 3.7b can be approximated by a constant resistance of about 0.5 ohm in series with a constant voltage of about 0.25 volt. These numbers will change if we make the approximate model fit a different range of forward current.

Finally, we should note that the metal-semiconductor contacts and the lead wires (inside as well as outside the encapsulation of the diode) have some resistance which may contribute significantly to a linear V-I relationship at high forward currents.

4.2 CARRIER GENERATION AND RECOMBINATION IN THE SPACE-CHARGE LAYER

One of the assumptions which defines the idealized pn-junction diode model is that the hole and electron component currents are constant throughout the space-charge layer. Consequently, a diode will deviate from the idealized model if the current that is accounted for by the recombination of carriers in the space-charge layer is comparable to, or greater than, the current accounted for by recombination in the neutral regions. Such deviations are observed in silicon diodes both for forward and reverse bias.

Under forward-bias conditions, holes from the p-type region and electrons from the n-type region recombine in the space-charge layer. The current accounted for by this recombination adds to the forward current given by the idealized model, but does not follow the $e^{qV/kT}$ dependence of the neutral region currents, because inside the space-charge layer the excess carrier concentrations do not vary as $e^{qV/kT}$. Furthermore, the dependence of recombination rate on the excess carrier concentrations is different from the simple linear dependence which holds in the neutral regions. In Fig. 2.5, comparison of the carrier concentrations under forward-bias conditions (solid curves) with the equilibrium concentration (broken curves) shows that each excess carrier concentration is weakly dependent on V at the edge of the space-charge layer where it is the majority carrier, but strongly dependent ($e^{qV/kT}$) at the edge where it is the minority carrier. Near the center of the region both carrier concentrations vary approximately as $e^{qV/2kT}$. The net result is that the current associated with recombination in the space-charge layer, which is proportional to the integral of the recombination rate over the space-charge layer, varies as $e^{qV/mkT}$, where m is usually about 2.*

Most pn-junction diodes in which the recombination currents from the space-charge layer and from the neutral regions are comparable exhibit a current dependence between $e^{qV/kT}$ and $e^{qV/2kT}$. The neutral region currents tend to dominate at large forward bias because they rise faster with voltage. Because the forward current of *any* diode rises very rapidly with voltage, measurements must be made over a wide range of current to sort out these effects. Figure 4.1 is the measured V-I characteristic of a silicon diode which shows the effect of space-charge layer recombination current at low levels, as well as the effect of series resistance at high levels.

The effect of recombination in the space-charge layer is usually not seen in germanium diodes at room temperature. However, as the temperature decreases, the rate of recombination in the neutral region decreases faster than does the rate in the space-charge layer, and space-charge layer currents may dominate. Consequently, the low temperature V-I characteristic of a ger-

---

* These effects are treated in detail in Ref. 4.1.

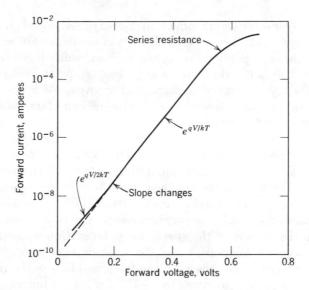

Fig. 4.1. The effect of recombination in the space-charge layer on *pn*-junction diode *V-I* characteristics (From Sah, Noyce, and Shockley, *Proc. IRE*, **45**, 1228-43, 1957).

manium diode may resemble that of a silicon diode at room temperature.

Space-charge layer currents also affect the reverse characteristics of a diode. These effects are discussed in the next section.

4.3 DEVIATIONS FROM REVERSE-CURRENT SATURATION

The idealized diode model predicts a reverse current resulting from the thermal generation of carriers near the junction, which is sensibly independent of the reverse-bias voltage and which increases nearly exponentially with temperature. Most diodes have reverse current in excess of that predicted by the idealized model because of surface leakage effects and also because of carrier generation in the space-charge layer.

Surface leakage occurs because the entire reverse-bias voltage is developed across the space-charge layer, thereby producing very large electric fields at the surface as well as in the volume. Surface leakage mechanisms are complicated and not well understood.

They may involve ionic conduction and may also depend on surface conditions which vary with the history of the device. In any case, surface leakage produces a reverse current which increases with reverse bias and which is usually less temperature-dependent than the volume saturation current. Improvements in the device fabrication art have tended to minimize the importance of surface leakage in modern devices.

Under reverse-bias conditions, nearly all of the space-charge layer is depleted of mobile carriers. Therefore, the rate of generation of carriers is essentially equal to the rate at which carriers are generated by thermal mechanisms, which is, of course, independent of bias voltage. The total current accounted for by generation in the space-charge layer is proportional to the rate of generation and to the volume of the space-charge layer. Consequently, this reverse-current component has the same dependence on $-V$ as does the width of the space-charge layer, and falls in the range of $(-V)^{\frac{1}{2}}$ for abrupt junctions to $(-V)^{\frac{1}{3}}$ for graded junctions. This current is also less temperature-sensitive than the volume saturation current because the rate of generation in the space-charge layer increases less rapidly with temperature than does the corresponding rate in the neutral regions.

These deviations from reverse-current saturation, and the corresponding anomalous temperature dependence of the reverse current, are more apparent in silicon devices than in germanium diodes. In most germanium diodes at room temperature the volume saturation currents dominate the reverse current. However, in germanium devices at low temperatures and in silicon diodes, these volume currents, which are proportional to n_i^2, are smaller so that surface currents and space-charge layer currents can be observed. These effects are summarized in Fig. 4.2, which illustrates the voltage dependence and the temperature dependence of the reverse current of typical germanium and silicon diodes.

Inasmuch as the reverse current of a real diode may exceed that calculated on the basis of our idealized model, better agreement between the V-I relationship of a real diode and the idealized diode equation (Eq. 3.19) in the *forward-bias region* can often be obtained by deducing I_s from the measured forward characteristics rather than the measured reverse characteristics. The other components of the junction current are less important when very much in for-

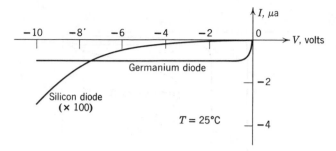

(a) Reverse-bias diode characteristics

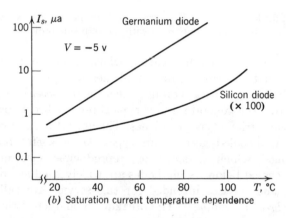

(b) Saturation current temperature dependence

Fig. 4.2. Deviations from reverse-current saturation and anomalous temperature dependence of the saturation current caused by surface leakage and carrier generation in the space-charge layer. Note that the current scale is expanded by a factor of 100 for the silicon diode.

ward bias, where carrier injection into the bulk neutral regions dominates.

4.4 JUNCTION BREAKDOWN

In all real diodes there is a limiting value of reverse voltage beyond which the reverse current increases greatly without significant increase of reverse voltage. In poorly cooled germanium diodes, particularly those using point contacts or small wire con-

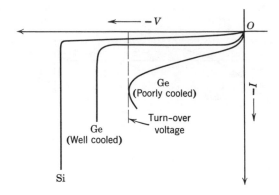

Fig. 4.3. Types of diode breakdown. The current scale of the silicon diode has been greatly expanded to permit comparison with the germanium diodes.

tacts, the effect is complicated by heating, which raises the satura-tion current so that the curves, on actual measurement, have a negative slope beyond a critical voltage called the *turn-over voltage.*

Figure 4.3 shows the general form of typical reverse breakdown characteristics for various types of diodes. The abrupt breakdown of silicon and well-cooled germanium types has a useful non-destructive range, which depends on reproducible electronic mechanisms discussed below. Such diodes are widely used as volt-age regulators, and devices intended for this service are called *Zener diodes* or *breakdown diodes.* The breakdown characteristic of point contact or poorly cooled wire-contact germanium diodes is usually outside the desirable operating range of the device because of the high temperature at the junction.

There are two electronic breakdown mechanisms in the bulk semiconductor which can cause a voltage-saturated breakdown—Zener breakdown, and avalanche breakdown. Zener breakdown is a direct disruption of interatomic bonds in the space-charge layer by very high electric fields (greater than 10^6 volts/cm), which produces mobile hole-electron pairs. It is the mechanism of breakdown in good crystalline insulators and it occurs in abrupt junctions be-tween highly doped regions. Avalanche breakdown occurs when the acceleration of carriers in the space-charge region is great enough to cause ionizing collisions with atoms, thus producing mobile hole-electron pairs. Since avalanche multiplication can occur at electric fields appreciably lower than those required for Zener breakdown, avalanche breakdown will occur before the Zener voltage can be reached, except in diodes with very large impurity concentrations. Silicon voltage-regulator diodes which break down above 8 volts probably use the avalanche mechanism, whereas those which break down below 5 volts work by Zener breakdown. Between 8 and 5 volts the dominating mechanism depends on the exact impurity distribution at the junction. Both mechanisms can be present in the same diode. Note that the term *Zener diode* is often used without regard to the mechanism to identify a diode intended to operate at breakdown.

4.4.1 *Theory of Avalanche Multiplication*

Avalanche multiplication occurs when the electric field in the space-charge layer is large enough so that carriers traversing the region acquire sufficient energy to break covalent bonds in their collisions with the crystal structure. Every such ionizing collision produces a hole and an electron, each of which is accelerated by the field and has a possibility of producing another ionizing collision before it leaves the space-charge region. Neglecting recombination in the layer, all the carriers produced will contribute to the total reverse current.

The total current is then a multiplication within the space-charge region of a primary current of carriers traversing some or all of the region. In germanium diodes, as in the idealized diode model of Chapter 3, the primary current originates outside the space-charge region. For many silicon diodes most of the primary current is produced by generation inside the region. If the primary current is I_s, the total reverse current is $I_s M$, where M is a multiplying factor which depends on the rate at which carriers have ionizing collisions. If $I = I_s M$ is to remain finite, M must be finite, and thus the average rate at which the hole and electron pair produced by an ionizing collision produces another pair must be less than unity in the sense discussed below.

We illustrate the mechanism of avalanche multiplication by considering a diode where most of the saturation current consists of holes collected from the n-type region ($N_D \ll N_A$). On the average, each hole from the n-type region produces P_{1h} pairs of holes and electrons in traversing the space-charge region. Each secondary hole-electron pair produces, *on the average*, P_2 additional pairs, each of which in turn produces, on the average, P_2 additional pairs, and so forth. Consequently, the total current is:

$$I = I_s[1 + P_{1h}(1 + P_2 + P_2{}^2 + P_2{}^3 \cdots)] \qquad (4.4)$$

The series $P_{1h} (1 + P_2 + P_2{}^2 + P_2{}^3 + \cdots)$ converges (because $P_2 < 1$) so that

$$M = \frac{I}{I_s} = \frac{1 + P_{1h} - P_2}{1 - P_2} \qquad (N_A \gg N_D) \qquad (4.5a)$$

A similar multiplication factor given by

$$M = \frac{1 + P_{1e} - P_2}{1 - P_2} \qquad (N_D \gg N_A) \qquad (4.5b)$$

can be calculated for diodes where $N_D \gg N_A$ and the primary carriers supplied by the saturation current are electrons collected from the p-type region. In both cases, M approaches infinity when P_2 approaches unity.

We define the avalanche breakdown voltage of a junction as $-V_a$, the voltage at which M is infinite. Experiments on asymmetrically doped abrupt junctions in silicon and germanium show that V_a decreases as the doping on the lightly doped side increases, as shown in Fig. 4.4. These experiments show that V_a depends on the impurity concentration on the lightly doped side, but is independent of whether it is n-type or p-type. This seems plausible because P_2 is a property of a secondary hole-electron pair and not of the type of primary carrier.

The dependence of breakdown voltage on the impurity concentration of the lightly doped side of the junction can be understood from the space-charge layer analysis of Sec. 2.3. The data of Fig. 4.4 are obtained from diodes with highly asymmetrical doping, so that the portion of the depleted region on the highly doped side is negligible compared to the portion on the lightly doped side. A carrier traversing the entire depleted region then has most of its path length in the lightly doped region. Consequently, the average rate at which it has ionizing collisions with the lattice depends on the field strength and path length in the lightly doped side.

Equations 2.13 and 2.14 describe the maximum field and the widths of the depleted regions. They include the equilibrium

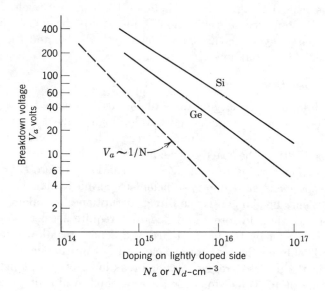

Fig. 4.4. Avalanche breakdown voltage versus impurity concentration for asymmetrically doped step junctions (from S. L. Miller, *Phys. Rev.*, **93**, p. 1238, 1955; and **105**, p. 1248, 1957).

built-in voltage ψ_0, which is less than 1 volt in most diodes and thus negligible compared with V over most of the range of voltage plotted in Fig. 4.4. If we neglect ψ_0 and assume highly asymmetrical doping in which the p-type side is much more heavily doped than the n-type side:

$$\mathcal{E}_0 \cong - \left[\frac{2qN_D}{\epsilon} (-V) \right]^{1/2}$$

$$l_n \cong \left[\frac{2\epsilon}{qN_D} (-V) \right]^{1/2}$$

(4.6a,b)

From Eq. 4.6a we can see that the breakdown voltage would vary inversely with the impurity concentration on the lightly doped side if the avalanche breakdown phenomenon were characterized by a certain critical field. However, Fig. 4.4 shows that V_a does not fall as fast as $1/N$, which demonstrates that the average rate at which pairs are produced by impact ionization depends not only on the electric field, but also on the distance the carrier travels. Thus when the impurity concentration is increased, the width of the space-charge layer decreases, as shown by Eq. 4.6b, and the peak electric field at breakdown increases.

4.4.2 *Zener Breakdown*

Diodes with very large values of impurity concentration have narrow space-charge regions and develop high fields at low applied voltage. As the reverse voltage increases, both the electric field and the width of the space-charge layer increase. The field reaches a large enough value to cause Zener breakdown before the width of the space-charge region is sufficient to permit avalanche break-down. Zener breakdown is the direct disruption of covalent bonds by the electric field force, and does not require acceleration of a primary carrier by the field. Hence, the Zener breakdown voltage depends only on the maximum field and not on the length of the path in the depleted region. Zener breakdown occurs at fields of the order of 10^6 volts/cm, which are reached in abrupt junctions in silicon when the doping is about 10^{18} atoms/cm^3 and the reverse bias is about 5 volts. In such a diode, both Zener and avalanche

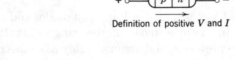

Definition of positive V and I

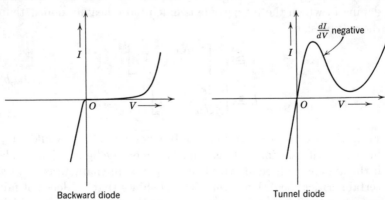

Backward diode   Tunnel diode

Fig. 4.5. Backward and tunnel diode V-I characteristics.

breakdown occur simultaneously. As the doping is further increased, the path length at breakdown drops, and only the Zener mechanism prevails. A calculation for diodes with doping of 10^{18} atoms/cm^3 or greater cannot neglect the built-in voltage, ψ_0. Thus, for a silicon diode with an N_D of 10^{18} donor atoms/cm^3 and an N_A of 10^{19} acceptor atoms/cm^3, the built-in potential ψ_0 calculated from Eq. 2.8 is 1 volt. If we calculate the maximum field $\mathcal{E}_0$ for this diode from Eq. 2.13b, with 4 volts of reverse bias, we find a field of 1.2×10^6 volts/cm. Such a diode has a Zener breakdown at about 4 volts reverse bias. At these high doping levels the built-in voltage is a significant fraction of the breakdown voltage. As doping level increases, it becomes a larger part of $\psi_0 + (-V)$.

A very reasonable question at this point is whether N_A and N_D can be increased to a point where the field associated with the built-in potential barrier, ψ_0, *alone* will cause Zener breakdown so that the diode will be a short circuit with no applied voltage. While we have not studied the theory needed to understand such devices in detail, they do indeed exist. Diodes which break down at $V = 0$, or at slight reverse bias, are called *backward diodes* because they conduct by Zener breakdown with small reverse voltage, but do not begin to show much normal diode forward conduction until an appreciable fraction of a volt of forward bias is applied. Hence, over a small voltage range, they appear like diodes which conduct when the n-type side is made positive. More heavily doped diodes which are still in breakdown with some forward bias are called *Esaki* or *tunnel diodes*. Until enough forward bias is applied they conduct well, as though still in breakdown. As forward bias increases, a point is reached at which $(\psi_0 - V)$ no longer is large enough to provide the conducting mechanism and forward current *falls* with increasing forward bias. Consequently, there is a negative resistance region. The current falls to a low value and then rises as the diode enters the region of normal conduction. Figure 4.5 shows the V-I characteristics of backward and tunnel diodes.

4.5 OHMIC CONTACTS

The idealized pn-junction diode model assumed that the metal contacts which afford external connection to the semiconductor provide no barrier to majority-carrier flow in either direction, so that there is no appreciable change in the height of the contact potential barrier at the metal-semiconductor interface in the presence of current. The practical device-fabrication art can approximate such contacts, known as *ohmic contacts*. They are by no means the only type of metal-semiconductor contact, and it is possible to produce contacts with rectifying properties similar to those of a *pn* junction.*

The difference between an ohmic contact and a rectifying contact can be understood in terms of the contact potential difference between the metal and the semiconductor. Just as at a *pn* junction, a contact potential must exist at a metal-semiconductor interface to oppose the diffusive tendencies that result from the differences in composition. Unlike the contact potential at a *pn* junction, how-ever, the contact potential at a metal-semiconductor interface may have either polarity, depending on both the type of metal and the conductivity type of the semiconductor.†

Thus, if a metal in contact with an *n*-type semiconductor has a lower electrostatic potential than does the semiconductor, the built-in electric field associated with the contact potential barrier must originate on positive charge in the semiconductor and termi-nate on negative charge in the metal, as shown in Fig. 4.6a. Such a dipole charge distribution is created by *depletion* of the conduction electron population in the *n*-type semiconductor near the interface, leaving behind positively charged donor ions. This situation is reminiscent of the space-charge layer at a *pn* junction, in that both regions are nearly depleted of mobile charge. Because of the scarcity of mobile charge in the semiconductor near the interface, a metal-semiconductor junction of the depleting type has rectifying properties.

If a different metal having a positive contact potential with respect to the *n*-type semiconductor is used, the built-in electric field at the interface is directed from the metal to the semiconduc-tor. The positive charge on which this field originates is provided

* Experiments on various semiconductor contacts are described in ISP, Ap-pendix, Sec. 5.

† The *V-I* characteristics of metal-semiconductor contacts are investigated in the SEEC film entitled *Minority Carriers in Semiconductors*, by J. R. Haynes and W. Shockley. Arrangements for the distribution of SEEC films are de-scribed in the Foreword.

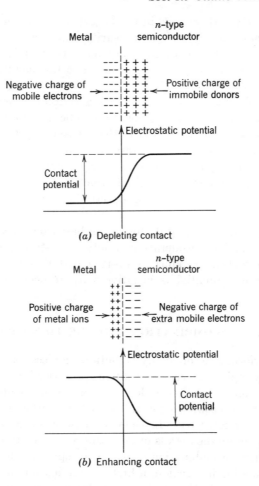

(a) Depleting contact

(b) Enhancing contact

Fig 4.6. Contact potentials and space charge at metal-semiconductor contacts.

by the metal ions while the negative charge on which this field terminates is produced by *enhancement* of the electron concentration in the semiconductor, as shown in Fig. 4.6*b*. The portion of the space-charge layer which lies in the metal is nearly depleted of electrons. However, this region is extremely thin because the charge density provided by the metal ions is very large. The semiconductor portion of the space-charge layer at an enhancing contact is well supplied with mobile carriers, and large currents can flow with relatively little change in the height of the contact potential barrier. Consequently, any nonlinearity which exists in the *V-I* characteristic of the metal-semiconductor contact is usually unimportant because operation is confined to the small region near the origin.

If a metal which gives an enhancing contact is not available, the resistance of the depleting contact can be minimized by doping the layer of semiconductor next to the contact very heavily, which causes the depth, and thus the resistance, of the depleted layer to drop. This technique of making a nearly ohmic contact is widely employed and is considered good practice. Alloyed contacts in which the alloy contains an appropriate impurity are good examples of this technique.

Although the preceding discussion is based on an *n*-type semiconductor, similar considerations apply for *p*-type material. Enhancing contacts are produced on *p*-type material by using a metal whose contact potential is negative with respect to the *p*-type semiconductor.

4.6 SURFACE RECOMBINATION AND THE THIN-BASE DIODE

The performance of many junction devices is significantly affected by regions of very low minority-carrier lifetime. In some cases, the volume lifetime is low over an entire region. In other cases, the high recombination rates occur at surfaces or at metal-semiconductor interfaces. In each of these cases it is often convenient to ignore the details of flow and recombination within the region of high recombination rate and to represent the total effect of recombination in a region of high recombination or at a surface by defining an *effective surface recombination velocity* S_r. If the excess minority-carrier concentration at a surface is p_n', then the minority carrier *particle* current density flowing *into* that surface is $S_r p_n'$. The *surface* in question may be either an actual surface of the semiconductor or the boundary between a region of high recombination and the rest of the semiconductor. The parameter S_r, which has the dimension of a velocity, describes the recombination rate at a surface in the same manner that the lifetime τ describes the recombination process in a volume of semiconductor. If p_n' is negative, the recombination velocity at the surface determines the rate at which carriers are generated at the surface.

The concept of surface recombination velocity occurs in a structure referred to as the *thin-base diode*. One or both of the neutral regions in such a device is so thin (measured with respect to a diffusion length) that most of the excess carriers injected at the junction survive until they reach the metal-semiconductor contact where they disappear by recombination in the thin high-recombination region associated with the contact. A structure of this type is shown in Fig. 4.7a. We consider first the thin n-type region between the junction and the contact. The excess concentration $p_n'(0)$ at the junction space-charge layer edge is established by the bias voltage applied to the junction. We assume that recombination in the thin n-type region is negligible compared with recombination at the surface between the n-type region and the contact, and characterize that recombination by a surface recombination velocity. Under static conditions the hole current must therefore be constant everywhere in the n-type region, so that the hole concentration gradient is constant, and has the value:

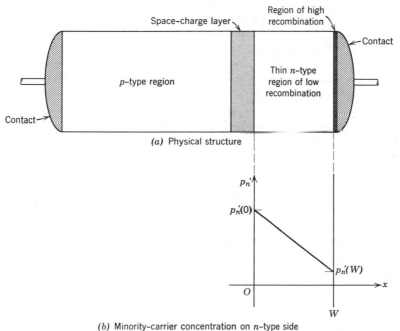

(a) Physical structure

(b) Minority-carrier concentration on n-type side

Fig. 4.7. The thin-base diode in which the thin n-type region is terminated in a region of high recombination.

$$\frac{dp_n'}{dx} = -\frac{p_n'(0) - p_n'(W)}{W} \tag{4.7}$$

where $p_n'(W)$ is the excess hole concentration at the high-recombination surface, as shown in Fig. 4.7b. The hole current density absorbed by the surface at $x = W$ is, from our definition for S_r:

$$J_h(W) = qS_r p_n'(W) \tag{4.8}$$

The diffusion current in the thin n-type region is:

$$J_h = -qD_h \frac{dp_n'}{dx} \tag{4.9}$$

Equating the diffusion current to the surface recombination current, and using Eq. 4.7 yields:

$$qD_h \frac{p_n'(0) - p_n'(W)}{W} = qS_r p_n'(W) \tag{4.10}$$

which can be solved for $p_n'(W)$ and J_h

$$p_n'(W) = \frac{(D_h/W)p_n'(0)}{D_h/W + S_r}$$

$$J_h = q\,\frac{p_n'(0)}{W/D_h + 1/S_r} \tag{4.11a,b}$$

The excess concentration $p_n'(0)$ at the space-charge layer edge is determined by the bias voltage in accordance with Eq. 3.11. Consequently, the hole current-voltage relationship for the thin-base diode is:

$$I_h = \frac{qA p_{no}}{W/D_h + 1/S_r}\,(e^{qV/kT} - 1) \tag{4.12}$$

The complete V-I relationship of the thin-base diode is obtained by adding the electron current injected into the p-type region to the hole current given by Eq. 4.12.

REFERENCE

4.1 A. K. Jonscher, *Principles of Semiconductor Device Operation*, 1960, John Wiley and Sons, New York, Chapters 2 and 4.

PROBLEMS

P4.1 Assuming that Zener breakdown occurs when the peak electric field in the space-charge layer reaches 10^6 volts/cm, estimate the doping concentration of a *symmetrical* $(N_A = N_D = N)$ germanium diode which exhibits Zener breakdown at 3 volts reverse bias.

P4.2 This problem is concerned with the minority carrier distributions and currents in the n-type region of the diode shown in Fig. 4.7a, and treats the case in which the width W of the thin region is large enough so that recombination in that region cannot be neglected. To simplify the algebra, assume that the effective surface recombination velocity S_r at $x = W$ is so large that the excess hole concentration at $x = W$ is equal to zero regardless of $p_n{}'(0)$. That is, assume that $p_n{}'(W) = 0$.

   (a) Solve the diffusion equation for holes in the n-type region for the case in which volume recombination is *not* negligible. Designate the excess concentration at $x = 0$ (the edge of the space-charge layer) as $p_n{}'(0)$.

   (b) Determine the hole current at $x = 0$ and at $x = W$. Why is $J_h(W)$ less than $J_h(0)$?

   (c) Show that your results for $p_n{}'(x)$ and $J_h(x)$ reduce to Eqs. 3.14 and 3.15 if $W \gg L_h$, but reduce to Eqs. 4.11 (with $S_r \to \infty$) if $W \ll L_h$.

The following *three* problems are based upon the configuration shown in Fig. 4.8.

Assumptions:

1. The diode is one-dimensional, of area A.
2. There is no recombination, *except* at the contacts at $x = \pm W$.
3. The surface recombination velocity at $x = \pm W$ is infinite, i.e., there are no *excess* carriers at $x = \pm W$.
4. All the diffusion constants are equal to D.
5. $N_O = N_A = N_D \gg n_i$, i.e., the material is strongly extrinsic.
6. The space-charge layer width is much less than W.

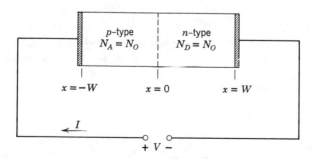

Fig. 4.8.

P4.3 For the diode described in Fig. 4.8, determine the dc volt-ampere characteristic $I = I(V)$ under low-level injection conditions.

P4.4 For the diode described in Fig. 4.8 compute the series resistance R_s, as defined by Eq. 4.3. Show that your result can be interpreted very simply in terms of the bulk resistance of the neutral regions. Would this interpretation be possible if the electron diffusion constant were different from the hole diffusion constant?

P4.5 The diode described in connection with Fig. 4.8 has a narrow beam of light applied to the n-type side at $x = W/2$. This light beam produces G_o hole-electron pairs per unit area per unit time in a slab of negligibly small width which is parallel to the junction. Assume low-level injection.

(a) If the terminals are *short-circuited* (i.e., $V = 0$, sketch and dimension the carrier concentrations in the neutral regions of the diode.

(b) Under the same conditions used in part (a , sketch and dimension the drift and diffusion components of the hole and electron currents.

(c) What is the magnitude and direction of the current I under *short-circuit* conditions?

(d) What is the magnitude and polarity of the voltage V under *open-circuit* conditions?

P4.6 The measurements tabulated below apply to a silicon diode at room temperature.

Diode voltage V, mv	Diode current I, μa
+250	+12.3
260	17.9
270	26.7
280	40.0
290	59.0
300	90.1
310	134
320	203
330	300
340	445
350	675

(a) Do these data fit the idealized diode equation? *Suggestion*: Plot $\log I$ versus V.

(b) What is the saturation current I_s?

5

Dynamic Behavior of
pn-Junction Diodes

5.0 DYNAMIC EFFECTS IN DIODES

In this chapter we investigate the performance of *pn*-junction diodes with time-dependent voltages and currents. There are two reasons why the dynamic behavior of a diode differs from the static or dc behavior considered in Chapter 3. First, under dynamic conditions, portions of the minority-carrier currents injected across the space-charge layer are associated with *changes* in the concentrations of excess carriers stored in the neutral regions. This is in contrast to the dc situation where *all* the injected currents are associated with the recombination or generation of excess carriers. Second, whenever the junction voltage changes with time, there must be an additional component of terminal current which causes changes in the dipole layer of space charge that straddles the metallurgical junction. This current is accounted for by the flow of majority carriers in the neutral regions and appears as a *displacement current* at the center of the space-charge layer. This current is frequently the dominant component of the diode current under ac reverse-bias conditions. It is usually masked by injected minority-carrier currents under forward-bias conditions. We consider first the dynamics of excess minority carriers and then take up dynamic effects in the space-charge layer.

In our discussion of time-dependent minority-carrier phenomena, we focus attention on holes in the n-type region. We assume that the p-type region is doped much more heavily than the n-type region, so that the total current associated with minority carrier injection in this *asymmetric diode* is approximately equal to the injected hole current. The behavior of electrons in the p-type region is entirely analogous to that of the holes in the n-type region. In diodes where both hole and electron currents at the space-charge layer are important, the component currents are simply added, as in Sec. 3.3.

5.1 THE DYNAMICS OF EXCESS MINORITY CARRIERS

The distribution and flow of the excess holes in the homogeneous n-type region is governed by the minority-carrier diffusion equation. It is, from Sec. 3.2.1:

$$D_h \frac{\partial^2 p_n'}{\partial x^2} = \frac{\partial p_n'}{\partial t} + \frac{p_n'}{\tau_h} \qquad (5.1)$$

The hole-current density is proportional to the gradient of the excess hole concentration because minority carriers move solely by diffusion in homogeneous material under low-level injection conditions. That is,

$$J_h = -qD_h \frac{\partial p_n'}{\partial x} \qquad (5.2)$$

The excess hole concentration at the space-charge layer edge $(x = 0)$ is related to the junction voltage v.* We assume that the relationships derived in Sec. 2.3.3, on the basis of quasi-equilibrium in the space-charge layer, are valid under dynamic conditions. That is, on the n-type side:

$$p_n'(0) = p_{no}(e^{qv/kT} - 1) \qquad (5.3)$$

---

* Lower-case symbols (small letters) for *terminal* voltage and current designate instantaneous values of time-dependent quantities, while corresponding upper-case symbols (capital letters) denote dc steady-state quantities.

Although this result was obtained on the basis of static considerations, it holds for time-dependent conditions if the voltage does not change too rapidly. Carriers move through the space-charge layer at speeds approaching the mean thermal speed, because the concentration gradients and the electric field in the space-charge layer are enormous. Inasmuch as the mean thermal speed of carriers at room temperature is about 10^7 cm/sec, and the width of the space-charge layer is usually less than 10^{-4} cm, the time required for a carrier to traverse the layer is, at most, of the order of 10^{-11} sec. The two-way random flow of carriers throughout the space-charge layer, on which Eq. 5.3 is based, is not impeded if the times during which the voltage changes are long compared with this transit time.

The excess carrier concentration at the other boundary of the neutral region is determined by the diode structure. If the contact is several diffusion lengths away from the junction, the excess concentration must approach zero for large x, as in Eq. 3.12. On the other hand, if the contact is near the junction, the boundary condition at the contact involves a proportionality between hole current and excess hole concentration. This boundary condition can be expressed in terms of an effective surface recombination velocity, as in Eq. 4.8.

The minority carrier diffusion equation can readily be solved once the current (which fixes $\left.\dfrac{\partial p_n'}{\partial x}\right|_{x=0}$ through Eq. 5.2) or the voltage (which fixes $p_n'(0)$ through Eq. 5.3) is specified. Unfortunately, the closed-form solution is expressed in functions which may be unfamiliar and difficult to visualize (e.g., error functions). Therefore, in this book we will not obtain exact solutions, but will discuss several general conclusions about diode dynamics and investigate two important classes of problems qualitatively and with approximate techniques.

One general conclusion is apparent from Eqs. 5.2 and 5.3. It is possible to change the injected current rapidly because this requires only a change in the *slope* of the excess hole distribution at $x = 0$. A slope change can occur quite rapidly because it requires the motion of very few holes. On the other hand, the diode voltage cannot be changed rapidly without enormous currents because a voltage change requires a change in the *concentration* of excess holes at $x = 0$. If the concentration at the space-charge layer edge changes so rapidly that the change is not propagated into the neutral region by diffusive transport, the slope at $x = 0$, and thus the current, will be very large. Therefore, the relationship between the injected hole current and the junction voltage is similar to the current-voltage relationship of a capacitor, in that the current can change rapidly without large voltage changes, whereas large voltage changes must be accomplished slowly unless a large current can be supported. This loose analogy cannot in general be developed further because of the essential nonlinearity of the diode and because the excess holes are distributed over a portion of the neutral region several diffusion lengths wide.

We may gain additional insight into the consequences of the diffusion equation by casting that equation in a different form. If Eq. 5.1 is multiplied by $qA\,dx$, where A is the cross-sectional area of the diode, and is integrated with respect to x over the n-type region, we obtain:

$$qAD_h\left[\frac{\partial p_n{}'}{\partial x}(W) - \frac{\partial p_n{}'}{\partial x}(0)\right] = \frac{d}{dt}\int_0^W qAp_n{}'\,dx$$

$$+\frac{1}{\tau_h}\int_0^W qAp_n{}'\,dx \quad (5.4)$$

where $x = W$ denotes the location of the contact. If we use Eq. 5.2 for the hole current, this result becomes:

$$A[J_h(0) - J_h(W)] = \frac{dq_h}{dt} + \frac{q_h}{\tau_h} \quad (5.5)$$

where

$$q_h = \int_0^W qAp_n{}'\,dx \quad (5.6)$$

denotes the *total excess hole charge* stored in the neutral region, which extends from $x = 0$ to $x = W$. Equation 5.5 states simply that the net rate of influx of hole charge into the neutral region, which is $A[J_h(0) - J_h(W)]$, equals the rate at which the stored hole charge increases plus the rate at which holes vanish by recombination. In other words, holes which are injected into the neutral region across the space-charge layer at $x = 0$ either augment the *store* of excess holes in the region, or vanish by recombination in the region, or flow out at the contact $(x = W)$.* Of course, if the contact is far removed, no holes flow out there because both the excess hole concentration and its gradient are zero at the contact.

The result expressed by Eq. 5.5 is simply a restatement of the continuity relationship for holes, and could have been used as the basic formulation of that important physical principle. Although the relationship between the diode current $i = AJ_h(0)$ and the total hole store q_h is a simple one indeed, this simplicity does not extend to the relationship between i and the diode voltage v because q_h is not uniquely related to v, except under static conditions when q_h is proportional to $p_n'(0)$.

We now consider two problems of diode dynamics which are governed by the time-dependent distribution and flow of minority carriers. The first of these involves the response of the diode to large excursions of voltage and current, as in pulse circuits and computer switching applications. The second is concerned with the response of the diode to small sinusoidal voltage perturbations.

5.2 JUNCTION DIODE SWITCHING TRANSIENTS

In many practical circuits the transient drive applied to a junction diode is provided by a source whose Thevenin equivalent output impedance is very large. Therefore, we will investigate diode turn-on and turn-off transients, assuming that the diode current is constrained by the circuit in which the diode is connected. In addition, we base our discussion on a "long-base" diode in which the contact is several diffusion lengths away from the junction. Similar considerations hold for thin-base diodes.

5.2.1 *Turn-on Transient*

We consider the circuit shown in Fig. 5.1. The symbol used to represent the diode is standard notation. The arrow points in the direction of easy current flow, i.e., from p-type to n-type. For $t < 0$, the switch is open and the diode is in equilibrium at zero bias. When the switch closes at $t = 0$, the diode forward current

---

* Most contacts represent surfaces of high recombination. Consequently, holes which "flow out" at the contact actually vanish by recombining with majority carriers there. Nevertheless, this current represents a flow out of the n-type neutral region which must be accounted for explicitly in Eq. 5.5.

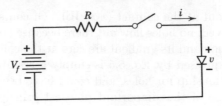

Fig. 5.1. Circuit used in discussing the turn-on transient of a diode.

immediately increases to I_f. Inasmuch as the diode forward-voltage drop is assumed to be small compared with V_f, the current I_f is approximately equal to V_f/R. At $t = 0$, $\dfrac{\partial p_n{}'}{\partial x}\bigg|_{x=0}$ assumes the value $-I_f/qAD_h$, dictated by Eq. 5.2, and stays constant thereafter. (A is the cross-sectional area of the diode.) Figure 5.2 shows the spatial distribution of p_n at various intervals of time after

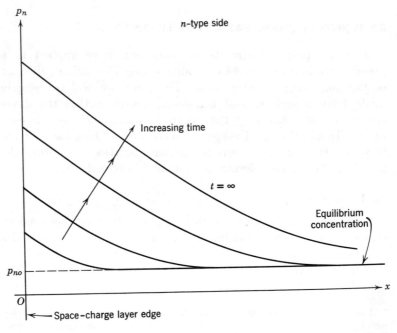

Fig. 5.2. The hole distribution in the *n*-type region of a diode during the transient following application of a constant forward current.

$t = 0$. The constant current of holes flows in at $x = 0$ and diffuses into the n-type region. Early in the turn-on process most of the holes which flow in increase the store of holes because the recombination term, q_h/τ_h, is small when q_h is low. When the hole store approaches its static value, most of the input current must supply recombination, and the fraction going into storage decreases. The region close to $x = 0$ rises toward its equilibrium hole concentration more rapidly than deeper regions. The diode voltage depends

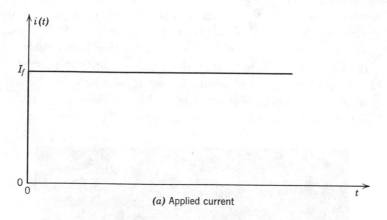

(a) Applied current

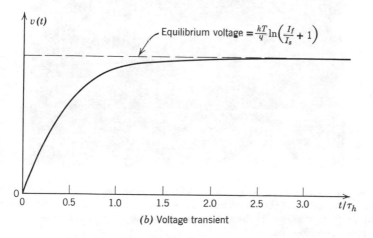

(b) Voltage transient

Fig. 5.3. The turn-on transient for an idealized junction diode.

on $p_n'(0)$ through Eq. 5.3. Figure 5.3 is a plot of v versus t/τ_h obtained by applying Eq. 5.3 to an exact solution of Eq. 5.1. It shows that there is an initial rapid rise of v through most of its excursion, followed by a much slower approach to equilibrium as the regions remote from $x = 0$ approach their final values of excess concentration.

Although we have described the turn-on transient in terms of the minority-carrier holes, electron currents exist as well. The current from the terminal applied to the n-type region is made up of electrons flowing in to supply recombination, and of electrons required to neutralize the charge of the increasing store of holes.

It is important to note that the voltage transient plotted in Fig. 5.3 is that of an idealized diode having negligible series resistance at the levels of current involved and operating under low-level injection conditions. Any series resistance, R_s, will produce an

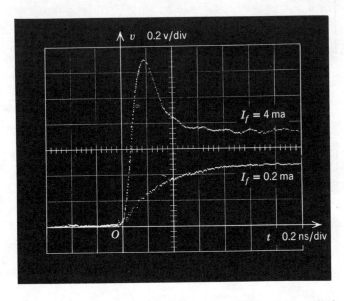

Fig. 5.4. Measured turn-on transients of an FD100 silicon planar diode. The initial rate of rise of the transient for $I_f = 4$ ma, which shows the effect of conductivity modulation, is limited by the rise-time of the pulse generator and sampling oscilloscope.

instantaneous step of voltage of magnitude $I_f R_s$ added to the plot of Fig. 5.3. More important, useful operating points for many real diodes exceed the low-level injection assumption. In such diodes, the excess majority-carrier concentration, which increases in order to balance the excess minority-carrier concentration, provides additional carriers for majority-carrier drift flow, and hence reduces at least a portion of the series resistance as the minority-carrier concentration increases. This phenomenon is called *conductivity modulation*. Conductivity-modulated diodes show a voltage turn-on transient quite different from that of Fig. 5.3, with an initial voltage rise due to series resistance, which *decreases* with time as the minority-carrier store increases and penetrates the n-type region. Typical measured turn-on transients illustrating this effect are shown in Fig. 5.4.

5.2.2 *Turn-off Transient*

We consider the circuit shown in Fig. 5.5, in which the switch is in position 1 for $t < 0$ and the diode is in the dc steady state with $i = I_f \cong V_f/R$. At $t = 0$, the switch changes to position 2. For large values of R, the diode current is again constrained by the circuit and is nearly equal to $-V_r/R$. That is:

$$i = \begin{cases} I_f \cong V_f/R & t < 0 \\ -I_r \cong -V_r/R & t \geq 0 \end{cases} \tag{5.7}$$

Inasmuch as the diode is in a steady state with $i = I_f$ for $t < 0$, the excess hole distribution falls off exponentially in the x-direction from a value of $I_f L_h/qAD_h$ at $x = 0$, as shown in the top curve of Fig. 5.6. At $t = 0$ the diode current reverses and becomes $-I_r$. The only instantaneous change is a reversal of $\partial p_n'/\partial x$ at $x = 0$

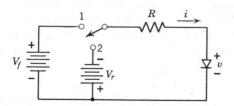

Fig. 5.5. Circuit used in discussing the turn-off transient of a diode.

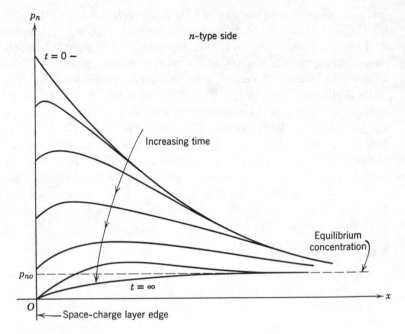

Fig. 5.6. The hole distributions in the n-type region of a diode during the turn-off transient following application of a reverse current.

from $-I_f/qAD_h$ to I_r/qAD_h. The reverse current across the junction consists of holes being withdrawn from the n-type region into the p-type region. Initially there can be little change in $p_n'(0)$, and hence little change in v. The diode remains with a forward-bias voltage, although the current has reversed. Figure 5.6 shows successive plots of p_n as time proceeds. The hole concentration slope at $x = 0$ remains fixed, but the hole concentration declines everywhere, because holes are being removed across the junction and because they are recombining everywhere at the rate p_n'/τ_h. At some point in time, $p_n'(0)$ drops to zero and v reverses. Some time later, there is an insufficient hole store to support the hole concentration slope I_r/qAD_h at $x = 0$ and I_r cannot be maintained. A true current supply for I_r would then force $-v$ to its reverse breakdown value. A supply of moderate voltage and internal resistance such as that shown in Fig. 5.5 delivers less current as $-v$ rises. Figure 5.7 illustrates the form of the electrical turn-off transient when I_r is supplied through a resistor from a voltage source whose open circuit voltage is less than the diode breakdown voltage. After some time, the voltage reverses and $-v$ rises as reverse current drops. The reverse current does not drop to its steady-state value of I_s for some time, during which excess holes stored deep in the n-type region are being removed, and the charge stored in the space-charge layer is changing.

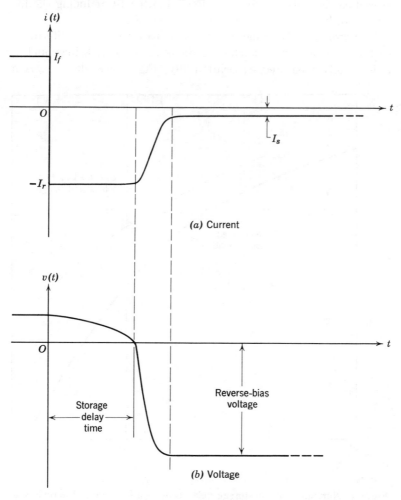

(a) Current

(b) Voltage

Fig. 5.7. The turn-off transient in a diode.

The period of time during which the diode voltage remains positive is called the *storage delay time*, t_s. This delay time, which occurs whenever a diode is switched from forward conduction to reverse bias, and which is a consequence of the storage of excess minority carriers in the neutral regions of the diode, is of great practical importance in the application of diodes in fast-switching circuits. The storage delay time can be reduced by removing the stored carriers faster, which is effected either by reducing the lifetime τ_h or by increasing the reverse current I_r.

The storage-delay time can be used to estimate the lifetime τ_h of the semiconductor of which a diode is fabricated, inasmuch as t_s is readily measured experimentally. Figure 5.8 shows t_s/τ_h as

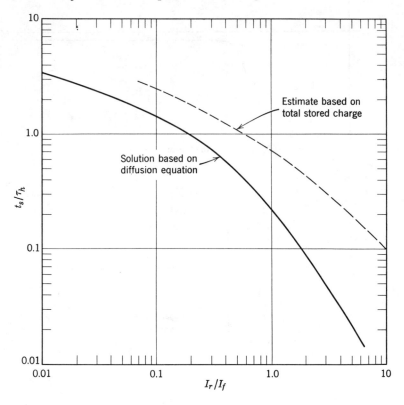

Fig. 5.8. Normalized diode storage delay-time as a function of the reverse-to-forward current ratio (asymmetrically doped junction with $N_A \gg N_D$).

a function of I_r/I_f. It was obtained from an exact solution of Eq. 5.1 (see Reference 5.1). Figure 5.8 shows that, if only small values of I_r/I_f can be provided by the circuit, we must wait about $3\tau_h$ for v to reverse, but we can reduce t_s to $0.2\tau_h$ by providing $I_r = I_f$. A convenient method for the experimental estimation of τ_h is to measure t_s at $I_r/I_f = 0.2$, where $t_s = \tau_h$.

We can *estimate* the storage delay time of the idealized diode by using the formulation of the continuity relationship which puts the total stored charge in evidence, i.e., Eq. 5.5. The hole current at the contact, $J_h(W)$, is approximately zero because we are dealing with a long-base diode $(W \gg L_h)$. Consequently, for $t < 0$ we have:

$$I_f = AJ_h(0) = \frac{q_{hf}}{\tau_h} \qquad (5.8)$$

whereas for $0 \leqslant t < t_s$ we have:

$$-I_r = AJ_h(0) = \frac{dq_h}{dt} + \frac{q_h}{\tau_h} \qquad (5.9)$$

The general solution of this linear ordinary differential equation for q_h is:

$$q_h(t) = -I_r\tau_h + Ce^{-t/\tau_h} \qquad (5.10)$$

where C is a constant of integration. For $t = 0$, we must have q_h equal to q_{hf} (see Eq. 5.8) because the stored charge cannot change instantaneously. Thus C is determined and:

$$q_h(t) = \tau_h[-I_r + (I_f + I_r)e^{-t/\tau_h}] \qquad (5.11)$$

If the stored charge changed very slowly, the excess minority-carrier distribution would appear as a succession of steady states, i.e., exponentials in x. Furthermore, the diode voltage would change sign when $q_h = 0$ because under steady-state conditions $q_h = 0$ when $p_n'(0) = 0$. We can estimate the storage delay time by determining the time at which $q_h(t)$, given by Eq. 5.11, equals zero. The time thus determined is in excess of the actual storage delay time because the diode recovers before all of the stored charge is removed, as shown by Fig. 5.6. Solving Eq. 5.11 for the time at which $q_h = 0$ yields:

$$t_s = \tau_h \ln\left(1 + \frac{I_f}{I_r}\right) \qquad (5.12)$$

This approximate result is shown in Fig. 5.8 as the dotted curve for comparison with the accurate solution.

5.3 SMALL-SIGNAL SINUSOIDAL BEHAVIOR OF THE JUNCTION DIODE

If the diode voltage v contains an ac component, the excess hole concentration at $x = 0$, $p_n'(0)$, contains ac components. If the ac component of the voltage is small enough (less than 5 mv at room temperature; see Sec. 3.3.3), the incremental component of $p_n'(0)$ is directly proportional to the incremental component of the voltage. More precisely, if $v = V + \Delta v$, where V is the dc bias voltage and Δv is the ac component, $p_n'(0)$ is, from Eq. 5.3:

$$p_n'(0) = p_{no}[e^{q(V+\Delta v)/kT} - 1]$$

$$\simeq p_{no}[e^{qV/kT} - 1] + (p_{no}e^{qV/kT}) \frac{q\Delta v}{kT} \qquad (5.13)$$

The ac component of $p_n'(0)$ is given by the second term in this equation:

$$\Delta p_n'(0) \cong (p_{no}e^{qV/kT}) \frac{q\Delta v}{kT} \qquad \text{if} \qquad \Delta v \ll \frac{kT}{q} \qquad (5.14)$$

Clearly, if Δv is a sinusoid, $\Delta p_n'(0)$ will be sinusoidal and will have the same frequency. If we employ the conventional complex notation for sinusoids, the incremental component $\Delta p_n'(0)$ may be written as:

$$\Delta p_n'(0, t) = \text{Re}\,[\Delta P(0)e^{j\omega t}] \qquad (5.15)$$

where $\Delta P(0)$ is a complex amplitude and ω is the angular frequency of the sinusoidal component.

Inasmuch as the diffusion equation for excess minority carriers, Eq. 5.1, is *linear*, it must be satisfied separately by the dc and incremental components of $p_n'(x,t)$. Therefore, the incremental component $\Delta p_n'(x, t)$ must satisfy:

$$D_h \frac{\partial^2 \Delta p_n'}{\partial x^2} = \frac{\partial \Delta p_n'}{\partial t} + \frac{\Delta p_n'}{\tau_h} \qquad (5.16)$$

The incremental component of the excess hole concentration at $x = 0$ is sinusoidal. Because of the linearity of the diffusion equation, the incremental component of the excess hole concentration is sinusoidal for *all* values of x. That is,

$$\Delta p_n'(x, t) = \text{Re}\,[\Delta P(x)e^{j\omega t}] \qquad (5.17)$$

The magnitude and phase of $\Delta p_n'$ are functions of x, so that the complex amplitude $\Delta P(x)$ varies with position. This use of a position-dependent complex amplitude to represent a function of position and time whose time variation is sinusoidal is entirely analogous to conventional complex notation in networks. Instead of dealing with the complex amplitudes of a few node pair voltages or mesh currents we are concerned with the complex amplitude at all positions, which we designate as $\Delta P(x)$.

If we postpone the linear operation of taking the real part and substitute $\Delta P(x)e^{j\omega t}$ into Eq. 5.16 we obtain:

$$D_h \frac{d^2\Delta P(x)}{dx^2}\, e^{j\omega t} = \left(j\omega + \frac{1}{\tau_h}\right)\Delta P(x)e^{j\omega t} \qquad (5.18)$$

The *ordinary* differential equation which governs the complex amplitude $\Delta P(x)$ is thus:

$$D_h\tau_h \frac{d^2\Delta P}{dx^2} = (1 + j\omega\tau_h)\Delta P \qquad (5.19)$$

This ac diffusion equation is of particular interest because it has the same form as the dc diffusion equation (Eq. 3.7) if we replace the diffusion length $L_h = \sqrt{D_h\tau_h}$ with the *ac diffusion length* Λ_h, given by

$$\Lambda_h = \frac{L_h}{\sqrt{1 + j\omega\tau_h}} \qquad (5.20)$$

That is, Eq. 5.19 may be written as:

$$\Lambda_h{}^2 \frac{d^2\Delta P}{dx^2} = \Delta P \qquad (5.21)$$

which has a solution of the form:

$$\Delta P(x) = C_1 e^{-x/\Lambda_h} + C_2 e^{+x/\Lambda_h} \qquad (5.22)$$

If we write the reciprocal of the ac diffusion length as:

$$\frac{1}{\Lambda_h} = a + jb \qquad (5.23)$$

the complex amplitude ΔP has the form:

$$\Delta P(x) = C_1 e^{-ax - jbx} + C_2 e^{+ax + jbx} \qquad (5.24)$$

This result shows that the *magnitude* dependence of the complex amplitude of the ac component of the excess hole concentration is exponential in x, with a characteristic length determined by the real part of $1/\Lambda_h$. The *phase* dependence of ΔP is linear in x, with a phase constant determined by the imaginary part of $1/\Lambda_h$. Both the real part and the imaginary part of $1/\Lambda_h$ increase as ω increases. Consequently, the ac component of $p_n{'}$ decays with increasing x more rapidly at high frequencies than it does for low frequencies. If $\omega \gg 1/\tau_h$, the complex diffusion length Λ_h is approximately:

$$\Lambda_h \cong \sqrt{D_h/j\omega} \qquad \text{if} \qquad \omega \gg 1/\tau_h \qquad (5.25)$$

The real part of $1/\Lambda_h$ is then approximately $\sqrt{\omega/2D_h}$ so that the characteristic length which governs the exponential dependence of the magnitude of $\Delta P(x)$ is $\sqrt{2D_h/\omega}$ *which is independent of the lifetime* τ_h. That is, for high-frequency excitations, the magnitude of the ac component of the excess hole concentration decays exponentially with x at a rate which is much greater than that set by the diffusion length L_h, and which is independent of the recombination process.

The physical mechanism which accounts for this behavior can be understood in terms of the diffusion of ac disturbances into the neutral regions of the diode. With high-frequency excitations, an increase of the excess concentration at $x = 0$ is followed very rapidly by a decrease in the excess concentration. Therefore, large local concentration gradients are set up and the peaks and valleys in the ac component of $p_n{'}$ tend to be smeared out by diffusing into each other during the time they diffuse away from the junction. Because of this smearing out of the ac component of $p_n{'}$, the disturbance decays at a rate which is considerably greater than the rate set by the recombination process. For high enough frequencies the decay rate is, in fact, independent of the lifetime because, at every value of x, the ac hole current which results from changing the stores of excess carriers is much greater than the ac hole current that feeds recombination of these hole stores.

Although the analysis presented in this section can be used to evaluate the small-signal ac admittance of the junction diode, we shall use it principally as a qualitative guide to the frequency limitations of the transistor model which we develop in Chapter 7. All we require there is the recognition that at high frequencies, the ac component of the excess hole concentration has an exponential magnitude dependence with a characteristic length given by $\sqrt{2D_h/\omega}$, which may be much less than L_h.

5.4 DYNAMIC CHANGES IN THE CHARGE STORED IN THE SPACE-CHARGE LAYER

We found in Sec. 2.3 that the space-charge layer of a pn-junction diode contains a dipole layer of charge produced by the immobile impurity ions. The charge stored in either half of this dipole layer depends on the bias voltage. When the junction is reverse-biased, the depleted regions expand into the neutral regions and the charge in either half of the layer increases because some majority carriers have been removed, leaving behind immobile impurity ions. Forward bias has the opposite effect. The general form of the relationship between the charge q_j stored in either half of the dipole layer and the junction voltage v is shown in Fig. 5.9. The charge at zero bias is that associated with the equilibrium width of the space-charge layer.

The majority-carrier currents which accompany changes in q_j produced by changes in v may be an important component of the total diode current for rapid changes in the voltage. Although this component of the diode current is usually most important for

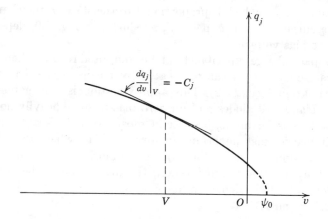

Fig. 5.9. Charge in the space-charge layer as a function of junction voltage.

reverse-bias conditions where it is not masked by currents resulting from minority-carrier injection, in some cases it is significant for forward bias.

The current associated with changes in q_j is:

$$i_j = -\frac{dq_j}{dt} = -\frac{dq_j}{dv} \cdot \frac{dv}{dt} \qquad (5.26)$$

where the minus sign is required because the mobile carriers that accomplish the charge change have the opposite sign from the immobile charges that comprise the dipole layer. At the p-type edge of the space-charge layer the current i_j is the result of majority-carrier hole motion, while at the n-type edge it consists of a flow of majority-carrier electrons. At the center of the space-charge layer there is no charge flow and i_j is a displacement current.

If the junction voltage v consists of a bias voltage V on which is superimposed an incremental component Δv, and if the incremental component is small enough, the current i_j may be described at the terminals of the diode by an incremental space-charge capacitance C_j, given by:

$$C_j = -\frac{dq_j}{dv} \qquad (5.27)$$

This capacitance, which is proportional to the slope of the charge-voltage curve at the bias point V, as shown in Fig. 5.9, depends upon the bias voltage.

The space-charge capacitance can be computed readily whenever the space-charge layer can be treated by means of the depletion approximation (Sec. 2.3.2). This approximation is reasonable for reverse bias in all diodes and for zero bias in some heavily doped diodes. This is fortunate, because in most cases the space-charge capacitance is least important in forward bias, where the diode current is dominated by the injected minority-carrier currents. Using the depletion approximation, the magnitude of the charge in either half of the depletion layer of an *abrupt* junction is from Eqs. 2.13a and 2.14:

$$q_j = qAl_nN_D = qAl_pN_A = A\left[2q\epsilon\frac{(\psi_0 - v)}{(1/N_D + 1/N_A)}\right]^{\frac{1}{2}} \qquad (5.28)$$

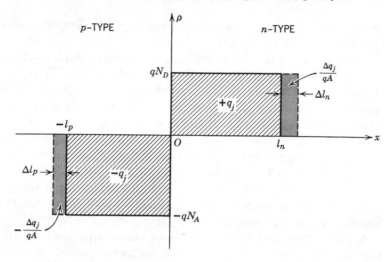

Fig. 5.10. Distribution of space charge in the dipole layer of an abrupt *pn* junction (based on the depletion approximation).

This charge is illustrated in Fig. 5.10. The space-charge capacitance* is:

$$C_j = -\frac{dq_j}{dv} = \frac{A}{2}\left[\frac{2q\epsilon}{(\psi_0 - V)(1/N_A + 1/N_D)}\right]^{\frac{1}{2}} \quad (5.29)$$

If the reverse bias applied to the diode is large compared with the contact potential, the capacitance varies as $(-V)^{-\frac{1}{2}}$.

Physically, when the *reverse* bias $-v$ is increased by $-\Delta v$, l_n and l_p increase and an amount of charge $qAN_D\Delta l_n = qAN_A\Delta l_p$ is added to the depletion layer, as shown in Fig. 5.10. This increase in depletion-layer charge is the result of the *removal* of an equal amount of mobile majority-carrier charge which occupied the regions $A\Delta l_n$ and $A\Delta l_p$ before $-\Delta v$ was applied. For a small voltage change, the charge change occurs entirely at the *edge* of the depletion layer. Consequently, the space-charge capacitance is exactly that of a parallel-plate capacitor of area A, spacing $l_n + l_p$, and dielectric permittivity ϵ.

$$C_j = \frac{\epsilon A}{l_n + l_p} \quad (5.30)$$

* When computed this way, the space-charge capacitance is frequently referred to as the *depletion-layer capacitance*.

This result is confirmed by substituting Eq. 2.13a into Eq. 5.30, thereby obtaining Eq. 5.29.

The dependence of space charge capacitance on junction voltage can be modified by changing the impurity distribution. Figure 5.11 shows an impurity distribution which makes the space-charge capacitance relatively independent of the reverse-bias voltage. At some small reverse bias, all of the lightly doped region between $-w_p$ and w_n is depleted. For larger reverse bias, a relatively large change in voltage is required to cause further penetration of the space-charge layer into the heavily doped material. The junction then behaves very much like a true parallel-plate capacitor because, over a wide range of voltage, charge is added or removed at locations separated by approximately $(w_p + w_n)$.

A distribution intermediate between the abrupt junction and the junction shown in Fig. 5.11 is the linearly graded junction, which has a space charge capacitance of the form

$$C_j = K(\psi_0 - V)^{-\frac{1}{3}} \tag{5.31}$$

REFERENCE

5.1 R. H. Kingston, "Switching Times in Junction Diodes and Junction Transistors," *Proc. IRE*, **42**, 829–834, (1954).

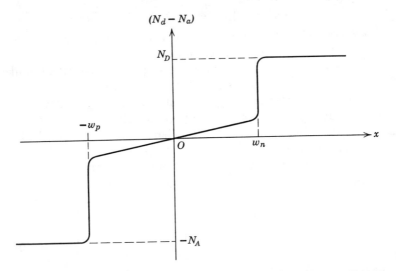

Fig. 5.11. A *pn*-junction impurity distribution which makes the space-charge capacitance relatively independent of bias voltage.

PROBLEMS

P5.1 One approximate method of treating the large-signal transient behavior of a diode is based upon the assumption that the changing excess charge distributions during a transient may be regarded as a succession of steady states. Although the transients predicted by this method differ somewhat from actual diode behavior, this approximation is simple to apply and offers considerable insight into dynamic effects in diodes.

We consider an asymmetrically doped long-base junction diode with $N_A \gg N_D$, and focus attention on the behavior of holes in the n-type region. We use the approximate method to estimate the diode response to a step in forward current.

(a) Solve Eq. 5.5 for $q_h(t)$ when i_h has the form shown in Fig. 5.3a. Assume that the diode is in equilibrium for $t < 0$ so that $q_h(0) = 0$.

(b) Prove that with the diode in the *steady state* the excess hole charge is given by

$$q_h = qAL_h p_n{}'(0)$$

where $p_n{}'(0) = p_{no}(e^{qV/kT} - 1)$.

(c) Assume that the steady-state relationship of (b) applies *during the transient*, and compute the diode voltage $v(t)$.

P5.2 This problem is concerned with the spatial dependence of the complex amplitude of the ac component of the excess hole concentration in the n-type region of a junction diode. The complex amplitude at the space-charge layer edge is $\Delta P(0)$, and the frequency is ω.

(a) If $\omega \tau_h = 0.1$, sketch and dimension the magnitude and phase of $\Delta P(x)/\Delta P(0)$ for $0 < x < 4L_h$.

(b) Repeat part (a), using the same coordinates, for $\omega \tau_h = 10$.

(c) What physical mechanism accounts for the differences between the results in (a) and (b)?

P5.3 Use the analysis of Sec. 5.3 to compute the small-signal admittance of an asymmetrically doped long-base diode. That is, compute:

$$Y(\omega) = \frac{\Delta I}{\Delta V}$$

where ΔI is the complex amplitude of the hole current at $x = 0$ and ΔV is the complex amplitude of the small ac component of the junction voltage. Express the bias point dependence of $Y(\omega)$ in terms of $(I + I_s)$, and compare your result with Eq. 3.27.

P5.4 Prove that the depletion-layer capacitance of an abrupt pn junction may be written

$$C_j = \frac{\epsilon A}{l}$$

where $l = l_n + l_p$ is the total width of the depleted region. Note that this capacitance is that of a parallel-plate capacitor of area A and spacing

l. This result is true regardless of the detailed nature of the impurity distribution in the depletion layer.

P5.5 Calculate the depletion-layer capacitance as a function of reverse-bias voltage ($-V$) for an abrupt pn-junction diode having $N_D = 10^{16}$ cm^{-3} and $N_A = 10^{18}$ cm^{-3} and an area of 1 mm^2. Neglect ψ_0 in comparison with $-V$. Sketch and dimension your result on logarithmic coordinates for $3 < (-V) < 20$ volts.

P5.6 Show that the incremental space-charge elastance of an *abrupt* junction diode is linearly related to q_j. Is this linear relationship true of diodes having graded impurity distributions?

P5.7 Derive an expression for the depletion-layer capacitance of a linearly graded junction, neglecting the portion of the contact potential that appears outside the depletion region. Let the net impurity concentration near the metallurgical junction be of the form:

$$N_d - N_a = ax$$

Show that your result can be written in the form

$$C_j = \frac{\epsilon A}{l}$$

where l is the total width of the depletion region. Note that this is in accord with the idea that the depletion-layer capacitance is the consequence of two sheets of charge separated by l (a parallel-plate capacitor).

P5.8 For the diode described in Fig. 4.8:
   (a) Calculate the charge stored in either half of the depletion layer when the reverse bias is much larger than the contact potential. Express your result in terms of q, N_o, A, V, and ϵ.
   (b) The reverse-bias battery is suddenly removed by *open-circuiting* the diode. Determine about how long it takes the diode to return to equilibrium. Make reasonable approximations and state them.

6

Lumped Models for

Junction Diodes

6.0 INTRODUCTION

Our treatment of the physical behavior of junction diodes has been based upon resolution of the idealized diode into a space charge layer sandwiched between neutral p-type and n-type regions. We have used the continuity equation (Eq. 3.4) together with appropriate boundary conditions to describe the distribution and flow of excess minority carriers as continuous functions of space and time.

This continuum approach to diode behavior was relatively simple to apply under dc or static conditions, as in Chapter 3, because in the dc steady state the *partial* differential equation of continuity reduced to an *ordinary* differential equation. However, the continuum treatment is more difficult to apply to the dynamic behavior of the diode, as evidenced by our decision in Chapter 5 to avoid solving in detail the continuity equation.

The question thus arises whether approximations can be made which preserve the principal features of the diode physics and yield useful and reasonably accurate descriptions of diode performance, but which simplify the mathematics involved in the solution of partial differential equations. We might suspect that the problem could be simplified if we are willing to inquire about the carrier concentrations at only a few carefully chosen planes in the neutral regions rather than at every point in those regions. An analogous situation occurs in our use of lumped electric-circuit techniques rather than electromagnetic field theory to characterize the interconnection of resistors, inductors, and capacitors. By accepting a knowledge of a few well-chosen node potentials in place of a complete knowledge of the electric and magnetic fields, we obtain an enormous simplification of the mathematics involved in analysis of the system.

We now demonstrate that analogous *lumped models* for the distribution and flow of charge carriers in semiconductor devices can be developed, and show that these lumped models enable us to answer questions regarding diode performance which would be more difficult to answer with continuum mathematics. These ideas and techniques are applicable in many other physical situations, where a lumped treatment of a distributed system permits us to replace a partial differential equation with a set of ordinary differential equations.

6.1 A LUMPED MODEL FOR A JUNCTION DIODE

As in Chapter 5, we consider an asymmetrically doped one-dimensional idealized diode structure in which the current crossing the space-charge layer is almost entirely the result of hole flow in the n-type neutral region. We first focus attention on the neutral n-type region.

6.1.1 *Carrier Distribution and Flow in the Neutral Region*

We station ourselves at a plane located at x_1 in the n-type neutral region and apply the ideas of carrier continuity to the volume bounded by planes located at $(x_1 - \Delta x/2)$ and at $(x_1 + \Delta x/2)$, as shown in Fig. 6.1a. The excess hole distribution is shown for two times t_1 and t_2, which differ by $\Delta t = t_2 - t_1$.

The continuity equation requires that holes which flow into the slice of width Δx in time Δt do one of three things: (1) they flow out again, (2) they recombine, (3) they are stored. That is,

$$(i_h)_{\text{in}}\Delta t = (i_h)_{\text{out}}\Delta t + q\left[\frac{\overline{p_n'}}{\tau_h}\,(A\Delta x)\right]\Delta t + q\Delta\overline{p_n'}(A\Delta x) \quad (6.1)$$

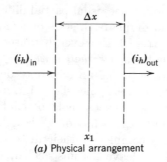

(a) Physical arrangement

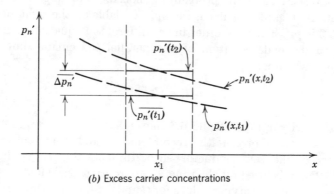

(b) Excess carrier concentrations

Fig. 6.1. Representation of carrier concentrations in a region of finite width.

where $\overline{p_n'}$ denotes the *average* excess hole concentration in the slice. Consequently, $\Delta\overline{p_n'}$ designates the change in the average excess hole concentration which occurs in the time interval Δt, as shown in Fig. 6.1b. Inasmuch as $(A\Delta x)$ is the volume of the slice, the second term on the right is the total recombination charge in time Δt because $\overline{p_n'}/\tau_h$ is the recombination *rate*. The third term on the right is the total change in the hole store. If we rearrange terms, divide both sides of Eq. 6.1 by Δt, and take the limit as $\Delta t \to 0$, we get:

$$(i_h)_{\text{in}} - (i_h)_{\text{out}} = \left(\frac{qA\Delta x}{\tau_h}\right)\overline{p_n'} + (qA\Delta x)\frac{d\overline{p_n'}}{dt} \qquad (6.2)$$

This limit has the effect of converting the second term into an average recombination current while the third term becomes an average storage current.

If our goal were to obtain the usual partial differential equation of continuity, we would divide both sides of Eq. 6.2 by $A\Delta x$ and proceed to the limit as $\Delta x \to 0$. However, because we wish to avoid partial differential equations, *we shall leave Δx finite* and regard the average concentration $\overline{p_n'}$ as an adequate description of the hole concentration throughout the slice. Inasmuch as $A\Delta x\overline{p_n'}$ correctly represents the total excess hole population in the slice, Eq. 6.2 describes correctly the behavior of the total population of excess holes but ignores completely their distribution within the slice. For the present we leave Δx unspecified, postponing until later a discussion of the problem of choosing a lump size.

With Δx regarded as fixed, the only variable on the right side of Eq. 6.2 is $\overline{p_n'}$. This first order linear differential equation is analogous to the node equation of the parallel GC circuit shown in Fig. 6.2, which is:

$$i_{\text{in}} - i_{\text{out}} = Gv + C\frac{dv}{dt} \qquad (6.3)$$

The similarity of Eqs. 6.2 and 6.3 shows that a *lumped circuit model* can be used to represent the recombination and storage of excess carriers in the semiconductor slice. In fact, the GC circuit of Fig. 6.2 may be used by choosing an appropriate scale factor relating $\overline{p_n'}$ to v and specifying values for G and C properly. Rather than using the circuit of Fig. 6.2 directly, we introduce a lumped model for Eq. 6.2 in which $\overline{p_n'}$ appears directly as the node variable. Our lumped model also uses symbols different from G and C to represent recombination and storage. Although the use of unfamiliar symbols may at first cause some minor confusion, the new symbols empha-

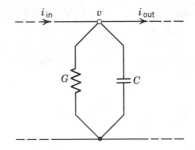

Fig. 6.2. An RC analogue for the lumped continuity equation.

size that we are dealing with the behavior of excess carriers in a semiconductor and *not* with currents and voltage in a *GC* network. Furthermore, they avoid serious confusion later when we will insert lumped models of diodes and transistors into electric circuits containing resistors and capacitors.

In order to develop our lumped model for the continuity equation we rewrite Eq. 6.2:

$$(i_h)_{\text{in}} - (i_h)_{\text{out}} = H_c\overline{p_n'} + S\frac{d\overline{p_n'}}{dt} \tag{6.4}$$

where

$$H_c = \frac{qA\,\Delta x}{\tau_h}$$

$$S = qA\,\Delta x \tag{6.5a,b}$$

The coefficient H_c, which contains only geometrical factors and material parameters, emphasizes the linear dependence of *recombination current* on average excess hole concentration. This coefficient is called a *combinance*. It is analogous to the conductance in the *GC* circuit. The coefficient S similarly depends only on geometrical factors and material parameters. It stresses the linear dependence of *storage* current on the rate of change of the average excess hole concentration, and is called a *storance*. It is analogous to the capacitance in the *GC* circuit.

A schematic representation of the minority-carrier behavior in the lump is obtained by defining symbols which represent the recombination process and the storage mechanism. Equation 6.4 shows that the current which results from the recombination of excess holes with excess electrons is related to the average excess concentration by

$$i_{hr} = H_c\overline{p_n'} \tag{6.6a}$$

The representation of the combinance H_c by means of a two-terminal lumped element is shown in Fig. 6.3a. The current in the element depends only on the variable at the upper node, which is the average excess hole concentration in the lump. Because recombination involves both holes and electrons in equal numbers, its representation by a two-terminal element is quite appropriate. We think of the current in the upper lead as hole flow, whereas the equal current in the lower lead is electron flow.

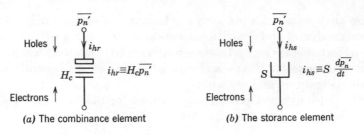

(a) The combinance element   (b) The storance element

Fig. 6.3. Basic lumped elements.

The current which results from the storage of excess carriers is, according to Eq. 6.4, related to the average excess concentration by

$$i_{hs} = S \frac{d\overline{p_n}'}{dt} \tag{6.6b}$$

The symbolic representation of the storance S is shown in Fig. 6.3b. The storage current depends on the rate of change of the variable at the upper node. However, the two-terminal nature of the element emphasizes that carrier storage involves the simultaneous build-up of *both* hole and electron concentrations. The total excess charge q_h stored in S is the time integral of the storage current i_{hs}. That is,

$$q_h = \int i_{hs}\, dt \tag{6.7a}$$

Therefore,

$$q_h = S\overline{p_n}' \tag{6.7b}$$

The symbols for the combinance and storance elements are two-terminal, but not symmetric, to remind us that the current flowing in the element is dependent on the average concentration at *one end* only. In fact, the node variable at the other end has not yet been defined. The current in the lead attached to the controlling node is the result of minority-carrier flow, while the current in the other lead is the result of majority-carrier flow.

These lumped elements can be combined to describe minority-carrier continuity in the lump completely, as shown in Fig. 6.4. Because of the two-terminal nature of the lumped elements, the model of Fig. 6.4 represents continuity of the majority carriers as well. The majority-carrier continuity equation is merely a statement of charge conservation at the lower node.

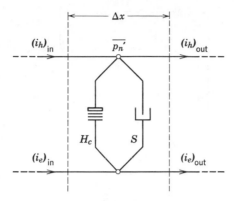

Fig. 6.4. Schematic representation of the continuity equation for a single lump.

Now that we have developed a lumped representation for the re-combination and storage of excess carriers in a slice of semi-conductor of finite width, it is necessary to account for the flow of excess carriers between adjacent slices or lumps. Inasmuch as we are focusing attention on low-level injection effects in homogeneous extrinsic semiconductors, the minority-carrier current flows prin-cipally by diffusion, and its drift component is entirely negligible in any situation where the minority-carrier current is a significant fraction of the total current. We consider the flow of excess minor-ity carriers between the two adjacent slices of semiconductor illus-trated in Fig. 6.5a. The actual continuous excess hole concentra-tion at some arbitrary time t_1 is shown as the broken line, and the average excess concentrations in the two slices or lumps are shown by the solid lines. The actual hole diffusion current which flows between the slices is

$$i_h\big|_{x=x_p} = -qAD_h \frac{\partial p_n'(x, t_1)}{\partial x}\bigg|_{x=x_p} \tag{6.8}$$

If the lump widths Δx_1 and Δx_2 are small enough, the hole diffusion current may be approximated by:

$$i_h\big|_{x=x_p} = -qAD_h \frac{\overline{p_n'(x_2)} - \overline{p_n'(x_1)}}{\Delta x_{21}} \tag{6.9}$$

where $\Delta x_{21} = x_2 - x_1$ is the distance between the centers of the two lumps. This approximation to the diffusion current is accurate if the slice widths are small enough so that the excess hole distribu-

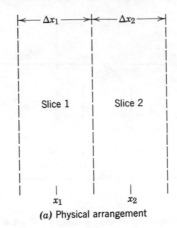

(a) Physical arrangement

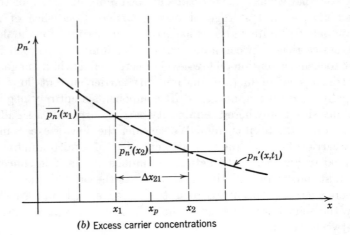

(b) Excess carrier concentrations

Fig. 6.5. Lumped representation of carrier concentrations for two adjacent slices.

tion is nearly linear over the distance Δx_{21}. If we regard Δx_{21} as a fixed constant, the hole diffusion current between the lumps may be written as

$$i_h|_{x=x_p} = -H_D[\overline{p_n'}(x_2) - \overline{p_n'}(x_1)] \tag{6.10}$$

where

$$H_D = \frac{qAD_h}{\Delta x_{21}} \tag{6.11}$$

The coefficient H_D, which depends only on material parameters and geometrical factors, is called the *diffusance*. Inasmuch as $i_h|_{x=x_p}$ is equal to the hole current which flows *out* of lump 1 and thus to the hole current which flows *into* lump 2, we can use Eq. 6.10, which is a lumped approximation to the diffusion current, to tie together the slices or lumps which comprise our model. Such a multiple-lump representation is shown in Fig. 6.6a. The diffusance element defined by Eq. 6.10 is different from the combinance and storance elements because the current through it represents minority-carrier flow at *both* terminals of the element and because its

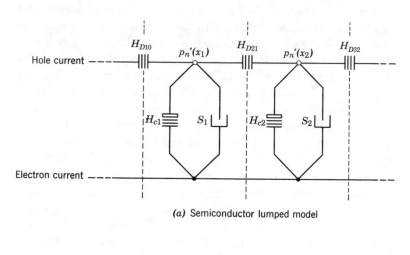

(a) Semiconductor lumped model

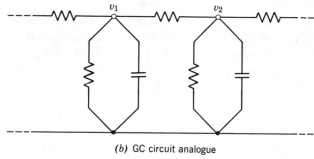

(b) GC circuit analogue

Fig. 6.6. Multiple-lump model for a one-dimensional semiconductor and its *GC* analogue.

current depends on the average carrier concentration at *both* ends. For this reason the diffusance symbol is symmetrical.

This lumped model for the distribution and flow of excess minority carriers is analogous to the *GC* circuit shown in Fig. 6.6*b*. Consequently, analysis of the lumped model of the semiconductor is entirely parallel to analysis of the electric circuit, and intuition developed by experience with the electric circuit can be applied to the lumped model.

It is important to understand the implications of our lumped representation of *majority*-carrier flow in this model. The electron line in the model merely emphasizes the continuity of majority carriers (and, therefore, of total current). The combinance and storance elements are connected to the electron line to emphasize that recombination involves the mutual annihilation of a hole and an electron, and that the storage of excess carriers involves the mutual accumulation of holes and electrons. We have not assigned a variable to the nodes on the electron line. This representation of majority-carrier phenomena is entirely consistent with the physical fact that in a homogeneous extrinsic semiconductor under low-level injection conditions the behavior of the *minority* carriers can be determined independently of the detailed motion of the majority carriers, and the *majority* carriers distribute themselves and flow in whatever manner is necessary to preserve space-charge neutrality and continuity of the total current. It follows that our lumped representation is limited, like essentially *all* of the analysis of this book, to low-level injection conditions in homogeneous extrinsic semiconductors.*

This completes our approximate lumped representation of the neutral regions of a junction diode. Before we devise a lumped schematic representation for the effects of the space charge layer, we shall illustrate the use of our lumped model for the neutral region with a simple example.

---

* Less restricted lumped models have been developed which characterize semiconductors without limitations on homogeniety, doping level, and injection level. Although the models may no longer be linear, they nevertheless permit the treatment of simultaneous *ordinary* differential equations in place of *partial* differential equations. The interested reader should examine References 6.1 and 6.2.

6.1.2 *An Illustrative Example*

Let us suppose that we illuminate uniformly a block of homogeneous n-type semiconductor, thereby creating excess hole-electron pairs. We assume that the light has been turned on for a long time so that the excess hole concentration is not changing with time and is in fact *uniform* throughout the block.† We wish to determine, by using a lumped model, how the excess hole concentration behaves when the light is suddenly turned off (at $t = 0$).

The excess hole distribution is uniform for $t < 0$, and there is no reason why it should become nonuniform for $t > 0$. Therefore, the entire block of semiconductor can in this case be represented by a *single lump*. This lump must have a combinance

$$H_c = \frac{qU}{\tau_h} \tag{6.12a}$$

where U is the volume of the block. The storance of the lump must be:

$$S = qU \tag{6.12b}$$

Equations 6.12 should be compared with Eqs. 6.5, where the volume of the semiconductor comprising the lump was written as $A\Delta x$ rather than U.

Inasmuch as there is no mechanism for the flow of excess holes into or out of the block, the ordinary differential equation which describes the average excess hole concentration $\overline{p_n'}$ must be simply (see Eq. 6.4):

$$0 = H_c\overline{p_n'} + S\frac{d\overline{p_n'}}{dt} \tag{6.13}$$

The solution of this equation is:

$$\overline{p_n'}(t) = Ae^{-H_c t/S} \tag{6.14}$$

where A is a constant of integration determined by the average excess hole concentration for $t = 0$. Now,

$$\frac{H_c}{S} = \frac{qU/\tau_h}{qU} = \frac{1}{\tau_h} \tag{6.15}$$

† The assumption of a uniform distribution is certainly open to question and is perhaps physically unreasonable because the photons are absorbed and excess carriers are produced in a thin skin very near the surface. However, the assumed uniformity simplifies our illustrative example.

consequently, the average excess hole density in the block may be written as

$$\overline{p_n'}(t) = \overline{p_n'}(0)e^{-t/\tau_h} \tag{6.16}$$

This simple example emphasizes the role of the recombination process, described by the combinance, in annihilating stored excess concentrations, represented in terms of the storance. Because of the linearity of the physical mechanisms involved, the combinance discharges the storance in an exponential mode.

6.1.3 *A Lumped Representation of the Space Charge Layer at a pn Junction*

Our description in Chapter 2 of phenomena in the space-charge layer emphasized that the principal effects, insofar as the neutral regions are concerned, of applying a voltage to the layer are changes in the *minority* carrier concentrations at the edges of the layer. For low-level injection and negligible voltage drops in the neutral regions and end contacts, the excess minority-carrier concentrations *at the edges* of the space charge layer are (see Eqs. 2.19):

$$p_n'\big|_{\text{edge}} = p_{no}(e^{qV/kT} - 1)$$
$$n_p'\big|_{\text{edge}} = n_{po}(e^{qV/kT} - 1) \tag{6.17a,b}$$

as illustrated in Fig. 6.7*a*. Inasmuch as the hole and electron currents crossing the space-charge layer are *constant* throughout the layer, because of our assumption of no recombination or generation of carriers in the layer, the flow of carriers through the layer and the minority-carrier concentrations at the edges of the layer may be represented diagrammatically by the symbol of Fig. 6.7*b*. We have added the subscript *E* in the excess minority concentrations to emphasize that these concentrations apply at the *edges* of the space charge layer.

This representation for the space-charge layer accounts for both the separate continuity of hole and electron currents throughout the region and the effect of a bias voltage on the excess minority carrier concentrations at the edges of the region. It can be extended to include the effects of the bias voltage on the width of the space-charge layer as reflected by charge changes in the dipole layer. Because the current on either side of the junction associated with the displacement of charge in the corresponding half of the dipole

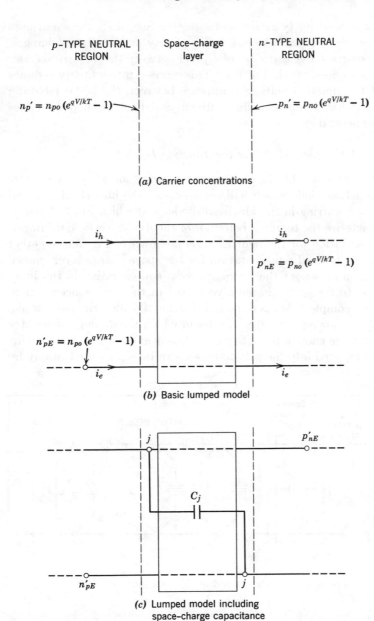

(a) Carrier concentrations

(b) Basic lumped model

(c) Lumped model including
space-charge capacitance

Fig. 6.7. Lumped representation of the space-charge layer.

layer is a majority-carrier current (see Sec. 5.4), these currents can be represented, at least for relatively small voltage changes, by a space-charge capacitance C_j tied between the majority-carrier flow lines, as shown in Fig. 6.7c. This representation tacitly assumes that the junction voltage V appears between the nodes labeled j and j', which is not in conflict with our assignment of node variables in the neutral regions.*

6.1.4 *A Complete Model for the Junction Diode*

We are now able to construct a lumped model for the entire *pn*-junction diode which will represent all the important physical effects occurring in the idealized diode, and which can be used to characterize the terminal behavior of the diode. To tie our lumped representation for the neutral region, shown in Fig. 6.6, together with the lumped representation for the space charge layer, shown in Fig. 6.7c, we set the average excess concentration in the lump closest to the space charge layer equal to the edge concentration.

The complete lumped model for an asymmetric *pn*-junction diode is shown in Fig. 6.8. Diodes in which the doping asymmetry is not large enough to justify complete neglect of the electron currents injected into the *p*-type region can be represented simply by

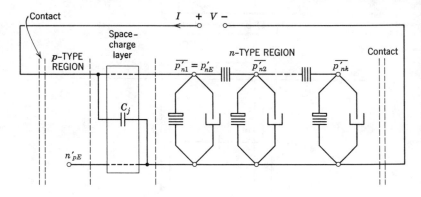

Fig. 6.8. Complete lumped model for a junction diode.

* The junction voltage V does *not* appear between the nodes designated p'_{nE} and n'_{pE}. To emphasize this, the carrier flow lines are shown dotted as they pass through the junction.

adding to the structure a lumped representation for the minority-carrier electrons in the p-type region.

This lumped model implies the existence of some interesting effects at the contacts of the diode, but does not describe them explicitly, just as in Chapter 3 we chose to describe the contact only by postulating no voltage drops there in the presence of current flow. Actually, at the contact to the p-type region, electrons in the external terminal wires must be freely converted into majority-carrier holes in the p-type semiconductor. At the other contact, electrons in the metal terminals must be interchanged for majority-carrier electrons in the semiconductor. All this action must occur without significant voltage drops.

The lumped model of Fig. 6.8 can be analyzed by using Kirchoff's current law to write a set of simultaneous node equations, one for each node. These simultaneous coupled equations can be solved for all the currents in the model by conventional methods, once the boundary conditions are specified. For the long-base diode, these boundary conditions are provided by the junction relations of Eqs. 6.17.

Before discussing the choice of lump number and size and before illustrating the use of the model in circuit calculations, it is desirable to point out several features of the physical electronics of junction diodes that are made very evident by the lumped model:

(1) All of the diode current is the consequence of changes in the dipole layer charge at the junction, recombination in the neutral regions, or storage in the neutral regions.

(2) The diode terminal characteristics are nonlinear *only* because of the exponential relationship between excess minority-carrier concentrations at the edges of the space-charge layer and the junction voltage. More precisely, the relationships between excess carrier concentrations and current are *entirely linear*.

(3) The semiconductor current near the terminals is entirely the result of majority-carrier flow. All injected minority carriers recombine in the neutral regions.

(4) The total diode current may be computed by adding the hole current crossing the space-charge layer, the electron current crossing the space-charge layer, and the displacement current characterized by C_j.

6.2 USE OF THE LUMPED MODEL

Before the lumped model of Fig. 6.8 can be used to predict junction diode behavior, it is in principle necessary to decide upon the number of neutral-region lumps to be used, to choose their widths, and to fix the values of the combinances, storances, and diffusances. The discussion of Sec. 6.1 shows that the lumped model can be made arbitrarily accurate by using many slices and making each thin. We are certainly justified in using a straight-line approximation for the concentration gradient if the width of each slice is small compared with a diffusion length. However, the use of a very large number of lumps is not particularly convenient, because the labor required in analysis of the lumped model increases enormously as the number of lumps (and thus the number of coupled equations) increases. Also, a model with many lumps may provide far more detail about carrier-concentration distribution *in space* than is necessary, if our principal concern is with *electrical behavior at the terminals.* Consequently, it may often be wise to give up entirely the idea of associating each node of a lumped model uniquely with a particular physical slice, and instead simply choose the number and value of the lumps according to the maximum complexity, detail, and accuracy desired in representing the terminal behavior of the device under consideration.

In any case, *we should use the smallest number of lumps that permits a sufficiently accurate description of the electrical behavior of the device at its terminals.* For example, if we are interested only in the dc or slow behavior of the diode, the single-lump model shown in Fig. 6.9a will suffice. This model contains a storance which can be chosen to represent correctly the total storage of carriers in the n-type neutral region and a combinance which can be chosen to reflect the total recombination current in this region. That is, choosing $\Delta x = L_h$ so that

$$H_c = \frac{qAL_h}{\tau_h}$$

and   (6.18a,b)

$$S = qAL_h$$

makes the equivalent excess carrier store Sp'_{nE} the same as the actual excess carrier store in a long-base diode, and makes the total

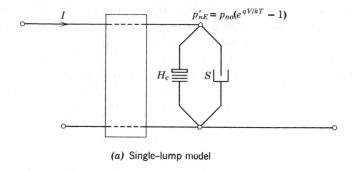

(a) Single–lump model

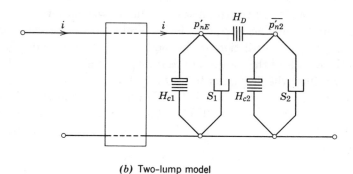

(b) Two-lump model

Fig. 6.9. One-lump and two-lump models.

equivalent recombination current $H_c p'_{nE}$ identical to the actual steady-state recombination current. The diode current i is:

$$i = H_c p'_{nE} + S \frac{dp'_{nE}}{dt}$$

where

$$p'_{nE} = p_{no}(e^{qv/kT} - 1) \qquad (6.19a,b)$$

Thus, the steady-state current-voltage relationship is:

$$I = H_c p'_{nE} = qA \frac{p_{no}L_h}{\tau_h} (e^{qV/kT} - 1) \qquad (6.20)$$

which, of course, agrees with the result of the continuous analysis, Eq. 3.19, because we chose H_c so that it would! While this single-lump model represents correctly the dc and slow-speed behavior of the diode (slow-speed implying that the excess carrier distribution changes as a succession of steady states), it says very little about the dynamic behavior of the diode.* Our discussions of Chapter 5 have shown that the carrier distribution changes shape under dynamic conditions and no single-lump model can possibly characterize the consequences of these shape changes.

A two-lump model, such as that shown in Fig. 6.9*b*, should provide a much better characterization of dynamic effects in a diode because it allows for the transient flow of minority carriers between the two nodes, which is certainly necessary if we are to represent the effects of dynamic changes of shape in the excess minority-carrier distribution. The five parameters in this model may be chosen in an infinite number of ways. Fortunately, if we use reasonable judgement, the predictions of the model are not strongly dependent on the details of the choice. For example, we will arbitrarily choose the width of the first lump to be $L_h/2$ (thereby storing half of the static excess-hole store in this lump), and shall take the width of the second lump to be $3L_h/2$. We take the distance between centers of the lumps, which determines the diffusance, to be L_h. The parameter values are thus:

$$H_{c1} = \frac{qAL_h}{2\tau_h} \equiv H$$

$$H_{c2} = \frac{3qAL_h}{2\tau_h} = 3H$$

$$H_D = \frac{qAD_h}{L_h} = \frac{qAL_h}{\tau_h} = 2H \qquad (6.21a\text{-}e)$$

$$S_1 = \frac{qAL_h}{2} \equiv S$$

$$S_2 = \frac{3qAL_h}{2} = 3S$$

---

* Because the single-lump model correctly represents the total excess-carrier store, it is entirely equivalent to the approximate stored-charge analysis of the diode outlined in Sec. 5.2.2.

The two differential equations of the neutral region, which are obtained by using Kirchoff's current law at the two nodes, are:

$$i = H_{c1}p'_{nE} + S_1 \frac{dp'_{nE}}{dt} + H_D(p'_{nE} - \overline{p'_{n2}})$$

$$0 = H_D(\overline{p'_{n2}} - p'_{nE}) + H_{c2}\overline{p'_{n2}} + S_2 \frac{d\overline{p'_{n2}}}{dt} \qquad (6.22a,b)$$

In terms of H and S, which are defined by Eqs. 6.21, the differential equations may be written as:

$$i = 3Hp'_{nE} + S\frac{dp'_{nE}}{dt} \qquad\qquad - 2H\,\overline{p'_{n2}}$$

$$0 = \qquad -2Hp'_{nE} \qquad + 5H\overline{p'_{n2}} + 3S\frac{d\overline{p'_{n2}}}{dt} \qquad (6.23a,b)$$

We shall illustrate the use of this two-lump model and shall partially check its accuracy by employing it to compute the *storage delay time* (see Sec. 5.2.2) of a diode. We assume that the diode is in the dc steady state with a forward current of $i = I_f$ for $t < 0$, and compute the response of the edge concentration p'_{nE} to a sudden reversal of the current at $t = 0$. That is, for $t > 0, i = -I_r$. Inasmuch as the diode voltage changes sign when $p'_{nE} = 0$, we define the storage delay time t_s as the time interval between the current reversal and when $p'_{nE} = 0$ (see Sec. 5.2.2.).

First, we find the value of p'_{nE} for $t < 0$. In this steady state, Eqs. 6.23 reduce to

$$I_f = \quad 3Hp'_{nE} - 2H\overline{p'_{n2}}$$

$$0 = -2Hp'_{nE} + 5H\overline{p'_{n2}} \qquad (6.24a,b)$$

When $\overline{p'_{n2}}$ is eliminated between these equations we obtain:

$$p'_{nE}\big|_{t<0} = \frac{5I_f}{11H} \qquad (6.25)$$

Similarly, the value that p'_{nE} would approach after the transient dies out *if the excess hole concentration were not required physically to be greater than* $-p_{no}$, is

$$p'_{nE}\big|_{t\to\infty} = -\frac{5I_r}{11H} \qquad (6.26)$$

The natural frequencies m_1 and m_2 of the model, which are the roots of the characteristic equation obtained by setting $i = 0$ in Eqs. 6.22, are obtained by solving

$$\begin{vmatrix} 3H + Sm, & -2H \\ -2H, & 5H + 3Sm \end{vmatrix} = 0 \tag{6.27}$$

for m. They are:

$$m_1 = -\frac{H}{S} = -\frac{1}{\tau_h}$$

$$m_2 = -\left(\frac{22}{6}\right)\frac{H}{S} \cong -\frac{3.7}{\tau_h} \tag{6.28a,b}$$

Consequently, the complete solution of Eqs. 6.23 for $p'_{nE}(t)$ is of the form:

$$p'_{nE}(t) = -\frac{5I_r}{11H} + Be^{-t/\tau_h} + Ce^{-3.7t/\tau_h} \tag{6.29}$$

where B and C are constants of integration. Two initial conditions on $p'_{nE}(t)$ are required to determine these constants. One condition is given by Eq. 6.25. The other is determined by recognizing that for $t = 0+$ *all* of the current change must be accommodated by the storance of the first lump because neither p'_{nE} nor $\overline{p'_{n2}}$ can change instantly. Therefore,

$$\left.\frac{dp'_{nE}}{dt}\right|_{t=0+} = -\frac{(I_f + I_r)}{S_1} = \frac{-(I_f + I_r)}{\tau_h H} \tag{6.30}$$

When B and C are evaluated with the aid of these initial conditions, we obtain

$$p'_{nE}(t) \cong -0.45\frac{I_r}{H} + 0.25\frac{(I_f + I_r)}{H}e^{-t/\tau_h}$$

$$+ 0.20\frac{(I_f + I_r)}{H}e^{-3.7t/\tau_h} \tag{6.31}$$

Therefore, the storage delay time t_s at which $p'_{nE} = 0$ is given by:

$$0 = -0.45I_r + 0.25(I_f + I_r)e^{-t_s/\tau_h} + 0.20(I_f + I_r)e^{-3.7t_s/\tau_h} \tag{6.32}$$

In order to compare the predictions of the two-lump model with the results of analysis of the distributed system, we have used Eq. 6.32 to compute t_s/τ_h as a function of I_r/I_f and have plotted the results together with the distributed solution in Fig. 6.10. The

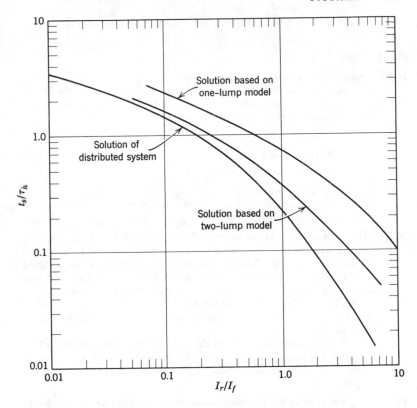

Fig. 6.10. Comparison of storage delay-time predictions.

results of a similar analysis applied to the single lump equivalent model of Fig. 6.9a are also shown for comparison.

While the two-lump model is clearly superior to the one-lump model in predicting storage-delay time, it is still substantially in error for large ratios of reverse to forward current. If closer agreement is required, more lumps must be used in the model.

This example has shown that a relatively simple lumped model can be used to obtain useful performance estimates without excessive difficulty. Alternate definitions of the lumps are considered in the Problems. If greater accuracy is required, more lumps can be used.

REFERENCES

6.1 J. G. Linvill and J. F. Gibbons, *Transistors and Active Circuits*, McGraw-Hill, New York, 1961.

6.2 J. G. Linvill, *Models of Transistors and Diodes*, McGraw-Hill, New York, 1963.

PROBLEMS

P6.1 Consider an asymmetric *pn*-junction diode which has $N_A \gg N_D$ so that substantially all of the diode current is the result of excess holes in the *n*-type region. A single-lump model for this diode is shown in Fig. 6.9a. The parameters of the model are:

$$p_{no} = 10^{11} \text{ cm}^{-3}$$
$$H_c = 10^{-17} \text{ amp-cm}^3$$
$$S = 10^{-24} \text{ coulomb-cm}^3$$

(a) What is the saturation current of this diode?

(b) What is the total stored excess-hole charge when the diode carries a steady forward current of 1 ma?

P6.2 If the *n*-type side of an asymmetrically doped diode is illuminated with light having sufficiently energetic photons, excess holes will be produced in this neutral region. This process can be represented in our lumped model by adding a current source as shown in Fig. 6.11. The light flux intensity is designated by F, and K is a constant of proportionality.

(a) What physical factors influence K?

(b) Determine the volt-ampere relationship $I = I(V, I_l)$ for the illuminated diode.

(c) If the saturation current I_s of the diode without illumination is $1\mu a$, and if I_l is equivalent to the breaking of 10^{16} bonds per second, compute the open-circuit voltage and the short-circuit current of the photodiode.

P6.3 The parameters of the two-lump diode model used in our storage delay-time calculations (see Eqs. 6.21) were chosen somewhat arbitrarily.

(a) Evaluate the dc current-voltage relationship of this two-lump model and determine the error with respect to the distributed calculation of dc behavior.

(b) How would you choose the lumps to eliminate this error?

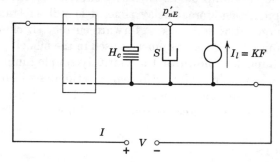

Fig. 6.11.

7

Structure and Operation
of Transistors

7.0 INTRODUCTION

The transistor is an electrical valve which works on the principle that a forward-biased junction control-element injects excess minority carriers into the region adjacent to it, and a reverse-biased junction, located in that same material, collects the injected carriers as part of its reverse current. The device consists of three layers of doped semiconductor, in either the *pnp* or *npn* configuration, with a lead attached to each layer. The middle layer, through which the minority carriers pass, must be very thin (*ca.* 10^{-3} cm) for effective performance, and the practical forms of the device represent various techniques for fabricating such a layer and making contact to it. The middle layer is called the *base*, one outer layer in which the minority carriers originate is called the *emitter*, and the other outer layer is called the *collector*.* Figure 7.1 shows, in approximate scale, two practical forms for real transistors, the

* The term "base" arose from the physical construction of the first transistors in which two closely spaced metal points contacted a base wafer of *n*-type germanium. One point contact acted as the emitter and the other as the collector.

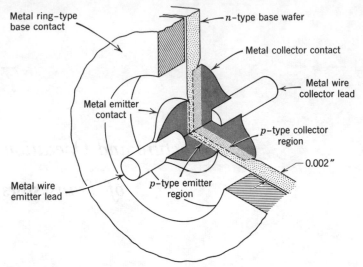

(a) *pnp* Germanium alloy transistor

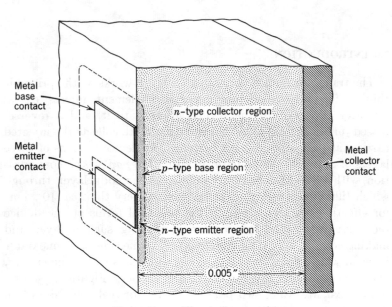

(b) *npn* Planar diffused silicon transistor

Fig. 7.1. Cross-sectional views of two representative transistor types, approximately to scale.

122

pnp alloy-germanium type and the *npn* planar-diffused silicon type. In each, the base is very uniform in thickness and is very thin in comparison with the smallest dimension of any region measured in a direction parallel to the metallurgical junctions. The external connections to the emitter and collector regions are metal contacts which cover an area comparable to the area of the emitter junction. Consequently, minority carriers flow essentially *normal* to the metallurgical junction planes.

In our initial analysis of transistor operation we will use the one-dimensional model of a *pnp* transistor which is shown in Fig. 7.2*a*. We assume that all three semiconductor regions are homogeneous

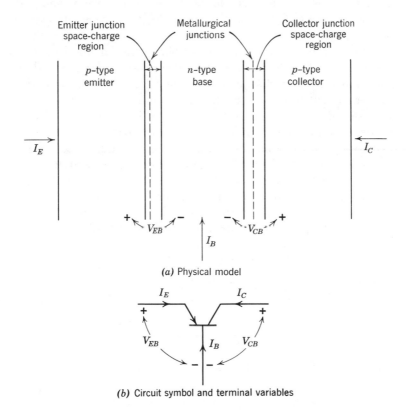

(a) Physical model

(b) Circuit symbol and terminal variables

Fig. 7.2. An idealized physical model of a *pnp*-junction transistor, showing polarities of terminal voltages and currents.

and extrinsic, and that the junctions are abrupt. This model preserves the principal physical features of the representative transistor structures shown in Fig. 7.1, and allows us to focus attention on the mechanisms that are basic to all types of transistors. The one-dimensional assumption, which neglects effects related to current flow in the transverse direction, fails to describe several important physical effects which limit the performance of very high-frequency and high-power transistors. These effects are discussed in Chapter 8 and in *CLT**. Although our discussion is entirely in terms of the *pnp* configuration, the operation of *npn* devices is similar in every respect if the roles of holes and electrons are interchanged. The polarities of the terminal currents and voltages are shown in Fig. 7.2*b*, which uses the standard circuit symbol for a *pnp* transistor.†

When a transistor is used as an amplifier, the emitter junction is forward-biased and the collector junction is reverse-biased, as shown in Fig. 7.3. Consequently, in the base region, the minority-carrier concentration at the edge of the emitter space-charge layer increases above the equilibrium concentration, and the minority-carrier concentration at the edge of the collector space-charge layer decreases to a negligible fraction of the equilibrium concentration. There is thus a gradient of minority-carrier concentration in the base and holes diffuse from emitter to collector, as shown in Fig. 7.4. Except for a small fraction which vanish by recombination in the base, all of the holes which are injected into the base at the emitter junction leave at the collector. Consequently, the collector current

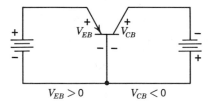

Fig. 7.3. Transistor bias polarities for operation of a *pnp* transistor as an amplifier.

* R. D. Thornton, David DeWitt, E. R. Chenette, and P. E. Gray, *Characteristics and Limitations of Transistors* (hereafter referred to as CLT), John Wiley and Sons, New York, 1964.

† The polarities used for the terminal variables are in accordance with the IEEE standard notation.

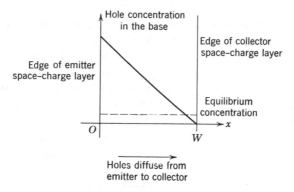

Fig. 7.4. Minority-carrier concentration in the base.

is much larger than the reverse current of an isolated *pn* junction and is under direct control of the emitter-base voltage, because that voltage determines the minority-carrier concentration at the emitter edge of the base, and thus controls the hole diffusion current.

The transistor is thus a valve, in which the collector current is controlled by the emitter-base voltage. We will later examine quantitatively the ratio of the controlled power in the collector circuit to the power needed to control the valve, and will conclude that power ratios in excess of 10^3 can be obtained. The transistor can be used as an amplifier because a small change in emitter-base voltage, requiring little power, can produce a large change in the collector current. Inasmuch as the collector current is sensibly independent of the collector-base voltage as long as the collector junction is reverse-biased, the associated change in collector-base voltage can be quite large, thus permitting the development of relatively large amounts of signal power in an appropriate load. The transistor can also be used to switch the current flowing in a load in series with the collector ON and OFF, by switching the emitter-base voltage a small fraction of a volt, using much less power than that controlled in the collector circuit.

7.1 TRANSISTOR OPERATION IN THE ACTIVE MODE

The mechanism of transistor operation introduced in Sec. 7.0 is called *active mode* operation because it provides the power-amplifying properties of an active component. Other modes of operation, such as those which provide the open-switch and closed-switch states, are discussed in Chapter 9.

In the present section we explore the principal features of active mode operation, and find that the relationships between the terminal currents and the junction voltages can be obtained by focussing attention on the distribution and flow of the *minority* carriers. We are studying an idealized transistor model, shown in Fig. 7.2, in which the neutral regions are homogeneous and extrinsic. Furthermore, in the active mode, the terminal currents are dominated by the flow of holes across the base. Therefore, these minority carriers flow almost solely by diffusion under low-level injection conditions. Consequently, our approach to a detailed description of active-mode operation starts with the minority-carrier concentrations established at the space-charge layer edges by the junction voltages, deduces the minority-carrier distributions, and finally evaluates the terminal currents by computing the minority-carrier diffusion currents.

7.1.1 *Minority Carrier Distributions*

With the emitter junction forward-biased, the minority-carrier concentrations at both edges of the emitter junction space-charge layer are increased above their equilibrium values. Conversely, the reverse-bias voltage applied to the collector junction causes the minority-carrier concentrations at both edges of the collector junction space-charge layer to be depressed well below the corresponding equilibrium values.

The general form of the minority-carrier distributions in all three neutral regions of our idealized *pnp* transistor is shown in Fig. 7.5a.* The excess electron distribution in the emitter and collector vary exponentially with position, exactly as in a junction diode, if the contacts are several diffusion lengths away from the junctions. However, the distribution of holes in the base is essentially linear. Inasmuch as very few holes vanish by recombination in traversing the base region (because $W \ll L_b$), the hole-current density is essentially constant; this requires a constant hole gradient, i.e., a

---

* The notation used in Fig. 7.5 is an extension of that introduced in Chapter 3. The subscripts e, b, and c refer to the three regions of the transistor. When these subscripts are used with a flow parameter, such as D, they refer to the *minority carriers* (see Note 1 in List of Symbols).

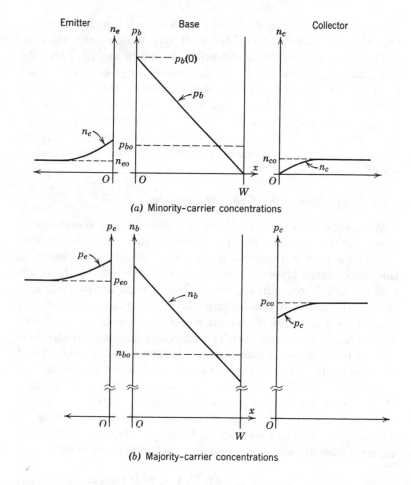

(*a*) Minority-carrier concentrations

(*b*) Majority-carrier concentrations

Fig. 7.5. Carrier concentrations in a *pnp* transistor biased in the active mode.

linear hole distribution, because the holes flow almost entirely by diffusion.

Figure 7.5 has not been drawn to scale. The minority-carrier concentration in the emitter is usually less than 1 per cent of the minority-carrier concentration in the base, because the emitter is doped much more heavily than the base. In many transistors the minority-carrier concentration in the collector is also small compared to the minority-carrier concentration in the base, as a consequence of asymmetric doping. Also, at typical operating currents $p_b(0)$ may be several orders of magnitude greater than p_{bo}.

The majority carrier distributions are shown in Fig. 7.5b. The *excess* majority-carrier concentration is at every point nearly equal to the *excess* minority-carrier concentration at that same point. However, under low-level injection conditions the fractional changes in the majority-carrier concentrations are entirely negligible, whereas the excess minority-carrier concentrations may be several orders of magnitude greater than the corresponding equilibrium values.

7.1.2 *Composition of the Terminal Currents*

We assume that there is no net recombination or generation of carriers in the space-charge layers of our idealized transistor model, so that the hole and electron component currents are constant in the space-charge layers. Therefore, the emitter current I_E is the sum of the injected minority-carrier currents at the two edges of the emitter-junction space-charge layer. Likewise, the collector current I_C is the sum of the extracted minority-carrier currents. The electron currents are usually negligible compared with the hole current because the emitter junction is asymmetrically doped and the thermally generated electron current extracted from the collector is small. If we designate the hole concentration in the base at the edge of the emitter-junction space-charge layer as $p_b(0)$, the hole gradient in the base is approximately $p_b(0)/W$, where W is the width of the neutral base region. Consequently, the emitter and collector currents are approximately equal and are given by:

$$I_E \cong (-I_C) = qAD_b\left(\frac{p_b(0)}{W}\right) = \frac{qAD_b p_{bo}}{W} e^{qV_{EB}/kT} \qquad (7.1)$$

where p_{bo} is the equilibrium hole concentration in the base, D_b is the diffusion constant, A is the cross-sectional area, and V_{EB} is the emitter-base voltage. In writing Eq. 7.1 we have used Eq. 2.19a to relate the hole concentration at the emitter edge of the base to the voltage. Note that the collector current I_C, as defined in Fig. 7.2, is *negative* because holes flow *out* of the base at the collector. Therefore, $(-I_C)$, which is *positive*, may be regarded as the magnitude of the collector current.

Equation 7.1 is valid for a wide range of collector-base voltage V_{CB}, because the minority-carrier concentration at the collector-junction space-charge layer edge is negligible compared with p_{bo} as long as the reverse-bias voltage on the collector is greater than about 100 millivolts $(4kT/q)$. Consequently, V_{CB} has no direct influence on the hole gradient in the base. We will see later that V_{CB} has an indirect effect on the emitter and collector currents because the width of the neutral base region W is weakly dependent on V_{CB}. For the present we neglect base-width changes and assume that W is a constant.

The base current I_B is very small compared with either the emitter current or the collector current. In fact, to the accuracy of Eq. 7.1 the base current is zero, because Kirchoff's current law requires $I_B = -(I_E + I_C)$ and $I_C \cong -I_E$. Although the base current is indeed small, it reduces the effectiveness of the transistor as an active device because it limits the power gain. Therefore, it is important to understand the mechanisms which produce base current.

Base current results from the flow of majority-carrier electrons in the base region. This is in contrast to the emitter and collector currents, which are dominated completely by the holes which are injected at the emitter and diffuse across the base. In the active mode, the base current I_B is usually *negative*, corresponding to the flow of electrons *into* the base region at the base terminal. This electron flow has three origins:

1. Some electrons are injected back into the emitter.
2. Electrons are required to recombine with the small fraction of the holes which vanish in the base.
3. Electrons are *extracted* from the collector region because the collector junction is reverse-biased.

These components of the base current are shown schematically in Fig. 7.6.

The electron current injected into the emitter can be determined by the static *pn*-junction diode theory of Chapter 3. If the emitter is several diffusion lengths wide, this current is:

$$I_{BE} = \frac{qAD_e n_{eo}}{L_e} (e^{qV_{EB}/kT} - 1) \qquad (7.2)$$

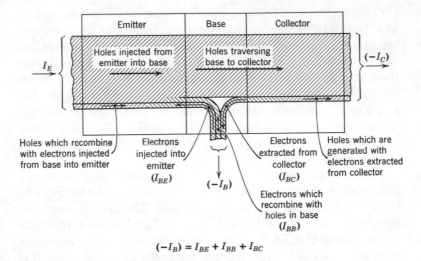

Fig. 7.6. Components of the terminal currents for active-mode operation.

where D_e is the electron diffusion constant in the emitter, L_e is the corresponding minority-carrier diffusion length, and n_{eo} is the equilibrium minority-carrier concentration in the emitter. This component of the base current can be minimized by doping the emitter very heavily, thus making n_{eo} small.

The electron current which supports recombination in the base can be evaluated easily because we know the approximate form of the hole distribution in the base. The volume recombination rate is p_b'/τ_b where $p_b' = p_b - p_{bo}$ denotes the excess hole concentration, and τ_b is the lifetime in the base. The total number of holes which recombine in the base per unit time is the integral of p_b'/τ_b over the volume of the neutral base region. Inasmuch as an electron is required for each hole which vanishes in the base, the current I_{BB} is:

$$I_{BB} = q \int_0^W \frac{p_b'}{\tau_b} A\,dx \qquad (7.3)$$

Since p_b varies linearly from $p_b(0)$ at $x = 0$ to 0 at $x = W$, Eq. 7.3 reduces to:

$$I_{BB} = \frac{qA}{\tau_b}\left[\frac{p_b(0)W}{2} - p_{bo}W \right] = \frac{qA p_{bo}W}{2\tau_b}\left(e^{qV_{EB}/kT} - 2 \right) \qquad (7.4)$$

Clearly, this component of base current can be minimized by making the base as thin as possible and by using for the base semiconductor material which has a relatively long lifetime. That is, the base width should be made small compared with the diffusion length for a hole. In some transistors, surface recombination is as significant as bulk recombination in determining I_{BB}. For these devices, Eq. 7.4 describes only a portion of the total base-region recombination current.

The approximation made in deriving the base recombination current is important and should be understood clearly. In evaluating the integral of Eq. 7.3 we assumed that the hole distribution in the base is *linear*, which is equivalent to saying that the hole current is constant, and thus that no recombination occurs in the base. Clearly, a linear hole distribution in the base is inconsistent with the existence of a recombination component of base current. In practical transistors, however, the deviations of the hole distribution from linearity and the resulting error in Eq. 7.4 are exceedingly small because 1 per cent or less of the holes vanish in the base. That is, I_{BB} is 1 per cent or less of $|I_C|$.

The electron current extracted from the collector can also be evaluated on the basis of the static diode theory of Chapter 3. If the collector region is several diffusion lengths wide, this current is:

$$I_{BC} = - \frac{qAD_c n_{co}}{L_c} \tag{7.5}$$

where D_c and L_c are the diffusion constant and the diffusion length in the collector, and n_{co} is the equilibrium minority-carrier concentration in the collector. This current component can be minimized by doping the collector heavily, thereby reducing n_{co}.

The total base current $(-I_B)$ is:

$$(-I_B) = I_{BE} + I_{BB} + I_{BC} \tag{7.6}$$

In the neutral base region this majority-carrier current flows transversely, normal to the minority-carrier flow. There is a transverse electric field associated with this majority-carrier current which causes the forward voltage drop across the emitter-junction space-charge layer to have a transverse variation, decreasing slightly with increasing distance from the metal contact applied to the base region. Because the effective bias voltage is lower at points removed from the base contact, the *longitudinal* minority-carrier current density *decreases* at points far from the base contact, and the flow of holes is crowded or concentrated near the base contact. For simplicity, we initially neglect the effects of this transverse voltage drop in the base.

We have now identified the components of the terminal currents of a transistor in the active mode, and have shown how those currents depend on the junction voltages. In summary, the emitter and collector currents are nearly equal in magnitude and increase exponentially with V_{EB}. The base current is much smaller than the other currents, and is also strongly dependent on V_{EB}. None of the currents depend significantly on the collector-base voltage V_{CB}.

7.2 THE TRANSISTOR AS AN AMPLIFIER

Many active mode applications of transistors involve *changes* in V_{EB} which are small enough so that the *changes* in current and voltage thereby produced are *linearly* related. With this broad class of applications a *small-signal linear model* of the transistor is desirable for use in circuit analysis. We begin our investigation of small-signal models for the active-region transistor by considering the consequences of a small *slowly applied* change of emitter-base voltage of magnitude ΔV_{EB}. That is, we assume that the transistor is biased in the active mode at an operating point defined by V_{EB} (which constrains I_C, I_E, and I_B) and determine the consequences of changing the emitter bias to $V_{EB} + \Delta V_{EB}$.

When ΔV_{EB} is applied, the hole concentration in the base at the edge of the emitter-junction space-charge layer increases. If ΔV_{EB} is less than about 5 millivolts, the change in $p_b(0)$ is found from Eq. 2.19a to be:

$$\Delta p_b(0) = p_b(0) \frac{q}{kT} \Delta V_{EB} \tag{7.7}$$

The hole distribution in the base changes as shown in Fig. 7.7. The minority-carrier electron distribution in the emitter also changes to accommodate the increased emitter-junction bias voltage. These changes have two consequences:

1. The collector current increases in magnitude [by $\Delta(-I_C)$] because the hole gradient in the base is greater.

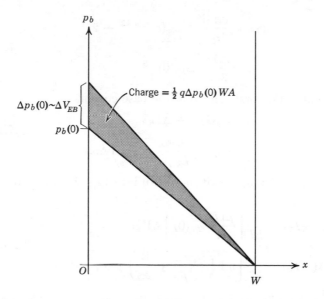

Fig. 7.7. The effect of a change in V_{EB} on the base minority-carrier concentration.

2. The base current increases in magnitude [by $\Delta(-I_B)$] because the increased store of holes in the base recombines at an increased rate, and because the current of electrons injected back into the emitter also increases.

The change in collector current can be evaluated from Eq. 7.1. It is:

$$\Delta(-I_C) = qAD_b\left(\frac{\Delta p_b(0)}{W}\right) \tag{7.8}$$

The change in base current can be evaluated from Eqs. 7.2 and 7.4 (I_{BC} does not change in response to ΔV_{EB}). The components are:

$$
\begin{aligned}
\Delta I_{BE} &= \frac{qAD_e n_{eo}}{L_e p_{bo}} \Delta[p_{bo}(e^{qV_{EB}/kT} - 1)] \\
&= \frac{qAD_e}{L_e} \frac{n_{eo}}{p_{bo}} \Delta p_b(0)
\end{aligned}
\tag{7.9a}
$$

and
$$\Delta I_{BB} = \frac{qAW}{2\tau_b} \Delta[p_{bo}(e^{qV_{EB}/kT} - 2)]$$

$$= \frac{qAW}{2\tau_b} \Delta p_b(0)$$
(7.9b)

Consequently, the total change in the base current is:

$$\Delta(-I_B) = \Delta I_{BE} + \Delta I_{BB}$$
(7.10)

$$= qA\left(\frac{D_e}{L_e}\frac{n_{eo}}{p_{bo}} + \frac{W}{2\tau_b}\right)\Delta p_b(0)$$

If we use Eq. 7.7 and substitute $\Delta p_b(0)$ into Eqs. 7.8 and 7.10, we obtain:

$$\Delta(-I_C) = \frac{q}{kT}\left[\frac{qAD_b}{W}p_b(0)\right]\Delta V_{EB}$$

$$\Delta(-I_B) = \frac{q}{kT}\left[qA\left(\frac{D_e}{L_e}\frac{n_{eo}}{p_{bo}} + \frac{W}{2\tau_b}\right)p_b(0)\right]\Delta V_{EB}$$
(7.11a,b)

This pair of equations, which express the changes in collector and base current in terms of the change in emitter-base voltage, are the results we desire. Note that the coefficients are proportional to $p_b(0)$ and thus vary with operating point. We can make this operating-point dependence more explicit by using Eq. 7.1 to express $p_b(0)$ in terms of $(-I_C)$, which we write $|I_C|$:

$$p_b(0) = \frac{W}{qAD_b}|I_C|$$
(7.12)

In terms of $|I_C|$ Eqs. 7.11 become:

$$\Delta(-I_C) = \frac{q}{kT}|I_C|\Delta V_{EB}$$

$$\Delta(-I_B) = \left(\frac{D_e}{D_b}\frac{W}{L_e}\frac{n_{eo}}{p_{bo}} + \frac{W^2}{2D_b\tau_b}\right)\frac{q}{kT}|I_C|\Delta V_{EB}$$
(7.13a,b)

which we rewrite as:

$$\Delta(-I_C) = g_m\Delta V_{EB}$$

$$\Delta(-I_B) = \delta g_m\Delta V_{EB}$$
(7.14a,b)

The coefficient g_m, given by

$$g_m = \frac{q}{kT}|I_C|$$
(7.15a)

is called the *transconductance*. At room temperature where $kT/q \cong$ 25 millivolts, the transconductance g_m is about 0.04 mhos per milli-ampere of quiescent collector current $|I_C|$. The dimensionless parameter δ given by

$$\delta = \frac{D_e W n_{eo}}{D_b L_e p_{bo}} + \frac{1}{2}\left(\frac{W}{L_b}\right)^2 \qquad (7.15b)$$

represents the effect of two *defects* in the transistor which give rise to base current. These defects are:

   (*a*) Minority-carrier injection into the emitter.
   (*b*) Recombination in the base.

This coefficient, which varies from 0.1 to 0.003 in various tran-sistors, can be made small by decreasing the base width and by doping the emitter more heavily than the base.

Figure 7.8 shows a transistor used as an amplifier in the common-emitter configuration. A signal source ΔV is connected so that it must supply increments of base current only. We assume that the reverse bias on the collector junction is in excess of 100 millivolts because of the bias battery V_C. The incremental currents and volt-ages caused by ΔV are, from Eqs. 7.14 and the circuit:

$$\Delta(-I_B) = \delta g_m \Delta V$$
$$\Delta(-I_C) = g_m \Delta V \qquad (7.16a,b,c)$$
$$\Delta V_{CE} = g_m R_L \Delta V$$

Therefore, the various gain factors of the transistor are:

The current gain: $\dfrac{\Delta(-I_C)}{\Delta(-I_B)} = \dfrac{1}{\delta}$

The voltage gain: $\dfrac{\Delta V_{CE}}{\Delta V} = g_m R_L \qquad (7.17a,b,c)$

The power gain: $\dfrac{\Delta V_{CE} \Delta I_C}{\Delta V \Delta I_B} = \dfrac{g_m R_L}{\delta}$

For a typical transistor biased at $|I_C| = 1$ ma and having $\delta = 0.02$, and for $R_L = 10^3$ ohms, we have:

$$\text{Current gain} = 50$$
$$\text{Voltage gain} = 40$$
$$\text{Power gain} = 2000$$

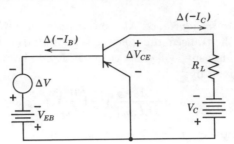

Fig. 7.8. The transistor as an amplifier.

This calculation implies that the voltage gain and power gain can be increased without limit by increasing R_L. The gain is limited, however, for large values of the load resistance by a second-order mechanism which causes the collector current to depend on the voltage at the reverse-biased collector junction. This limitation occurs because the instantaneous width of the field-free base, W, depends on the instantaneous collector-junction reverse-bias voltage, inasmuch as the length of the collector-junction space-charge region that penetrates the base changes with collector voltage. This effect, which will be considered in Chapter 8, typically becomes important when the voltage gain approaches 200.

The results of our small-signal analysis for slowly applied changes in V_{EB} can be interpreted in terms of the simple circuit model of Fig. 7.9. This circuit is clearly equivalent to Eqs. 7.14. Because this model represents the small-signal behavior of the transistor for relatively low voltage-gain and for slowly varying signals, it does not reflect any of the dynamic features of the transistor which become important when rapidly changing signals are applied. These matters are considered in Sec. 7.4, where a more complete model is obtained.

7.3 CURRENT-ACTUATED CIRCUIT MODELS

The discussion of the preceding section and the simple circuit model of Fig. 7.9 regard the incremental emitter-base voltage ΔV_{EB} as the controlling or independent variable. This is a powerful point of view, closely related to the operating mechanism of the transistor, and we will find much employment for it. There are,

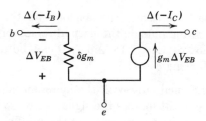

Fig. 7.9. A simple circuit model for the transistor in the active mode.

however, other equally useful ways of describing the action of the transistor, using the increment in either I_E or I_B as the independent variable.

The incremental components of the terminal currents are linearly related because they all depend linearly on the excess minority-carrier distributions, as shown by Eqs. 7.8 and 7.10. Consequently, the incremental current-gain from base to collector is:

$$\frac{\Delta(-I_C)}{\Delta(-I_B)} = \frac{\Delta I_C}{\Delta I_B} = \frac{\dfrac{qAD_b}{W}\Delta p_b(0)}{qA\left(\dfrac{D_e n_{eo}}{L_e p_{bo}} + \dfrac{W}{2\tau_b}\right)\Delta p_b(0)} = \frac{1}{\delta} \qquad (7.18)$$

Because the incremental emitter current is

$$\Delta I_E = -(\Delta I_B + \Delta I_C) \qquad (7.19)$$

the incremental current gain from emitter to collector is

$$\frac{\Delta I_C}{\Delta I_E} = \frac{-1}{1+\delta} \qquad (7.20)$$

It is important to recognize that these current gain expressions are *independent of the relationship between* $\Delta p_b(0)$ *and* ΔV_{EB}. That is, the incremental current gains of the transistor are constant over a wide range of operating-point current and are not limited by the principal nonlinearity of the transistor, which is the exponential relationship between emitter-base voltage and minority-carrier concentration in the base. In our idealized transistor model the defect δ is a constant, independent of $|I_C|$. Many transistors are designed so that δ is reasonably constant over a wide range of collector currents.* Consequently, as long as the collector-base voltage does not swing outside the normal region of operation, the current gain ratios of Eqs. 7.18 and 7.20 can be used with large signals in the following cases:

(a) We are concerned only with the incremental current ratios.

(b) The input current follows the signal source which drives the transistor, despite the presence of the nonlinear relationship between ΔV_{EB} and ΔI_B.

To check for satisfaction of condition (b) we express the signal source as a Thevenin equivalent. If the Thevenin equivalent source-voltage is much larger than ΔV_{EB}, the condition is satisfied. While the output voltage and current will follow faithfully the equivalent source-voltage at the input over large-signal excursions, the incremental emitter-base voltage will be quite distorted, appearing compressed at the high current peaks of the signal swing.

If the incremental component of emitter-base voltage is small enough so that it is linearly related to $\Delta p_b(0)$, Eqs. 7.18 and 7.20 may be interpreted, along with Eq. 7.14b, in terms of the current-actuated small-signal models of Fig. 7.10. These models are, of course, entirely equivalent to the voltage-actuated model of Fig. 7.9. The common-emitter current-gain factor $1/\delta$ is usually designated as β and the common-base current-gain factor $1/(1 + \delta)$ is usually designated as α, as indicated in Fig. 7.10.

7.4 A SMALL-SIGNAL DYNAMIC CIRCUIT MODEL

The circuit models of Figs. 7.9 and 7.10 are incomplete in that they do not account for the components of the terminal current which are associated with dynamic changes in the internal charge distributions. There are two types of change in internal charges:

(a) The excess minority-carrier charge store in the base region changes in response to increments in the emitter-base voltage. The change in the hole store, which is illustrated in Fig. 7.7, is accompanied by an equal change in the majority-carrier electron store.

---

* In silicon transistors at low current levels the defect δ increases strongly above its medium current value because of recombination in the emitter-junction space-charge layer. This effect has been neglected in our idealized model.

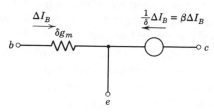

(a) Common–emitter model with generator
dependent upon incremental base current

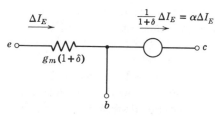

(b) Common–base model with generator
dependent upon incremental emitter current

Fig. 7.10. Current actuated low-frequency small-signal circuit models.

(b) The emitter- and collector-junction space-charge layers contain dipole layers of charge which change in response to increments in the junction voltages.

We will now investigate the consequences of dynamic changes in these charges and obtain a modified incremental model which includes these effects. As in Sec. 7.2, we are concerned with small variations about an operating point, and we use the variables shown in Fig. 7.11 to designate the instantaneous incremental com-

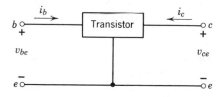

Fig. 7.11. Definition of incremental terminal variables.

ponents of the terminal voltages and currents.* We base our analysis on a common-emitter configuration, so that the emitter terminal is in common to the input and output loops.

For small increments, the relationships among the incremental variables will be *linear*. Therefore, the relationships between the incremental terminal variables can be expressed in terms of a pair of coupled ordinary differential equations.

$$i_b = \mathcal{Y}_i v_{be} + \mathcal{Y}_r v_{ce}$$
$$i_c = \mathcal{Y}_f v_{be} + \mathcal{Y}_o v_{ce}$$

(7.21a,b)

In these equations, the $\mathcal{Y}$'s represent linear differential operators.† $\mathcal{Y}_i$ is the input admittance operator, $\mathcal{Y}_o$ the output admittance operator, and $\mathcal{Y}_f$ and $\mathcal{Y}_r$ the forward and reverse transfer admittance operators, respectively.

We have chosen to express the currents in terms of the voltages because our basic point of view is that currents are produced by changes in internal charge distributions, which are the result of voltage changes at the junctions. We use the changes in the internal carrier distributions to compute the admittance operators directly, and then interpret the admittances in terms of a linear circuit model which involves resistors, capacitors, and dependent generators. The general form of this circuit model is shown in Fig. 7.12. This circuit is entirely equivalent to Eqs. 7.21 because its node equations are identical to those equations.

We initially neglect the currents associated with charge changes in the space-charge layer and compute the currents associated with excess charge stores in the neutral regions.

First, we determine $\mathcal{Y}_r$ and $\mathcal{Y}_o$, which account for the effects of v_{ce} on i_b and i_c. To evaluate these operators we set v_{be} equal to zero and compute i_b and i_c in response to v_{ce}. Figure 7.12 shows that with $v_{be} = 0$, $v_{cb} = v_{ce}$. However, the change in collector-base voltage v_{cb} has no effect on the minority-carrier distribution in the base

---

* The instantaneous incremental variables are designated by lower-case variables with lower-case subscripts, rather than by the Δ notation used earlier, in conformity with IEEE standard notation.

† In general, each linear differential operator is of the form $\mathcal{Y} = \left(a_o + a_1 \dfrac{d}{dt} + a_2 \dfrac{d^2}{dt^2} + \cdots \right)$, where the a's are constants.

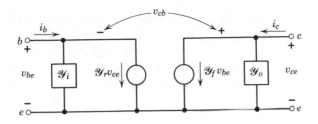

Fig. 7.12. The incremental admittance model.

because the hole concentration at the collector edge of the base is approximately zero as long as the collector junction is reverse-biased more than about 100 millivolts, and because we are at present neglecting changes in base width produced by v_{cb}. Consequently, i_b and i_c must be zero and we have:

$$\mathcal{Y}_r = 0$$
$$\mathcal{Y}_o = 0$$
$$(7.22a,b)$$

The other two admittance operators $\mathcal{Y}_i$ and $\mathcal{Y}_f$ can be evaluated by constraining v_{ce} to be zero and determining the consequences of v_{be}. Under these conditions $v_{cb} = -v_{be}$. However, v_{cb} has no effect on the minority-carrier concentrations, as evidenced by the discussion above, and we can focus directly on the changes produced by v_{be}.

The minority-carrier concentration at the emitter edge of the base changes in response to v_{be}, as shown by Eq. 7.7 (with $\Delta V_{BD} - -v_{be}$), so that the hole distribution in the base region must change. *We assume that v_{be} changes slowly enough so that the hole distribution in the base changes as a succession of steady states.* That is, we assume that the base hole distribution is approximately *linear*, even under dynamic conditions. Such a change is shown by the shaded area in Fig. 7.7.

Because the hole distribution is approximately linear under dynamic conditions, the change in collector current is proportional to the change in $p_b(0)$ and thus to v_{be}. Consequently, Eq. 7.14a is applicable and yields [with $i_c = -\Delta(-I_C)$]:

$$i_c = g_m v_{be} \qquad (7.23)$$

That is, the forward admittance operator $\mathcal{Y}_f$ is just a constant, g_m, given by Eq. 7.15a.

The base current has two components. One supplies electrons for the modified injection into the emitter and for the changed recombination in the base. The other supplies electrons which change the majority-carrier store to match the change in minority-carrier store shown in Fig. 7.7, thereby preserving neutrality. The first component has already been evaluated and is given by Eq. 7.14b. The second component is given by $-d\Delta q_b/dt$ where Δq_b is the shaded area shown in Fig. 7.7. The minus sign is necessary because the base current supplies the *electrons* which neutralize the hole charge represented by the shaded area. The charge change Δq_b is:

$$\Delta q_b = \tfrac{1}{2}q\Delta p_b(0)\,WA \qquad (7.24)$$

Using Eq. 7.7 with $\Delta V_{EB} = -v_{be}$, we have

$$\Delta q_b = -\frac{qA\,Wp_b(0)}{2}\frac{q}{kT}v_{be} \qquad (7.25)$$

or, expressing $p_b(0)$ in terms of $|I_C|$,

$$\Delta q_b = -\frac{W^2}{2D_b}g_m v_{be} \qquad (7.26)$$

The total base current is, therefore,

$$i_b = \delta g_m v_{be} + \frac{W^2}{2D_b}g_m\frac{dv_{be}}{dt} \qquad (7.27)$$

Therefore, the values of $\mathcal{Y}_f$ and $\mathcal{Y}_i$ are:

$$\begin{aligned} \mathcal{Y}_f &= g_m \\ \mathcal{Y}_i &= \delta g_m + \frac{W^2}{2D_b}g_m\frac{d}{dt} \end{aligned} \qquad (7.28a,b)$$

Figure 7.13a shows the incremental circuit model which our analysis yields. The forward transfer-admittance operator is represented by a dependent current generator. The recombination portion of the input admittance operator is represented by a conductance δg_m, and the term which is associated with changes in the stored base charge is represented by a capacitor $(W^2/2D_b)g_m$.

The effects of changes in the dipole layers at the two junctions are represented by adding space-charge capacitances between emitter-base and collector-base terminals, as shown in Fig. 7.13b.

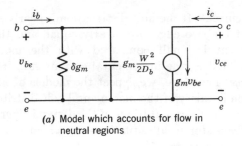

(a) Model which accounts for flow in
neutral regions

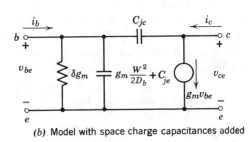

(b) Model with space charge capacitances added

Fig. 7.13. The small-signal circuit model for a transistor.

The models of Fig. 7.13 are based on the assumption that the hole distribution in the base is approximately linear, even under dynamic conditions. This assumption is certainly justified for very slowly changing incremental variables, because under nearly static conditions the shape of the hole distribution in the base is governed by the hole diffusion length L_b, which is much greater than the base width W. As the rate of change of v_{be} increases, the hole distribution in the base deviates from a straight line and the models derived on the basis of a straight-line approximation are in error.

The deviations from linearity of the base hole distribution which occur for higher-speed signals are closely coupled to the incremental base current. The slope at $x = 0$ (the emitter edge) of the instantaneous incremental component of the excess hole distribution is proportional to the instantaneous incremental emitter current. Similarly, the slope at $x = W$ (the collector edge) is proportional to the instantaneous incremental collector current. The *difference* between slopes is, therefore, proportional to the instantaneous incremental *base* current. If the hole distribution is nearly straight-line, the slopes at the two edges are nearly equal, and the incremental base current is small compared with the incremental collector current. That is, the incremental current gain from base to collector is *large*. Therefore, we expect the models of Fig. 7.13, which are based on linearity of the incremental hole distribution in the base, to be accurate representations of the dynamic incremental behavior of the transistor in all situations for which the base-to-collector current gain is large.

For sinusoidal small signals, we can estimate the frequency at which the current gain becomes small, and thus at which the model is in error, by using the model of Fig. 7.13a. If v_{be} is sinusoidal of complex amplitude V_{be}, the complex amplitudes of the collector and base current are:

$$I_b = \left(\delta g_m + j\omega g_m \frac{W^2}{2D_b} \right) V_{be}$$
$$I_c = g_m V_{be} \tag{7.29a,b}$$

where ω is the frequency. Consequently, the base-to-collector current gain, usually designated as β, is:

$$\beta = \frac{I_c}{I_b} = \frac{g_m}{\delta g_m + j\omega g_m (W^2/2D_b)} = \frac{1}{\delta + j\omega(W^2/2D_b)} \tag{7.30}$$

For low frequencies, β approaches the value $1/\delta$, which agrees with our previous low-frequency analysis (see Eq. 7.18). As the frequency increases, the current gain decreases in magnitude. For a frequency of

$$\omega_\tau = \frac{2D_b}{W^2} \tag{7.31}$$

the *magnitude* of the current gain is nearly unity. At this frequency we expect the model to be appreciably in error because here the instantaneous incremental hole distribution in the base is not well-approximated by a straight line. For frequencies appreciably less than ω_τ, the current gain is large and the errors in the model which result from inaccuracies in the representation of the dynamic hole distribution are small.

An alternative interpretation for the frequency ω_τ can be obtained by considering the behavior of the ac diffusion length Λ_b in the base, which governs the incremental hole distribution there. The *magnitude* of the incremental hole distribution varies exponentially with x, with a characteristic length given by $(\mathrm{Re}\,[1/\Lambda_b])^{-1}$. For high frequencies, this characteristic length is approximately $\sqrt{2D_b/\omega}$, which is equal to the base width W for $\omega = \omega_r$. Therefore, at ω_r it is not surprising that the incremental hole distribution deviates significantly from a straight line.

The broad applicability of the quasi-static approximation to transistor dynamics is in sharp contrast to its very limited usefulness in analysis of the dynamics of pn-junction diodes. In transistors the requirement that there be *incremental gain* limits operation to frequencies low enough to justify the straight-line approximation. Consequently, it is seldom necessary to consider the details of the base hole distribution for frequencies or rates of change which cause appreciable deviations from the straight-line distribution. On the other hand, the interesting rates of change for diode dynamic analysis are not limited by gain considerations and are usually high enough so that the dynamic excess carrier distribution cannot be treated as a slowly changing static distribution, and some analysis of the distributed system is necessary.

PROBLEMS

P7.1 Use the analysis of Sec. 7.1.2 to obtain expressions for I_E, I_B, and I_C in the active mode which account for *all* components of these currents. Show that the currents can be written in the following form:

$$I_E = I_1(e^{qV_{EB}/kT} - 1) + I_2$$
$$I_C = -(aI_E + I_3)$$

where a, I_1, I_2, and I_3 are constants.

P7.2 Near room temperature, the collector current I_C and the base current I_B (with polarities defined in Fig. 7.2) are both normally negative for a *pnp* transistor biased in the active mode. If the collector current is held constant while the temperature is increased, I_B decreases in magnitude, passes through zero, and becomes *positive*. What physical effects account for this behavior? Is the small-signal behavior of the transistor influenced by this reversal of the dc base current?

P7.3 Consider a *pnp* transistor which is biased in the active mode and which is illuminated in the collector space-charge layer. The radiation produces hole-electron pairs in the space-charge layer at a total rate of r pairs per unit time.

    (a) Describe the behavior of the carriers produced by the ionizing radiation. That is, indicate briefly the flow of these carriers.

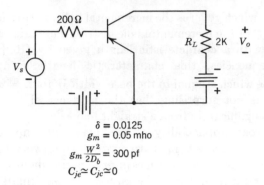

$$\delta = 0.0125$$
$$g_m = 0.05 \, \text{mho}$$
$$g_m \frac{W^2}{2D_b} = 300 \, \text{pf}$$
$$C_{je} \approx C_{jc} \approx 0$$

Fig. 7.14.

(b) Can the effects of the pairs produced by radiation be represented by modifying the small-signal model of Fig. 7.9? If so, indicate the required modification on a schematic circuit model.

(c) Compute the change in I_C produced by the pairs resulting from the radiation, if the emitter-base circuit is incrementally shorted, i.e., if $\Delta V_{EB} = 0$.

(d) Repeat (c) if the base circuit is incrementally open, i.e., if $\Delta I_B = 0$.

P7.4 The transistor used in the circuit in Fig. 7.14 has the parameters indicated at the operating point.

(a) Compute the incremental voltage gain V_o/V_s as a function of frequency. At what frequency is the voltage gain 3 db down from its low-frequency asymptote; i.e., what is the break frequency of the voltage gain?

(b) The incremental power gain may be defined as the ratio of the power delivered to the load resistor R_L to the power supplied by the signal source V_s. Compute the incremental power gain as a function of frequency. At what frequency is the power gain 3 db down from its low frequency asymptote?

(c) What is ω_τ for this transistor? Assuming that the model is valid at ω_τ, compute the power gain at that frequency.

P7.5 Show that the models of Fig. 7.10 are equivalent to the model of Fig. 7.9.

P7.6 The incremental behavior of a *pnp* transistor may be represented by the circuit model shown in Fig. 7.15. For a temperature of 300°K, the sketches of Fig. 7.15 show the dependence in the active region of:

(a) dc collector current I_C on dc base current I_B;

(b) stored minority-carrier charge in the base, q_b, on I_C;

(c) charge q_{jc} in either half of the collector-junction space-charge layer on collector-to-base voltage V_{CB}. Estimate numerical values for g_m, g_π, C_π, and C_μ at an operating point of $I_C = 2 \, \text{ma}$, $V_{CE} \cong V_{CB} = -10$ volts. Assume that the *emitter* space-charge layer capacitance is a negligible component of C_π, and neglect charge storage in the emitter.

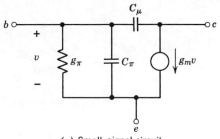

(a) Small–signal circuit

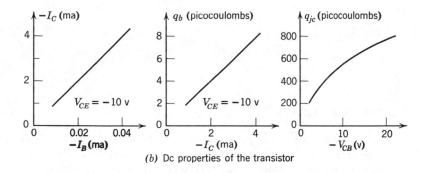

(b) Dc properties of the transistor

Fig. 7.15.

8

Small-Signal Transistor
Models

8.0 INTRODUCTION

Our development in the previous chapter of a small-signal model for the transistor contains two important restrictions. First, we neglected the consequences of base-width changes produced by changes in the collector-to-base voltage, and thereby obtained $\mathcal{Y}_r = \mathcal{Y}_o = 0$. Second, we ignored voltage drops in the base region produced by the transverse flow of majority-carrier currents there.

The objectives of this chapter are to determine the effect of base width modulation on $\mathcal{Y}_r$ and $\mathcal{Y}_o$ (and to modify our calculations for $\mathcal{Y}_f$ and $\mathcal{Y}_i$ accordingly), and to find a circuit representation for the effects of transverse voltage drops in the base region. We first investigate the behavior of the minority carriers in the neutral regions, thereby determining the four admittance operators of the basic model, and then add space-charge capacitances and the effects of base voltage drops later.

8.1 COLLECTOR SIGNAL VOLTAGE AND BASE-WIDTH MODULATION

For a transistor biased in the active mode, the minority-carrier concentration at the collector edge of the neutral base region is always essentially zero if the collector junction is reverse-biased more than 100 mv. However, the width of the space-charge layer at the collector junction depends on the magnitude of the reverse-bias voltage, so that the width of the neutral base region depends on the collector-to-base voltage. This dependence of base width on the collector-to-base voltage is illustrated in Fig. 8.1*a* which is shown for constant emitter-to-base voltage. The sketch shows that a positive increment in collector-to-base voltage, represented by positive v_{cb}, causes a decrease in the magnitude of the reverse bias, thereby shrinking the width of the space-charge layer and causing an incremental increase in base width.

The increase in base width ΔW which accompanies v_{cb} has two effects, which can be seen in Fig. 8.1*a*. First, the collector current decreases because the slope of the hole distribution in the base decreases. Second, the charge store in the base increases, thereby increasing the base current. Our problem is to represent these incremental changes in collector current and base current in a circuit model.

The circuit configuration we have chosen to represent the transistor as a linear active two-terminal-pair device is the admittance model shown in Fig. 7.12. The coupled ordinary differential equations which characterize this model are (see Eqs. 7.21):

$$i_b = \mathcal{Y}_i v_{be} + \mathcal{Y}_r v_{ce}$$
$$i_c = \mathcal{Y}_f v_{be} + \mathcal{Y}_o v_{ce}$$

$$(8.1a,b)$$

We compute the operators $\mathcal{Y}_i$ and $\mathcal{Y}_f$ by determining the effect of v_{be} on i_b and i_c with $v_{ce} = 0$ and compute $\mathcal{Y}_r$ and $\mathcal{Y}_o$ by similarly investigating the effect of v_{ce} on the currents with $v_{be} = 0$. The two parts of this pair of calculations are really very similar, and we can demonstrate the similarity by finding an equivalent representation for the incremental base-width change shown in Fig. 8.1*a*.

8.1.1 *The Effect of Base-Width Modulation on Minority-Carrier Concentration*

Although the underlying physical mechanism involves a change in the width of the neutral base region, we can compute the collector-current and base-current changes produced by v_{cb} by representing the base-width change ΔW by an *equivalent* minority-carrier concentration change $\Delta p_b(W)$ as shown in Fig. 8.1*b*.

This sketch shows that the physical effect, which involves a shift in the location of the plane at which the minority-carrier

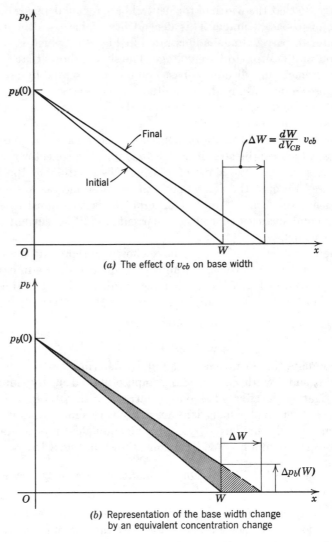

(a) The effect of v_{cb} on base width

(b) Representation of the base width change
by an equivalent concentration change

Fig. 8.1. The effect of collector-to-base signal voltage on the base minority-carrier distribution.

concentration is zero, can be represented by assigning a minority carrier concentration change $\Delta p_b(W)$ to the collector edge of the base *which is assumed to remain fixed in position* at the value of W corresponding to the quiescent operating point of the device. This representation by means of $\Delta p_b(W)$ is clearly equivalent to the actual situation insofar as the slope of the distribution is concerned. It is also equivalent in terms of the change in the base-charge store because the area of the small triangle of base ΔW and height $\Delta p_b(W)$ which we ignore, is a second-order differential in comparison with the larger shaded triangle.

The equivalent concentration change can easily be computed from the geometry of the base minority-carrier distribution. Inasmuch as the small triangle is similar to the large unshaded triangle (of base $W + \Delta W$), which represents the total base-hole store, we have:

$$\frac{\Delta p_b(W)}{\Delta W} = \frac{p_b(0)}{W + \Delta W} \simeq \frac{p_b(0)}{W} \tag{8.2}$$

However, for small changes in collector-to-base voltage we have:

$$\Delta W = \frac{dW}{dV_{CB}} v_{cb} \tag{8.3}$$

Consequently, the equivalent increment in hole concentration at the collector edge of the base is

$$\Delta p_b(W) = \frac{p_b(0)}{W} \frac{dW}{dV_{CB}} v_{cb} \tag{8.4}$$

It is interesting to compare this result with our previous calculation showing the dependence of the increment in hole concentration at the emitter edge of the base on v_{be}. From Eq. 7.7 that result is:

$$\Delta p_b(0) = -p_b(0) \frac{q}{kT} v_{be} \tag{8.5}$$

Rewriting Eq. 8.4 as:

$$\Delta p_b(W) = p_b(0) \frac{q}{kT} \left(\frac{kT}{q} \frac{1}{W} \frac{dW}{dV_{CB}} \right) v_{cb} = p_b(0) \frac{q}{kT} \eta v_{cb} \tag{8.6}$$

we see that *the effect of a change in collector-to-base voltage v_{cb} on the hole concentration at $x = W$, $\Delta p_b(W)$, is similar to the effect of a* *change in base-to-emitter voltage v_{be} on the hole concentration at $x = 0$, $\Delta p_b(0)$, except it is multiplied by the dimensionless factor*

$$\eta = \frac{kT}{q} \frac{1}{W} \frac{dW}{dV_{CB}} \tag{8.7}$$

This factor η, which we call the *base-width modulation factor*, is quite small for all transistors. At useful operating points, it typically lies in the range of 10^{-3} to 10^{-5}. Therefore, changes in collector-to-base voltage have a much smaller effect on the base minority-carrier distribution than equal changes in base-to-emitter voltage. Consequently, *base-width modulation effects are not important unless the voltage gain of the device approaches $1/\eta$.*

Our result, given by Eq. 8.6, is valid as long as the base minority-carrier distribution is well approximated by a straight line. This will be true as long as the small-signal base-to-collector current gain is reasonably large, as discussed in Sec. 7.4.

8.1.2 *Calculation of* $\mathcal{Y}_i$ *and* $\mathcal{Y}_f$

We compute $\mathcal{Y}_i$ and $\mathcal{Y}_f$ by constraining the incremental collector-to-emitter voltage, v_{ce}, to be zero and determining the effect of a change in base-to-emitter voltage v_{be}. With $v_{ce} = 0$, $v_{cb} = -v_{be}$ (see Fig. 7.12). That is, when we apply some v_{be} the hole concentration at the collector edge changes because the collector-to-base voltage changes by an amount exactly equal to v_{be}. In our analysis of Sec. 7.4, we neglected this change. We now see that this neglect was completely justified because the ratio of the change at $x = W$ to the change at $x = 0$ is equal to η, and η is extremely small. Therefore, Eq. 7.28 is still valid and we have*

$$\mathcal{Y}_f = g_m$$
$$\mathcal{Y}_i = \delta g_m + \frac{W^2}{2D_b} g_m \frac{d}{dt} \tag{8.8a,b}$$

8.1.3 *Calculation of* $\mathcal{Y}_o$ *and* $\mathcal{Y}_r$

We compute $\mathcal{Y}_o$ and $\mathcal{Y}_r$ by setting v_{be} equal to zero and determining the effect of v_{ce}. With this constraint, Fig. 7.12 shows that

---

* It is not necessary to include base-width modulation effects due to changes in *base-to-emitter* voltage because such effects at the emitter are second-order in comparison with the basic mechanism of minority-carrier injection at a forward-biased junction.

$v_{cb} = v_{ce}$. Figure 8.1b shows that the change in collector-to-base voltage produces a change in slope and thus in i_c, as well as a change in the hole store and thus in i_b. *The changes depicted in Fig. 8.1b are precisely analogous to those shown in Fig. 7.7*, except that i_c is positive rather than negative (collector current magnitude decreases) and i_b is negative (base current magnitude increases). Hence,

$$i_c = \eta g_m v_{ce}$$

$$i_b = -\eta \left(\delta_b g_m + \frac{W^2}{2D_b} g_m \frac{d}{dt} \right) v_{ce}$$

(8.9a,b)

where we have used δ_b instead of simply δ because there is no analogue to injection into the emitter in response to v_{ce}. The subscript b denotes that δ_b is the base portion of the defect, i.e., $\frac{1}{2}(W/L_b)^2$. Comparison of Eqs. 8.1 with Eqs. 8.9 shows that

$$\mathcal{Y}_o = \eta g_m$$

$$\mathcal{Y}_r = -\eta \left(\delta_b g_m + \frac{W^2}{2D_b} g_m \frac{d}{dt} \right)$$

(8.10a,b)

8.1.4 *Representation by a Circuit Model*

These four admittance operators can be used in the basic model of Fig. 7.12. While this model is a complete representation of the effects of minority-carrier flow in the transistor, it is somewhat inconvenient to use because it contains two dependent generators. An alternate form, which is exactly equivalent, is shown in Fig. 8.2a. The equivalence of these two models can be seen by expressing i_c and i_b in terms of v_{be} and v_{ce} for both circuits and comparing the expressions.

In Fig. 8.2b we show the modified admittance model with the admittance operators represented by circuit elements. Because $\mathcal{Y}_r$ is of the order of η times $\mathcal{Y}_i$ and even less than η times $\mathcal{Y}_f$, we have neglected $\mathcal{Y}_r$ in expressing $(\mathcal{Y}_i + \mathcal{Y}_r)$ and $(\mathcal{Y}_f - \mathcal{Y}_r)$. We have also not shown the capacitive component of $\mathcal{Y}_r$ where it appears as $\mathcal{Y}_o + \mathcal{Y}_r$ at the output terminals. The susceptance of this capacitor is of the same order of magnitude as other effects which have been neglected as a consequence of our assumption that the dynamic hole distribution is nearly straight-line. That is, this capacitor in the model has little effect at frequencies below ω_r.

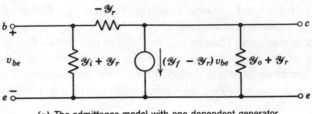

(a) The admittance model with one dependent generator

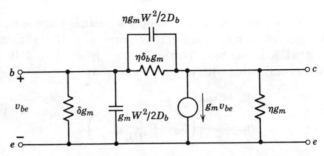

(b) The model with the admittances represented by circuit elements

Fig. 8.2. The small-signal model without space-charge capacitances and transverse voltage drops in the base.

8.1.5 *Exponential Excitations*

If the incremental signals are of the form Re $[Ae^{st}]$ where A is a complex amplitude and s is the complex frequency, the admittance operators can be given a simple interpretation. For example, if $v_{be} = $ Re $[V_{be}e^{st}], i_b$ is from Eq. 8.8b:

$$i_b = \mathcal{Y}_i v_{be} = \text{Re}\left[\left(\delta g_m + s\frac{W^2}{2D_b}g_m\right)V_{be}e^{st}\right] = \text{Re}\,[y_i V_{be}e^{st}] \quad (8.11)$$

where y_i is the complex input admittance at frequency s. This frequency domain interpretation is in complete accord with the interpretation of the admittance operators in terms of conductances, capacitances, and dependent generators. Inspection of Fig. 8.2b shows that the complex input admittance at frequency s is indeed $\delta g_m + s\dfrac{W^2}{2D_b}g_m$ (remember that $\eta \ll 1$).

8.2 BASE RESISTANCE — DC LARGE SIGNAL

The majority-carrier base current is a drift current which requires an electric field to drive it. It flows at right angles to the minority-carrier current. Figure 8.3 shows the path of base current in a typical planar transistor. There are two regions of interest, the active base region under the emitter, and the inactive base region near the base contact. All the base current must flow through the inactive region, and the current path is through material of finite conductivity. This portion of the path can be simulated by a fixed resistor in series with the base lead. It is called the *extrinsic* base resistance because it is outside the active region.

The potential drop needed to drive majority-carrier current in the active region has a polarity such as to reduce the forward bias on the emitter junction. This can be seen in Fig. 8.3, where the arrows indicate the direction of base-current flow in a *pnp* transistor. The potential drop to drive this current makes the upper portion of the active base region positive with respect to the lower portion. As a consequence of this voltage drop, the minority-carrier current density in the base falls off as we proceed from the edge of

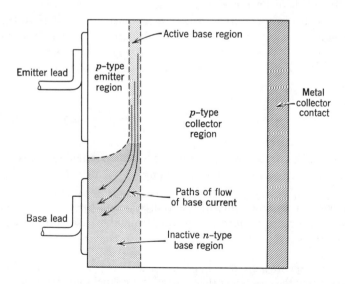

Fig. 8.3. Cross section of a *pnp* mesa transistor, showing the base current path.

the emitter adjacent to the base contact, deeper into the active region (*up* in Fig. 8.3). At very low currents, the effect is negligible. As current rises, this transverse voltage drop in the base becomes important. The collector current ceases to rise as fast as $e^{qV_{EB}/kT}$ Over a considerable range of current it is possible to represent the effect by an *intrinsic* base resistance added to the extrinsic base resistance. The intrinsic base resistance is not an identifiable lumped resistor like the extrinsic base resistance. It is the integrated effect of a distributed voltage drop. The intrinsic base resistance decreases with increasing dc current level for two reasons. First, the strong exponential dependence of collector current on the emitter junction voltage causes the bulk of the hole current to be carried by the portion of the active region close to the base contact at high current levels. Hence the transistor has its useful active base region narrowed at high currents and the effective resistive path length in the base is reduced. Second, at very high currents the low-level injection condition is exceeded, and the excess majority-carrier concentration in the base region increases the conductivity of the base material, also causing the intrinsic base resistance to drop.

The dc effect of base resistance is seen in Fig. 8.4, which shows measured collector current versus base-to-emitter terminal voltage over a wide current range. Up to 3 ma it is hard to see any deviation from the $e^{qV_{EB}/kT}$ law.* The deviation at higher currents can be ascribed to an equivalent dc large-signal base resistance, $R_B(I_C)$, defined by:

$$(-I_C) = I_o \exp \frac{q(V_{EB} + I_B R_B)}{kT} \qquad (8.12)$$

The scale factor, I_o, is determined for any particular transistor by measurements at currents low enough so that $I_B R_B$ is negligible.†

It is possible to erect the differential equation for $V_{EB}(y)$, where y is the position coordinate proceeding from the base contact edge of the active region *into* the active region. In the dc case, we obtain

---

* These data apply to a 2N1305 transistor operated with $V_{CB} = -15$ volts.
† In interpreting the analysis of this section it is essential to recognize that I_C and I_B are negative quantities for a *pnp* transistor biased in the active mode.

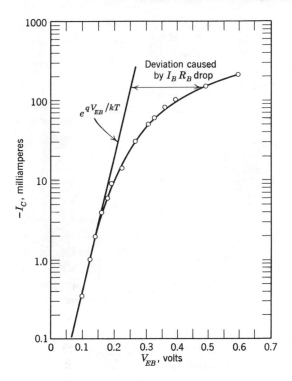

Fig. 8.4. I_C versus V_{EB} on semilogarithmic coordinates, showing the departures from the exponential relationship which occur in typical transistors at high currents.

a nonlinear differential equation because of the nonlinearity of $e^{qV_{EB}/kT}$ and because of the nonlinear nature of the conductivity modulation. The equation has a solution in a form which can be visualized only by plotting the results. It is possible then, with $V_{EB}(y)$ known, to calculate the collector current density as a function of y and integrate it to get the total collector current and the base current. This, in principle, permits calculation of the intrinsic component of R_B. The results of such calculations show that at low currents the minority-carrier current density across the emitter is nearly uniform, and at higher currents it falls off markedly as we proceed away from the base contact. The value of the intrinsic base resistance drops as collector current is increased, because the portion of the active region near the base contact carries most of the

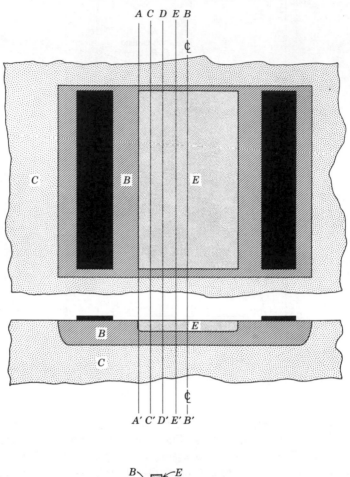

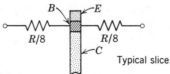

Typical slice

Fig. 8.5. Physical basis of a four-lump model for use in base voltage drop calculations.

collector current, reducing the length of base over which most of the base current must be driven by drift and because the conductivity is increased. The nonuniform distribution of the minority-carrier current density is sometimes called "emitter crowding," since the collector current is crowded toward the edge of the emitter nearest the base contact. This crowding effect does not influence the current gain of the transistor because the base current is determined by the total store of excess holes in the base region and is insensitive to the exact hole distribution.

Rather than use the formal analysis of the distributed base system, we will make a simple calculation for a typical transistor by slicing it into a number of smaller transistors and lumping the transverse resistance of the base layer external to the small transistors. For simplicity, we ignore conductivity modulation effects and use a constant value of conductivity for the base region. Figure 8.5 shows a planar transistor with symmetrical base contacts. Because of the symmetry we consider only half of it, up to the center line, and consider the emitter to be twice as long. The transverse resistance of the double-length active base layer between AA' and BB' is R. We neglect the shunting of R by base material outside the active region. The active region is sliced into four equal

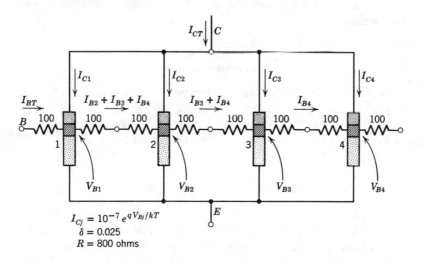

Fig. 8.6. Four-section lumped circuit model for base resistance calculations.

parts by the planes CC', DD', and EE'. Each of these parts is considered to have zero transverse base resistance internally, but to have an external resistance of $R/8$ ohms connected to each side of the slice, as shown in the sketch of a typical slice. The small transistors without base resistance behave in accordance with the models which ignore base resistance. We use four sections because that is a sufficient number to illustrate clearly the phenomena without too much calculation. Fewer sections may give good engineering answers in some practical problems; more may be required in others.

Figure 8.6 shows the four sections connected together with typical numerical values for a low-power germanium transistor assigned. We designate the voltage between the external base terminal (B) and the emitter terminal as V_{BE}. Each individual part has an I_o of 10^{-7}, so each draws a collector current of $-10^{-7} e^{qV_B/kT}$, where V_B is the emitter-base voltage of that part. δ is assumed to be 0.025, so the base current of each section is $0.025 I_C$. The total base current I_{BT} flows in from terminal B. The performance is calculated by assuming I_{C4} and then working back. Table 8.1 shows the various quantities for a range of total collector current from 0.4 ma to 8.5 ma. R_B is computed from Eq. 8.12, using 4×10^{-7} for I_o, since the complete transistor consists of all four sections.

TABLE 8.1

Currents in ma

$(-I_{CT})$	$(-I_{C1})$	$(-I_{C2})$	$(-I_{C3})$	$(-I_{C4})$	R_B
0.424	0.114	0.107	0.103	0.100	273 ohms
1.419	0.439	0.361	0.319	0.300	250
4.420	1.831	1.089	0.814	0.700	213
8.490	4.360	1.908	1.222	1.000	159

The significance of the data in Table 8.1 is:

1. At low currents the intrinsic base resistance is approximately $R/3$ ($= 267$ ohms) and there is very little crowding. That is, all four sections have nearly the same collector current.
2. As the collector current increases, the intrinsic base resistance drops below $R/3$, and marked crowding appears.

The four-section model is too coarse to follow the complete decrease of intrinsic base resistance with current because of the 100-ohm input lump. In any case, the typical transistor we selected would be in high-level injection at higher currents and the actual intrinsic base resistance would drop even faster because of conductivity modulation of the transverse base resistance. At high-current levels the intrinsic base resistance becomes small compared to the extrinsic component of base resistance, and R_B stays constant with increasing collector current.* Figure 8.7 shows a linear plot of V_{EB} versus I_C for the transistor of Fig. 8.4 at higher levels of

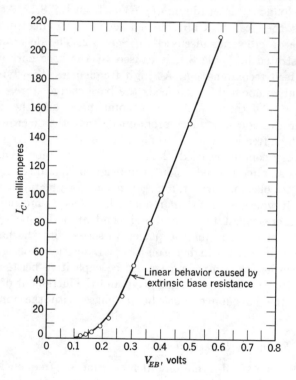

Fig. 8.7. I_C versus V_{EB} on linear coordinates, showing the effect of extrinsic base resistance at high currents.

* In many transistors there is sufficient minority-carrier injection in the *inactive* base region to cause conductivity modulation of the extrinsic base resistance. For these devices R_B continues to drop as I_C increases.

current. I_C increases almost linearly with V_{EB} instead of exponentially as at low-current levels. At these high-current levels, most of V_{EB} appears across R_B, so that I_B becomes proportional to V_{EB}. The current gain, $1/\delta$, is approximately constant, so I_C is proportional to V_{EB}.

8.3 SMALL-SIGNAL BASE-RESISTANCE EFFECTS

The resistance to lateral base-current flow modifies the small-signal circuit model. The modification at low frequencies is simple, and can be found by determining dI_C/dV_{EB} from Eq. 8.12. At high frequencies, there can be a pronounced ac crowding effect in addition to the dc crowding discussed in Sec. 8.2. The dc crowding effect, illustrated in Table 8.1, is caused by the base current required to feed recombination. At high frequencies, the dynamic base current component which feeds the base charge store can be much larger than the recombination component, and the consequent ac crowding can be more pronounced than the dc crowding. Hence, at high frequencies, only the portion of the dc active region near the base contact is used. This effective reduction in useful area causes an effective reduction in mutual conductance, and for a required ac collector current, a larger ac emitter-junction voltage is needed. If we retain a circuit model which has its mutual conductance proportional to I_C and independent of frequency, an appropriate impedance must be placed in series with the base to account for the actual higher small-signal junction voltage. At high frequencies, this impedance must be capacitive because the base-to-emitter impedance is capacitive and the increment of voltage across the impedance must be in phase with the junction voltage.

8.3.1 *Low-Frequency Base Resistance*

Figure 8.8 is a small-signal circuit model for low frequencies, to which a series base resistance, $r_b(I_C)$ has been added (compare Fig. 7.9). The model is appropriate for determining input impedance and short-circuit output current, and neglects y_r, because y_r is unimportant with a shorted output. The value of $r_b(I_C)$ can be determined from Eq. 8.12 by interpreting dI_C/dV_{EB}. The linear small-signal model shows the operation of the transistor for small

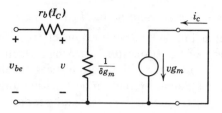

Fig. 8.8. Circuit model used to define the low-frequency base resistance.

current and voltage changes about a dc operating point, and was derived by differentiating the nonlinear dc equations. We recognize that r_b is a function of I_C, as Table 8.1 shows; and from Eq. 8.12, we obtain dI_C/dV_{BE}:

$$\frac{dI_C}{dV_{BE}} = -\frac{dI_C}{dV_{EB}} = \frac{1/\delta}{(1/\delta g_m) + R_B + I_C(dR_B/dI_C)} \quad (8.13a)$$

From the proposed circuit model of Fig. 8.8 we obtain the small-signal ratio, i_c/v_{eb}, which should equal dI_C/dV_{EB}.

$$\frac{i_c}{v_{be}} = \frac{1/\delta}{(1/\delta g_m) + r_b} \quad (8.13b)$$

By comparison of Eqs. 8.13a and 8.13b we find:

$$r_b = R_R + I_C\frac{dR_B}{dI_C} \quad (8.14)$$

Since R_B falls with increasing collector current, r_b is smaller than R_B, but approaches R_B for small values of I_C. Problem P8.6 uses the data of Table 8.1 to determine r_b from R_B and compares it with the value of r_b found by analyzing the circuit of Fig. 8.6 with each transistor represented by its circuit model. This problem simulates in lumped form the actual distributed nature of base resistance effects.

R_B and r_b are convenient circuit-model fictions, which reduce a distributed system to a simple lumped circuit, but since they vary with I_C in a way which is not simple mathematically, they must be used with caution. In some low-frequency small-signal applications of transistors, r_b is small compared to $1/\delta g_m$, and a rough approximation to its value suffices.

8.3.2 *Base Resistance Phenomena at High Frequency*

Figure 8.9 is a lumped representation of the distributed high-frequency circuit of the transistor, with the collector shorted. The device is sliced, as in Fig. 8.5, but into n slices. Each slice is represented by its small-signal circuit model without base resistance, and the circuits are joined by elements of base resistance. In general, there is dc crowding. Hence, y_1 and g_{m1} are larger than y_2 and g_{m2}, which are, in turn, larger than y_3 and g_{m3}. As the frequency rises to the range where the capacitive component of the input admittance of each section dominates, there is a significant change in performance. The y's close to the base terminal carry most of the ac base current, and the voltage, V_n, falls off rapidly as we move into the active base region (to the right in Fig. 8.9). This is the phenomenon of ac crowding. Sections further to the right, which may still be carrying significant dc current have very small values of V and contribute very little to I_c. In order to maintain a fixed value of I_c as frequency rises, V_{be} must be raised, because fewer of the $g_m V$ generators are used effectively. A circuit model which attempts to lump all the y's behind a single series base impedance and to lump all the g_m's in a single g_m, does not represent the physical situation, although a series base-impedance value exists and describes the circuit performance for each value of collector current and frequency. Because the circuit model of Fig.

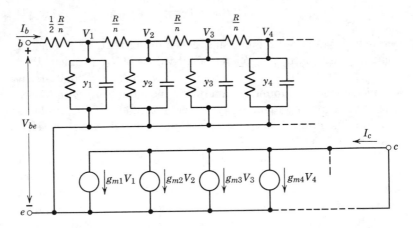

Fig. 8.9. A lumped representation of ac base-impedance effects.

8.2*b* has a wide range of usefulness in circuit analysis, we will examine the sort of fictitious series base impedance which must be added to the model to describe transistor performance in the presence of serious ac crowding. Our modified model retains the full input admittance and g_m, as calculated from $(q/kT)I_C$, at all frequencies, and is shown without base-width modulation effects in Fig. 8.10. z_b is determined as the difference between the true input impedance of the distributed system and the impedance of δg_m in parallel with $sg_m(W^2/2D_b)$. The current, $g_m V$, is correct because the values of δg_m and $sg_m(W^2/2D_b)$ are *chosen* so that the model produces the current gain versus frequency response of the actual transistor, which is that of the voltage developed across a conductance in parallel with a capacitance and which is characterized by a constant low frequency gain, followed by a transition to a high-frequency gain falling at 6 db per octave. For the case where dc crowding can be neglected, the circuit of Fig. 8.9 can be used to generate a linear differential equation by allowing n to approach infinity. The resulting differential equation can be solved, subject to the appropriate boundary conditions, and yields an input impedance in closed form. Unfortunately, the answer is in the form of a hyperbolic function of a complex variable and can only be used in our range of interest by calculating particular values. A normalized plot of the results cannot be applied to most transistor operating points because it neglects dc crowding and the effect of high-level injection on base resistance. For numerical work with any particu-

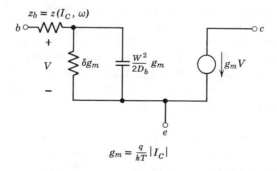

$$g_m = \frac{q}{kT}|I_C|$$

Fig. 8.10. Small-signal model which includes the base impedance. Base-width modulation effects are neglected.

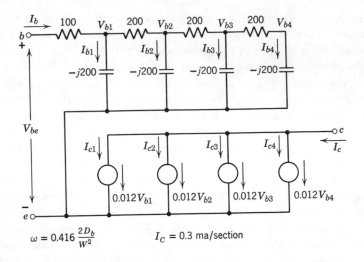

$$\omega = 0.416\, \frac{2D_b}{W^2} \qquad\qquad I_C = 0.3 \text{ ma/section}$$

Fig. 8.11. Four-section lumped-circuit model for use in ac base-impedance calculations. Resistances and reactances are in ohms, conductances in mhos.

lar transistor we must determine the input impedance at dc operating points of interest by measurement.

We can gain some insight into the form of z_b at high frequencies by making a four-lump approximation for the transistor of Fig. 8.5 at a convenient high frequency, and at a dc current level where dc crowding can be neglected. We operate the device at $I_C = 1.2$ ma, and assume that each section carries 0.3 ma. Table 8.1 shows that this is a reasonable assumption. We choose the operating frequency so that $2D_b/\omega W^2 g_m$ is exactly 50 ohms.* For 0.3 milliampere of collector current per section, the value of $1/\delta g_m$ is 3333 ohms. Consequently, we neglect this resistance in comparison with the $-j200$ ohm capacitive reactance. The circuit, shown in Fig. 8.11, is analyzed by assuming a unit incremental voltage at zero phase for V_{b4}, and then working up the ladder to the base terminal. The results are shown in Table 8.2.

The extent of ac crowding at this high frequency is clearly seen, with section 1 handling 6 times as much signal as section 4. The dc crowding at this current level (which we neglected) has section 1

* This frequency is about $\omega_r/3$ for this transistor. It may be a much smaller fraction of ω_r if R is smaller or if I_{CT} is larger.

TABLE 8.2

	Section 1	Section 2	Section 3	Section 4	Total
V_b	$-4 + j5$	$j3$	$1 + j1$	1	
I_b	$\dfrac{-5 - j4}{200}$	$\dfrac{-3}{200}$	$\dfrac{-1 + j1}{200}$	$\dfrac{j1}{200}$	$\dfrac{-9 - j2}{200}$
I_c	$\dfrac{-4 + j5}{83.3}$	$\dfrac{j3}{83.3}$	$\dfrac{1 + j1}{83.3}$	$\dfrac{1}{83.3}$	$\dfrac{-2 + j9}{83.3}$

$$Z_{\text{in}} = 100 + \frac{(-4 + j5) \times 200}{(-9 - j2)} = 161 - j125 \text{ ohms}$$

$$\text{Current Gain} = -j2.4$$

handling only 1.46 times the section 4 current. Also of interest is the phase shift from section to section. The V_b phasors are displayed in Fig. 8.12. z_b is obtained by subtracting the reactance of the input capacitance of all four sections from Z_{in}, so that z_b is $161 - j75$. The reactive portion of z_b accounts for the physical fact that the actual V_b on the first two sections is higher than the fictitious voltage across the frequency independent capacitor $g_m(W^2/2D_b)$ in the model. The first two sections with only half the g_m of the transistor, handle nearly all the signal and require about

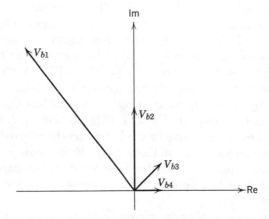

Fig. 8.12. Phasor diagram, showing transverse attenuation and phase shift of the small-signal emitter-base voltage.

twice the ac base voltage required by the total transistor in the absence of ac crowding. The resistive portion of z_b consists largely of the external 100 ohms. The balance is small because of the extreme crowding. As expected, the incremental current gain is independent of the ac crowding in the base because the base current depends only on the total excess hole store, and not on its distribution.

Although this illustrative example ignores the dc crowding and the conductivity modulation effects which are usually present at typical operating points, the base impedance is more nearly resistive and is less frequency-dependent when there is pronounced dc crowding. In such cases, the effective area of the transistor is reduced and most of the minority-carrier flow occurs very near the base contact edge of the base region, so that incremental ac-voltage drops are correspondingly smaller.

8.4 SMALL-SIGNAL MODELS WHICH INCLUDE SPACE-CHARGE CAPACITANCE

The junction space-charge layer capacitances must be added to improve our small-signal circuit model. The emitter space-charge capacitance C_{je} is simply added in parallel with the base charging capacitor $(W^2/2D_b)g_m$ as shown in Fig. 8.13, because it must be charged through the base impedance. The capacitance of the collector junction must be split into two parts, as suggested by Fig. 8.3. The portion which is in the active base region is denoted by C_{jc} and is connected as shown in Fig. 8.13 because it must be charged through the base impedance. The portion which lies outside the active base region is not charged through the base impedance. Consequently, it is connected directly between base and collector terminals and is designated as C_{sc}. This portion of the collector-junction space-charge capacitance is frequently referred to as the space-charge capacitance of the *overlap diode*, because the corresponding portion of the collector junction does not participate in transistor action but appears as a reverse-biased diode between base and collector.

This assignment of space-charge capacitance is not straightforward if there is severe crowding of the minority-carrier flow in the base. When the crowding is severe, the portion of the active

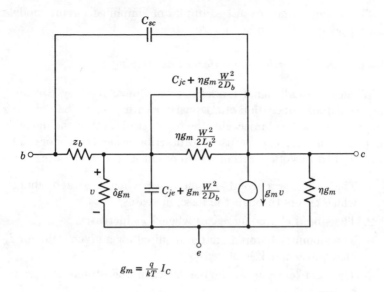

Fig. 8.13. Detailed small-signal circuit model.

base region far removed from the base contact is in fact *not active*, and the associated portion of C_{jc} in series with the corresponding portion of C_{je} appears directly between the collector and emitter terminals.

The detailed small-signal circuit model of Fig. 8.13, usually referred to as the *hybrid-pi model*, appears formidable indeed. Fortunately, there are very few applications in which *all* the elements appearing in the model need be considered simultaneously. Partial models containing fewer elements can frequently be used for the following reasons:

1. The signal source or load with which the transistor is operated makes the effects of one or more of the elements negligible.
2. Variations or uncertainties in a parameter make it unnecessary to use one or more elements because their effects are smaller than other uncertainties in the analysis.
3. Other physical factors which have not been included in arriving at the model of Fig. 8.13 introduce uncertainties greater than the effects of one or another element in the model.

These issues, and several examples of simplified circuit models are considered in detail in ECP.*

8.4.1 *Transistors with Nonuniform Base Doping*

While our small-signal model has been developed by considering the detailed operation of a transistor with uniform base doping operated in low-level injection, the topological form of the model is more general and can be used to describe other transistors. The primary features of operation which produced the model were:

1. The collector current I_C increases when a stored charge, which enters through the base, increases.
2. The stored charge increases when V_{EB} increases.
3. The amount of stored charge required for a given value of I_C increases when V_{CB} increases.
4. The base current I_B increases when the stored charge increases.

All of these primary features are present in a transistor in which minority-carrier transport is aided by a field in the base and does not completely depend on diffusion. The drift component of current is proportional to $\mu p_b \mathcal{E}$, and for any value of built-in field $\mathcal{E}$ requires an increase in p_b for an increase in current. Thus features 1, 2, and 4 are present. Feature 3 is always present because the base width must change when the collector space-charge region width changes. Even if there is a uniform distribution of minority carriers across the base, because all transport is by a large uniform field, the total stored charge will depend on the base width. Thus the general form of the model applies to transistors having graded-base structures, although the detailed dependence of the circuit parameters on the internal flow parameters may be different if the effects of the drift field are important.†

---

* C. L. Searle, A. R. Boothroyd, E. J. Angelo, Jr., P. E. Gray, and D. O. Pederson, *Elementary Circuit Properties of Transistors* (hereafter referred to as ECP), Chapter 3, John Wiley and Sons, New York, 1964.

† The relationships between manufacturing technology, transistor structure, and circuit performance are the subject of an SEEC film now in preparation. Upon completion, this film will be distributed as described in the Foreword.

8.4.2 *Determination of Circuit Model Parameters*

The circuit model of Fig. 8.13, obtained by consideration of the internal physics of the transistor, preserves a one-to-one correspondence between most of the circuit elements and the internal physical mechanisms.

Analysis of the internal physical behavior shows how the values of the elements depend on the properties of the semiconductor, the physical structure of the device, and the operating conditions. However, this analysis cannot, in general, be used as a basis for assigning numerical values to the parameters; the structures are too complicated and there are too many uncertainties introduced by changes in the material parameters during the manufacturing process, or by insufficient control over some of these processes. Furthermore, without destroying the transistor, it is not even possible to tell by physical observations after fabrication whether the design specifications are met. We cannot escape the need for electrical measurements made at the terminals of the device to establish satisfactorily the values of the elements in the model. *Which* terminal properties to measure is decided primarily by measurement convenience and the ease of relating the measurements to the model parameters. Problems of parameter determination are discussed in detail in ECP, Chapter 3.

REFERENCES

8.1 Early, J. M., "Effects of Space-Charge Layer Widening in Junction Transistors," *Proc. IRE*, **10**, pp. 1401–1406, November 1952.

8.2 Giacoletto, "The Study and Design of Alloyed-Junction Transistors," *1954 IRE Convention Record*, pt. 3, pp. 99–103.

PROBLEMS

P8.1 Our calculation of $\mathcal{Y}_o$ and $\mathcal{Y}_r$ in Sec. 8.1.3 was based on the analogy between the distribution change shown in Fig. 8.1 for $v_{be} \equiv 0$, $v_{ce} \neq 0$ and the distribution change shown in Fig. 7.7 for $v_{be} \neq 0$, $v_{cb} \equiv 0$. The admittances $\mathcal{Y}_o$ and $\mathcal{Y}_r$ can be computed directly from the area change and slope change depicted in Fig. 8.1b. Determine $\mathcal{Y}_o$ and $\mathcal{Y}_r$ by investigating the changes in area and slope apparent in Fig. 8.1b.

P8.2 The problem is concerned with the base width modulation factor

$$\eta = \frac{kT}{q} \frac{1}{W} \frac{dW}{dV_{CB}}$$

for an alloy-junction pnp transistor having a homogeneous base region. Designate the distance from the emitter edge of the neutral base region to the metallurgical junction as W_o, and let the actual width of the neutral base region be W. We must have $W = W_o - l_n$, where l_n is the width of the collector-junction space-charge layer on the n-type (base) side. Assume that the collector is so much more heavily doped than the base ($N_A \gg N_D$) that the space-charge layer extends entirely into the base.

(a) Using the depletion assumption derive an expression for W in terms of the reverse bias $(-V_{CB})$. Assume $(-V_{CB}) \gg \psi_0$.

(b) Compute the punch-through voltage V_p, which is defined as the value of reverse bias on the collector junction at which W is reduced to zero.

(c) Express W in terms of $-V_{CB}/V_p$ and calculate η. Sketch and dimension your result showing η as a function of $-V_{CB}/V_p$.

(d) Assume $V_p = 50$ volts and compute η at $-V_{CB} = V_p/2 = 25$ volts.

P8.3 Typical impurity profiles of an alloy transistor and a diffused transistor are shown in Fig. 8.14. Assuming that for each device the collector-junction depletion layer penetrates halfway into the metallurgical base region, as shown by the dotted line in the figure:

(a) How does the base-width modulation factor η of the diffused device compare with that of the alloyed structure?

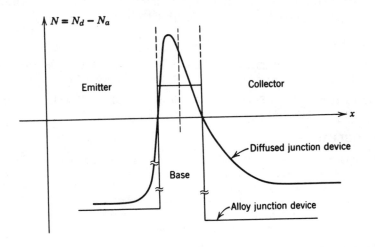

Fig. 8.14.

(b) How does the collector junction capacitance C_{je} of the diffused device compare with that of the alloyed device?

P8.4 Use the data of Fig. 8.4 to estimate the equivalent dc base resistance R_B, as defined by Eq. 8.12. Make estimates at $|I_C| = 2, 5, 10$, and 20 ma, and notice the dependence of R_B on I_C. Assume that the recombination defect δ is constant at $\delta = 0.025$.

P8.5 Use the data of Fig. 8.7 to estimate the extrinsic base resistance of the transistor. Assume $\delta = 0.025$.

P8.6 Equation 8.14 relates the small-signal low-frequency base resistance r_b to the large-signal dc equivalent base resistance R_B. Use the data of Table 8.1 to estimate the right side of Eq. 8.14 at $|I_C| = 1.4$ ma and at $|I_C| = 4.4$ ma. (Plot R_B versus I_C to estimate dR_B/dI_C at these two values of collector current. Compare the values of r_b obtained in this manner with the values calculated by direct analysis of a small-signal distributed model. That is, use a model like Fig. 8.9 having four sections and take $y_k = \delta g_{mk}$. Determine g_m for each of the sections by using the section currents tabulated in Table 8.1 and take $R/n = R/4 = 200$ ohms.

The Ebers-Moll Model

For Transistor Volt-Ampere

Characteristics

9.0 NONLINEAR TRANSISTOR OPERATION

Our analysis of transistors in the previous two chapters has been limited to *small-signal* situations. This limitation permitted linearization of the exponential carrier concentration-junction voltage relationship and of the nonlinear base width-junction voltage equation, and permitted us to develop linear incremental models for a transistor which is biased in the active or normal mode.

There are, however, many practical situations in which these small-signal models are not useful. For example, the transistor may be driven beyond the limits of the active mode by large signal swings, as in switching circuits. Or the signals may be so large that incremental models are not reasonable approximations, even though the transistor may remain entirely in the active mode, as in linear power amplifiers. We now wish to develop electric circuit models which approximate the nonlinear behavior of the transistor at its terminals for these *large-signal* situations.

Inasmuch as our models should be relatively convenient to use, we must make some simplifying approximations. We therefore focus attention on *low-frequency* or *slow-speed* conditions and neglect completely the components of the terminal currents which *change* the excess carrier stores in the transistor. Furthermore, we neglect the dependence of base width on the junction bias voltages; that is, we assume that the base width is constant. As usual, we consider only low-level injection and neglect ohmic voltage drops at the contacts and in the neutral regions.

The discussion in this chapter is phrased in terms of a *pnp* transistor. The physical mechanisms occurring in an *npn* transistor are, of course, fundamentally the same, and the involvement of charge carriers of the opposite type requires no significant changes in the method of analysis.

9.1 INTERNAL DC BEHAVIOR OF THE IDEALIZED TRANSISTOR

In addition to the assumptions described above, which define our idealized transistor model, we shall initially assume that the emitter, base, and collector regions are *homogeneous,* so that the impurity concentration is uniform in each region. Therefore, our initial results are valid for alloy transistors which have homogeneous bulk regions. Subsequently, in Sec. 9.4, we see that the large-signal model which we obtain is valid even if the bulk regions are not homogeneous but have graded impurity distributions. We employ the one-dimensional model shown in Fig. 7.2a, and use the definitions of terminal variables shown in Fig. 7.2b.

9.1.1 *Effect of Applied Voltages on Excess Carrier Concentrations*

The principal effect of the voltages applied to the two *pn* junctions of the transistor is to cause changes in the minority-carrier concentrations at the edges of the space charge regions. If the injection levels are low, so that the minority-carrier concentrations remain small compared with the corresponding equilibrium majority-carrier concentrations, the excess minority-carrier concentrations at the space-charge region edges are obtained from Eqs. 2.19 as follows:

The excess hole concentration in the *base* at the emitter edge (at $x = 0$ in the coordinate system shown in Fig. 9.1) is:

$$p_b'(0) = p_{bo}(e^{qV_{EB}/kT} - 1) \qquad (9.1a)$$

The excess hole concentration in the *base* at the collector edge ($x = W$) is:

$$p_b'(W) = p_{bo}(e^{qV_{CB}/kT} - 1) \qquad (9.1b)$$

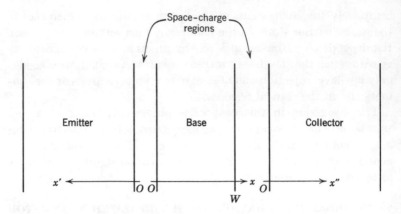

Fig. 9.1. Coordinate systems for the one-dimensional transistor model.

The excess electron concentration in the *emitter* at the edge of the space charge region ($x' = 0$) is:

$$n_e'(0) = n_{eo}(e^{qV_{EB}/kT} - 1) \qquad (9.1c)$$

The excess electron concentration in the *collector* at the edge of the space-charge region ($x'' = 0$) is:

$$n_c'(0) = n_{co}(e^{qV_{CB}/kT} - 1) \qquad (9.1d)$$

9.1.2 *Excess Carrier Concentration Distributions*

Because the applied bias voltages V_{EB} and V_{CB} establish excess concentrations at the edges of the neutral regions, there are distributions of excess carrier concentrations in the neutral regions, and junction currents result. The distribution of excess carriers in each of the three neutral regions of the transistor must satisfy the corresponding minority-carrier continuity equation.

Under low-level injection conditions, the excess minority-carrier concentrations in the homogeneous emitter, base, and collector are determined by solving the field-free diffusion equations subject to the boundary conditions of Eqs. 9.1. In the base region, the diffusion equation for the excess holes under dc steady-state conditions is:

$$D_b \frac{d^2 p_b'}{dx^2} = \frac{p_b'}{\tau_b} \qquad (9.2)$$

where D_b and τ_b designate the minority-carrier diffusion constant and the lifetime in the base. A solution of Eq. 9.2 that satisfies the boundary conditions of Eqs. 9.1a and b, can be obtained by straightforward application of the conventional techniques for solving linear ordinary differential equations. A solution that is adequate for our purposes can be obtained more directly by recognizing that in *all* transistors the base region is narrow enough so that a very small fraction of the minority carriers that are injected into it across the junction space-charge regions recombine in the base. Thus, *to a first approximation, recombination in the base may be neglected*, and the diffusion equation for holes may be written:

$$D_b \frac{d^2p_b'}{dx^2} \cong 0 \tag{9.3}$$

This approximate equation shows that the excess hole concentration $p_b'(x)$ varies almost linearly with position in the base. Consequently, the solution of Eq. 9.3 that satisfies the boundary conditions of Eqs. 9.1a and b is:

$$p_b'(x) = \frac{W - x}{W} p_{bo} (e^{qV_{EB}/kT} - 1) + \frac{x}{W} p_{bo}(e^{qV_{CB}/kT} - 1) \tag{9.4}$$

The general form of the excess hole distribution in the base is shown in Fig. 9.2. The exact distribution deviates slightly from the linear approximation because of the small amount of recombination that occurs in the base. Although Fig. 9.2 has been drawn for both bias voltages positive, similar results obtain for negative bias, when the excess concentration at the corresponding edge is negative.

The hole distribution in the base is very similar to the hole distribution in a diode having a thin n-type region, as discussed in Sec. 4.6. In that case, the excess concentration at $x = W$ was forced to be small by the recombination process at the surface. In the transistor, the concentration at either junction may assume a wide range of values, depending on the bias voltage applied to the junction.

The excess minority-carrier distributions in the emitter and collector neutral regions are exponential functions of distance from the junction, if the emitter and collector regions are wide compared with a diffusion length. If these regions are not wide, the distribu-

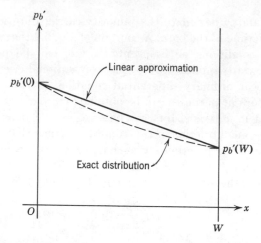

Fig. 9.2. Distribution of excess holes in the base with forward bias on both junctions.

tions are akin to that of the aforementioned thin-region diode. In any event, the distribution of excess minority carriers is determined by solving the diffusion equation subject to the boundary condition of either Eqs. 9.1c or d. If the emitter and collector regions are wide, the results are:

$$n_e'(x') = n_{eo}(e^{qV_{EB}/kT} - 1)e^{-x'/L_e} \qquad (9.5a)$$

$$n_c'(x'') = n_{co}(e^{qV_{CB}/kT} - 1)e^{-x''/L_c} \qquad (9.5b)$$

where L_e and L_c denote the minority-carrier diffusion lengths in the emitter and collector, respectively. The excess minority-carrier distributions are shown in Fig. 9.3, which applies when the voltage at each junction is positive.

9.1.3 *Dependence of Terminal Currents on Voltage*

Just as in the simple case of the *pn*-junction diode, the total current density crossing either junction is the sum of the hole and electron currents at that junction. Thus, *if carrier generation and recombination in the space-charge regions are negligible,* the component currents are constant throughout the space-charge regions and the total current density at either junction is the sum of the minority-carrier currents at the edges of the space-charge region. Since at present we are assuming that the neutral regions are homogeneous, these minority-carrier currents are diffusion currents.

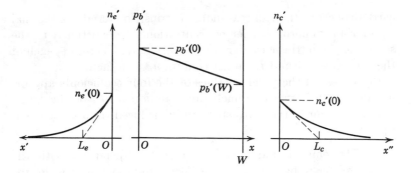

Fig. 9.3. Excess minority-carrier distributions with forward bias on both junctions.

Therefore, the emitter and collector currents of the one-dimensional transistor of area A may be written:

$$I_E = qA \left(-D_b \left.\frac{dp_b'}{dx}\right|_{x=0} - D_e \left.\frac{dn_e'}{dx'}\right|_{x'=0} \right) \quad (9.6a)$$

$$I_C = qA \left(+D_b \left.\frac{dp_b'}{dx}\right|_{x=W} - D_c \left.\frac{dn_c'}{dx''}\right|_{x''=0} \right) \quad (9.6b)$$

As we have already seen (Eqs. 9.4, 9.5), the excess minority-carrier concentrations p_b', n_e', and n_c' are *linearly dependent* on the voltage factors $(e^{qV_{EB}/kT} - 1)$ and $(e^{qV_{CB}/kT} - 1)$. It follows that the gradients of the carrier concentrations, and thus that the terminal currents I_E and I_C, are linearly dependent on the same voltage factors. In other words, the terminal currents must have the following general form:

$$I_E = I_{ES}(e^{qV_{EB}/kT} - 1) - \alpha_R I_{CS}(e^{qV_{CB}/kT} - 1) \quad (9.7a)$$

$$I_C = -\alpha_F I_{ES}(e^{qV_{EB}/kT} - 1) + I_{CS}(e^{qV_{CB}/kT} - 1) \quad (9.7b)$$

where $I_{ES}, I_{CS}, \alpha_F,$ and α_R are constants which depend on the diffusion constants, the diffusion lengths, the equilibrium minority-carrier concentrations, the area, and the base width. These coefficients can be evaluated for our idealized transistor model simply by evaluating the gradients in Eqs. 9.6, or they can be measured directly. One property of these coefficients is evident from the edge concentration factors given by Eqs. 9.1. Each of the voltage factors in these equations is multiplied by a thermal equilibrium minority-carrier concentration. In reasonably extrinsic material the thermal equilibrium minority-carrier concentration is proportional to the square of the intrinsic carrier concentration n_i^2. Therefore, each of the constants I_{ES} and I_{CS} must contain n_i^2 as a factor.

Regardless of the precise values of the four coefficients appearing in Eqs. 9.7, two extremely important features of the large-signal behavior of the transistor can be deduced from these equations:

(a) The emitter and collector currents depend on both the emitter-to-base and the collector-to-base voltages in the same general way that the current of a *pn*-junction diode depends on the voltage, except that each current depends on both voltages.

(b) For fixed voltages, the terminal currents are proportional to n_i^2, and are therefore as strongly temperature-dependent as the saturation current of a *pn*-junction diode.

Although we have based our discussion on a one-dimensional model, the resulting large-signal transistor equations, which are known as the *Ebers-Moll equations*, are valid for any transistor in low-level injection which has negligible voltage drops except at the junctions, *regardless of shape*. All that is required is that emitter and collector junction surfaces can be defined such that the excess carrier distributions are uniform on those surfaces and that the current components comprising the emitter and collector currents cross those surfaces.* Also, in Sec. 9.4, we show that the Ebers-Moll equations are valid for a transistor having a graded base region.

The Ebers-Moll equations satisfy a reciprocity condition in that the cross-coupling coefficients $\alpha_R I_{CS}$ and $\alpha_F I_{ES}$ are equal. We can demonstrate the plausibility of this requirement by considering the form of Eqs. 9.7 when the bias voltages V_{EB} and V_{CB} are small compared with the thermal voltage kT/q. In this case, Eqs. 9.7 reduce by series expansion to:

$$I_E = \quad I_{ES}\left(\frac{q}{kT}\right)V_{EB} - \alpha_R I_{CS}\left(\frac{q}{kT}\right)V_{CB} \left.\begin{array}{c}\\ \\ \\ \\ \end{array}\right| \quad V_{EB} \ll \frac{kT}{q}$$

$$I_C = -\alpha_F I_{ES}\left(\frac{q}{kT}\right)V_{EB} + \quad I_{CS}\left(\frac{q}{kT}\right)V_{CB} \left.\begin{array}{c}\\ \\ \end{array}\right| \quad V_{CB} \ll \frac{kT}{q}$$

$$\text{(9.8}a,b\text{)}$$

* See Reference 9.2.

These equations show that the transistor behaves as a *linear* two-terminal-pair device when the junction voltages are very small. On physical grounds we expect that for small enough applied voltages the transistor should behave as a piece of passive material with three leads attached, and should exhibit *linearity* and *reciprocity*. The linearity is evidenced by Eqs. 9.8. Reciprocity requires that:

$$\alpha_R I_{CS} = \alpha_F I_{ES} \tag{9.9}$$

Inasmuch as the coefficients do *not* depend on the junction voltages, Eq. 9.9 must apply for bias voltages of arbitrary polarity and magnitude.

The reciprocity condition of Eq. 9.9 can be confirmed for the idealized one-dimensional transistor by evaluating the coefficients of the Ebers-Moll equations directly. A more general argument shows that the reciprocity condition, like the Ebers-Moll equations themselves, applies for any transistor which meets the restrictions outlined in Sec. 9.0, regardless of the physical configuration.

The dependence of base current on the bias voltages can be determined from Eqs. 9.7 because the base current is simply:

$$I_B = -(I_E + I_C) \tag{9.10}$$

Clearly I_B is also linearly dependent on the exponential voltage factors.

9.1.4 *The Idealized Two-Diode Model*

The coupled equations which describe the large-signal *V-I* characteristics of the idealized transistor model can be given a simple and useful interpretation in terms of a circuit model that uses two dependent generators and two idealized exponential diodes. This model is shown in Fig. 9.4a. The diode symbols used in this model refer to idealized *pn*-junction diodes having *V-I* characteristics of the form

$$I = I_s(e^{qV/kT} - 1) \tag{9.11}$$

where I_s is the saturation current indicated below the symbol, and the current and voltage polarities are defined in Fig. 9.6b.

This model has a simple interpretation in terms of the internal mechanisms of the transistor. The emitter and collector currents can each be resolved into two components. The component which flows in the idealized diode is the consequence of minority-carrier

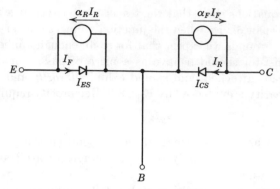

(a) Transistor model

$$I = I_s(e^{qV/kT} - 1)$$

(b) Idealized *pn*-junction diode symbol

Fig. 9.4. Two diode model for a transistor based on the Ebers-Moll equations.

injection at that junction while the other component, which is provided by the current source, is the consequence of minority-carrier injection at the other junction and transport across the base. Thus the first component of the emitter current $I_{ES}(e^{qV_{EB}/kT} - 1)$ results from diode action at the emitter junction. The second component $-\alpha_R I_{CS}(e^{qV_{EB}/kT} - 1)$ is the consequence of diode action at the collector junction and exists because a fraction α_R of that diode current is transported across the base to the emitter where it contributes to the total emitter current.

If the base region were made very wide (compared with a diffusion length) the fractions of the diode currents that could survive transport across the base without recombination would be very small (i.e., α_F and α_R would be very small), and the large-signal transistor model would degenerate to two diodes connected back-to-back with a common *n*-type terminal.

The four coefficients that appear in the Ebers-Moll model have simple physical interpretations which are suggested by Fig. 9.4. If the collector-base terminals are *shorted*, the emitter-base terminals have the volt-ampere characteristics of an idealized *pn*-junction diode having a saturation current of I_{ES}. Furthermore, the ratio of collector current to emitter current under these conditions is $-\alpha_F$. Therefore, I_{ES} is referred to as the *emitter-junction short-circuit saturation current*, and α_F is called the *forward short-circuit current gain*. Similar interpretations apply to the collector-junction short-circuit saturation current I_{CS}, and the *reverse* short-circuit current gain α_R. Methods of measuring the coefficients of the Ebers-Moll model are considered in detail in ECP, Chapter 2.

Both α_F and α_R are slightly less than unity for two reasons. First, not all of the current injected across a junction is comprised of holes injected into the base. Second, not all of the holes injected into the base diffuse to the other junction without recombining.

9.2 DC VOLT-AMPERE CHARACTERISTICS

If the two-diode model derived in Sec. 9.1 is a reasonable characterization of the dc terminal behavior of a transistor, we should be able to use it to generate the dc volt-ampere characteristic curves of typical transistors. A wide variety of characteristic curves is possible for any specific device because there are several ways of choosing dependent and independent variables.*

9.2.1 *Common-Base Characteristics*

Figure 9.5 shows the measured curves of I_E and I_C versus V_{EB} and V_{CB} for a germanium *pnp* alloy transistor.† These curves are referred to as *common-base* family because the two terminal-pair voltages used in this description of the transistor are measured with the base terminal as a common point. The predicted curves given by Eqs. 9.1 are also shown. The principal difference between the real curves and the curves given by the two-diode model is that the

---

* The transistor is defined electrically by three terminal currents and three terminal-pair voltages. Kirchoff's laws demand that only two currents and two terminal-pair voltages be independent. Therefore, a set of two currents and two terminal-pair voltages describes the transistor completely. The transistor imposes two independent functional relationships on these variables so that only two variables can be controlled independently in measuring characteristic curves. These two independent variables may be two currents, two voltages, or a mixed set.

† Type 2N1305.

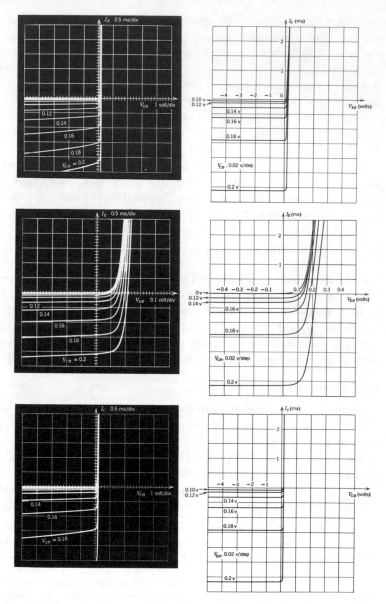

Fig. 9.5. Common-base transistor characteristics, showing the comparison between actual curves (left) and the predictions of the Ebers-Moll two-diode model (right).

collector or emitter driving-point characteristics of a real device are not current-saturated in the reverse bias region. The actual curves fan out and show a nonzero slope. This defect in the model is a consequence of our tacit assumption, made in writing Eqs. 9.4 and 9.6, that the base width W is constant. In real transistors the base width changes as the voltages applied to the junctions change, because the widths of the space-charge layers change with applied voltage. This base-width modulation effect is illustrated in Fig. 9.6 for a change in the collector-to-base voltage. Similar effects are caused by changes in the emitter-to-base voltage. These effects are most pronounced when the junction is reverse-biased, because the base-width changes are completely masked by the voltage dependence of the minority-carrier injection process in forward bias. It is clear that these changes in the effective base width influence the terminal currents even though the excess concentrations at the edges of the base may not change appreciably. The terminal currents change because they are the consequence of

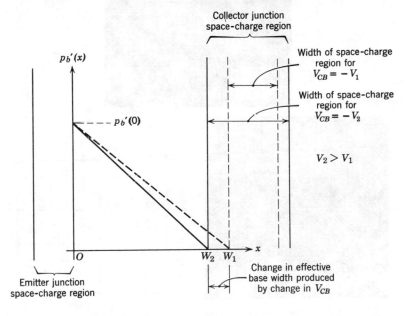

Fig. 9.6. The effect of a change in collector-to-base voltage on base width and on the base minority-carrier distribution.

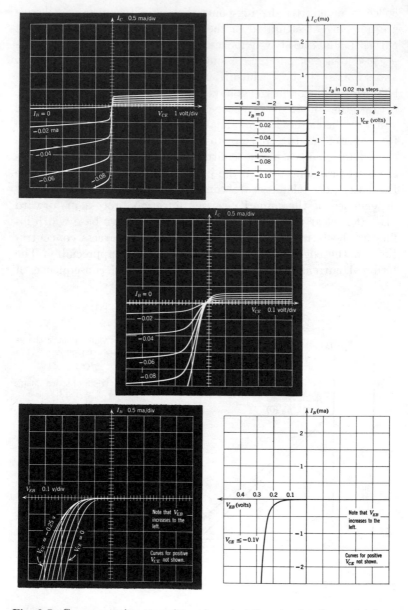

Fig. 9.7. Common-emitter transistor characteristics, showing the comparison between actual curves (left) and the predictions of the Ebers-Moll two-diode model (right).

diffusion (Eqs. 9.6), and the diffusion currents change because of the change in slope of the excess minority carrier distribution in the base.

9.2.2 *Common-Emitter Characteristics*

A very commonly used family of dc transistor characteristics are those in which I_C and V_{EB} are shown as functions of I_B and V_{CE}. These curves are known as the *common-emitter family* because the two node pair-voltages used in this description of the transistor are measured with the emitter terminal as a common point. Typical curves of this type are shown in Fig. 9.7 for the same *pnp* alloy transistor described by the curves of Fig. 9.5. The idealized curves computed from the two-diode model are also shown. Again the effects of base-width modulation in the real device are evident. The curves are not completely current-saturated for positive or negative values of V_{CE} large compared with kT/q, but fan out and have nonzero slope. Each of these discrepancies can be traced to changes in the effective base width that are produced by changes in the widths of the junction space-charge layers.

9.3 REGIONS OF OPERATION

The nonlinear model developed in this chapter describes the behavior of a transistor at its electrical terminals for arbitrary bias voltages. That is, either junction can be either forward- or reverse-biased. In many applications, the form of the circuit restricts the range of operation so that some bias combinations are not possible. In these cases simplification of the nonlinear model is possible. To illustrate this, we divide the volt-ampere characteristics of the transistor into four regions of operation and indicate the simplified form of the model in each case. We also consider the internal excess minority-carrier charge distributions that exist in each of the four regions.

The regions of operation of a transistor are usually defined by the states of the bias voltages on the two junctions. Because either junction may be either forward- or reverse-biased, only four combinations are possible.

9.3.1 *The Cut-Off Region*

The region of operation occurring when both junctions are reverse-biased is referred to as the *cut-off* region. The excess minor-

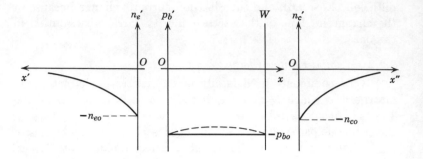

Fig. 9.8. Excess base minority-carrier concentrations in the cut-off region.

ity carrier concentration in the base is nearly equal to $-p_{bo}$, as shown in Fig. 9.8 and the terminal currents are constant and essentially independent of the magnitudes of the reverse bias voltages, if those voltages are in excess of a few kT/q. The approximate model for this case is shown in Fig. 9.9.

9.3.2 *The Normal Region*

The transistor is operating in the *normal region* when the emitter junction is forward-biased and the collector junction is reverse-biased. We have already encountered this region of operation in Chapters 7 and 8 where it was referred to as operation in the *active mode*, and have developed incremental models which describe *small*

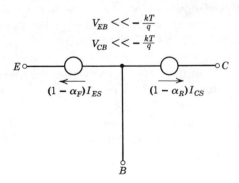

Fig. 9.9. Approximate large-signal model for the cut-off region.

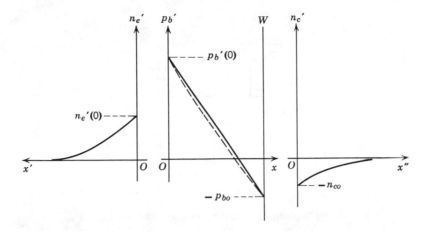

Fig. 9.10. Excess base minority-carrier concentrations in the normal region.

excursions in that region. The excess minority-carrier concentrations in this region are shown in Fig. 9.10, which should be compared with Fig. 7.5. If the collector junction reverse bias exceeds a few kT/q, the large-signal volt-ampere equations may be written as:

$$I_E = I_{ES}(e^{qV_{EB}/kT} - 1) + \alpha_R I_{CS}$$
$$I_C = -\alpha_F I_E - (1 - \alpha_F \alpha_R) I_{CS} \tag{9.12a,b}$$

These equations may be represented by either of the normal region circuit models shown in Fig. 9.11. In these models we have used the parameter I_{CO}, which is defined as:

$$I_{CO} = (1 - \alpha_F \alpha_R) I_{CS} \tag{9.13}$$

This *open-circuit* collector-saturation current is equal to the collector current that flows when the emitter is open-circuited ($I_E = 0$) and the collector is reverse-biased.

Frequently, the current source in parallel with the idealized diode in the models of Fig. 9.11 may be neglected because it is small in comparison with typical normal-region emitter currents.

9.3.3 *The Inverse Region*

If the collector junction is forward-biased and the emitter junction is reverse-biased, the transistor is operating in the *inverse region*. The behavior of the device is essentially the same as in the

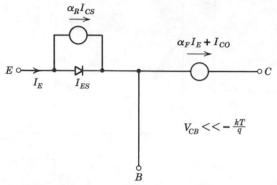

(a) Dependent generator actuated by emitter current

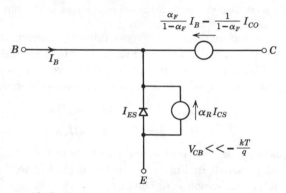

(b) Dependent generator actuated by base current

Fig. 9.11. Approximate large-signal models for the normal region.

normal region except that the roles of the collector and emitter are interchanged. The internal charge distributions and the approximate large-signal models change accordingly. Usually α_R is substantially less than α_F. In many transistors the area of the collector junction is considerably greater than the area of the emitter junction, as suggested by Fig. 7.1, to make the forward current gain α_F as large as possible. Consequently, a relatively large fraction of the holes injected into the base by a forward-biased collector recombine in the remote portions of the base and are not collected by the reverse-biased emitter junction. Thus the reverse current gain is low. In addition, the hole-injection efficiencies of the two junctions are usually different because the emitter and collector are doped differently.

9.3.4 *The Saturation Region*

The *saturation region* of operation is defined by forward bias at each junction. The excess minority carrier distributions in this case are shown in Fig. 9.12*a*. The excess hole concentration is positive throughout the base because both junctions are injecting holes into the base. The excess base hole concentration can be resolved into two components, which correspond to normal and inverse operation, as shown in Fig. 9.12*b*. The terminal currents can

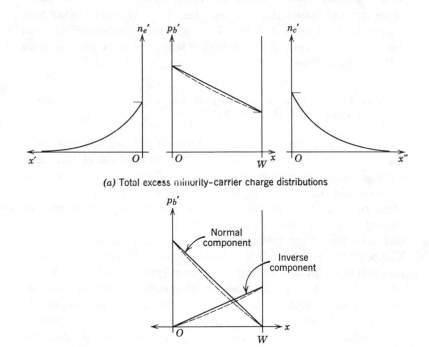

(a) Total excess minority-carrier charge distributions

(b) Resolution of base charge into normal and inverse components

Fig. 9.12. Excess base minority-carrier concentrations in the saturation region.

also be divided into similar additive normal and inverse components because of the linear relationships between currents and excess charge. Consequently, *insofar as excess charge and terminal currents are concerned, operation in the saturation region can be thought of as the superposition of operation in the normal region and operation in the inverse region.* We must emphasize that the terminal pair voltages cannot be thought of as the superposition of normal and inverse components because of the very nonlinear relationship between excess charge density and bias voltage. Because of this strong nonlinearity, the saturation-region model cannot be simplified, and the complete model of Fig. 9.7 must be used.

In some cases it is convenient to think of the saturation region as being divided into two regions. These are the *forward saturation region*, in which the emitter is more forward-biased than the collector, and the *reverse saturation region*, in which the collector is more forward-biased than the emitter. In the forward saturation region, internal current flow is from emitter to collector, whereas for the reverse saturation region, internal current flow is from collector to emitter.

9.4 THE EFFECTS OF A GRADED BASE ON LARGE-SIGNAL BEHAVIOR

The foregoing treatment of the internal physical electronics of the transistor has been restricted to a device model having a homogeneous base region. In the practical fabrication of devices, however, the techniques employed to achieve very thin base regions often result in the formation of a base region of nonuniform, or graded, impurity concentration. The impurity "profiles" of two distinct forms of graded-base structure are illustrated in Fig. 9.13. The profile in Fig. 9.13a is the consequence of forming the collector junction by diffusing impurities into p-type material, while the emitter junction is alloyed; the resulting structure exhibits a gradual variation of impurity concentration through the base and collector regions. In Fig. 9.13b *both* junctions are formed by the process of diffusing impurities into a wafer of p-type material, the emitter-base junction being formed by a second diffusion from a source of p-type impurities. Transistors made by these methods are referred to as being of single- and double-diffused structure, respectively.

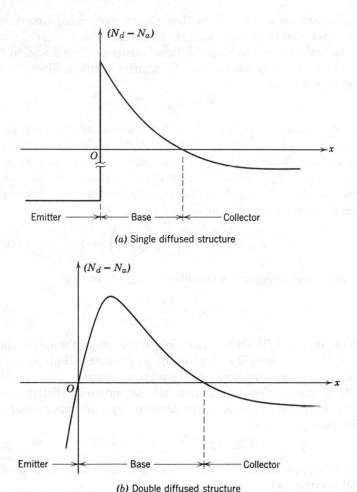

Fig. 9.13. Impurity distributions in transistors having graded base regions.

Because of the variation of impurity concentration with position in the base region, it is to be expected that conditions in a graded base are somewhat different from those in the homogeneous base region analyzed above. The space-charge layers within which the impurity concentration exhibits a gradual change through the junction also have characteristic properties. The purpose of this brief discussion is to show how the properties of graded-base devices differ in detail from those analyzed above.

We first discuss the single-diffused structure introduced in Fig. 9.13a to see the general effect of impurity grading. Since the net impurity density

$$N = N_d - N_a$$

is *not* constant, there must be a longitudinal electric field in the base. This is shown by the flow equation for the majority-carrier electrons in the base. The net longitudinal electron current in the base must be approximately zero if the emitter and collector are relatively heavily doped, so that the electron currents crossing the junctions are small. Thus we have

$$J_{ex} = q \left(D_{eb} \frac{dn_b}{dx} + \mu_{eb} n_b \mathcal{E} \right) = 0 \qquad (9.14)$$

Under low-level injection conditions $n_b \cong N$, so that

$$\mathcal{E} \cong - \frac{kT}{q} \frac{1}{N} \frac{dN}{dx} \qquad (9.15)$$

Thus there is a "built-in" field in the base region which is determined by the impurity distribution and which is independent of minority-carrier flow under low-level conditions.

In a single-diffused structure, the net impurity distribution is usually reasonably well-approximated by an exponential distribution.

$$N \cong N_o e^{-x/\mathcal{L}} \qquad 0 < x < W \qquad (9.16)$$

For this approximation, Eq. 9.15 shows that the field is *uniform* and is given by:

$$\mathcal{E} = \frac{kT}{q\mathcal{L}} \qquad (9.17)$$

Therefore, the minority-carrier hole current is:

$$J_h = qD_b \left(- \frac{dp_b}{dx} + \frac{p_b}{\mathcal{L}} \right) \qquad (9.18)$$

If we write the hole concentration p_b in terms of the excess concentration $p_b{}'$,

$$p_b(x) = p_{bo}(x) + p_b{}'(x) \qquad (9.19)$$

and recognize that the hole current must be zero in equilibrium when $p_b' = 0$, we see that the minority-carrier current is

$$J_h = qD_b \left(-\frac{dp_b'}{dx} + \frac{p_b'}{\mathcal{L}} \right) \tag{9.20}$$

This result shows that the minority-carrier current density in the graded base is a linear function of the excess hole concentration. If the conditions described in Sec. 9.0 as a definition of the idealized transistor are satisfied, the continuity equation for $p_b'(x)$ is linear. Because of this linearity both p_b' and J_h must be linearly dependent upon the junction voltage factors $(e^{qV_{EB}/kT} - 1)$ and $(e^{qV_{CB}/kT} - 1)$. It follows, therefore, that the large-signal volt-ampere characteristics of Eqs. 9.7 are valid for transistors having graded-base regions. The reciprocity relationship of Eq. 9.9 is likewise valid. All the large-signal models presented in this chapter are applicable to transistors having nonuniform base regions.

The general form of the minority-carrier distributions in the base of a single-diffused transistor is shown in Fig. 9.14. The excess carriers are distributed approximately exponentially with a characteristic length of $\mathcal{L}$ as a consequence of Eq. 9.20 (J_h is nearly constant in the base). It is evident that a given forward current requires less stored excess charge than a reverse current of the same value. This occurs because the built-in electric field aids normal flow but opposes inverse flow.

The internal behavior of the double-diffused structure of Fig. 9.13b differs from that of the single-diffused structure primarily because the flow of holes injected at the emitter is initially opposed by the built-in field near the emitter. Over the rest of the base region, holes injected at the emitter are aided by the built-in field. In typical double-diffused transistors the net effect of the field in the base is usually quite small, and the transport of holes to the collector is about the same as if the base were uniform and the holes were transported by diffusion only.

The analysis of this section has shown that while the detailed properties of the internal mechanisms of graded-base transistors may be significantly different from the details of the corresponding mechanisms in a transistor having a uniform base, the large-signal electrical circuit properties are very similar. The large-signal models developed in this chapter are valid, regardless of the exact nature of the impurity distribution in the base region.

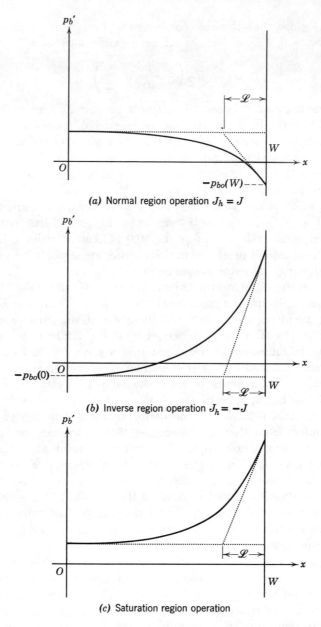

(a) Normal region operation $J_h = J$

(b) Inverse region operation $J_h = -J$

(c) Saturation region operation

Fig. 9.14. Excess base minority-carrier distributions for a graded base transistor.

REFERENCES

9.1 Shockley, W., "The theory of p-n junctions in semiconductors and p-n junction transistors," *Bell System Tech. J.*, **28**, pp. 435–489, July, 1949.

9.2 Ebers, J. J., and Moll, J. L. "Large-signal Behavior of Junction Transistors," *Proc. IRE*, **42**, pp. 1761–1772, Dec. '54.

PROBLEMS

P9.1 Solve the minority-carrier diffusion equation (Eq. 9.2) in the base region of the one-dimensional, homogeneous, idealized transistor for the case in which recombination is not negligible. Obtain a solution which satisfies the boundary conditions of Eqs. 9.1a and b. Show that your result reduces to Eqs. 9.4 if $W \ll L_b$.

P9.2 Demonstrate that the two-diode circuit model of Fig. 9.4 satisfies the equations (Eqs. 9.7) of the idealized transistor.

P9.3 This problem is concerned with the forward short-circuit current gain α_F, and its dependence upon the internal parameters of the one-dimensional, homogeneous, idealized transistor.

(a) Use the solution (with $V_{CB} = 0$) for $p_b'(x)$ obtained in P9.1 to compute the hole-current densities at each edge of the base region. That is, compute $J_{hb}(0)$ and $J_{hb}(W)$.

(b) Use the excess minority-carrier distributions in the emitter (Eq. 9.5a) to compute the electron-current density crossing the emitter space-charge layer: $J_{ee}(0)$.

(c) Compute the total emitter and collector currents that flow with $V_{EB} > 0$, $V_{CB} = 0$. These are:

$$I_E = A[J_{hb}(0) + J_{ee}(0)]$$
$$I_C = -AJ_{hb}(W)$$

Why is there no electron flow across the collector junction under these conditions?

(d) Compute the forward short-circuit current gain:

$$\alpha_F = \frac{-I_C}{I_E}$$

and show that it can be written

$$\alpha_F = \frac{(D_b p_{bo}/L_b)\ \text{csch}\ (W/L_b)}{(D_e n_{eo}/L_e) + (D_b p_{bo}/L_b)\ \text{coth}\ (W/L_b)}$$

(e) Show that α_F can be written as:

$$\alpha_F = \left[\operatorname{sech} \left(\frac{W}{L_b} \right) \right] \frac{1}{1 + \dfrac{D_e}{D_b} \dfrac{n_{eo}}{p_{bo}} \dfrac{L_b}{L_e} \tanh \left(\dfrac{W}{L_b} \right)}$$

and demonstrate that the first factor, which is usually called the *transport factor*, gives the fraction of the holes injected at the emitter which diffuse to the collector without recombining, and that the second factor, which is usually called the *emitter efficiency*, expresses the ratio of injected hole current to the total emitter current. Each of these factors is, of course, less than unity.

(*f*) Consider the practical case in which $W \ll L_b$, and $n_{eo} \ll p_{bo}$. Prove that in this case the forward short-circuit current gain may be written

$$\alpha_F \cong 1 - \delta$$

where δ is the recombination and emitter-injection defect given by Eq. 7.15*b*. Note that the current gain α defined in Fig. 7.10*b* is thus equal to α_F, since $\delta \ll 1$.

P9.4 Demonstrate that the normal-region circuit models of Fig. 9.11 satisfy the approximate large-signal equations, Eqs. 9.12, with $V_{CB} \ll -(kT/q)$.

P9.5 Prove for small-signal operation about an operating point in the normal region, that the model of Fig. 9.11*a* reduces to the small-signal model of Fig. 7.10*b*, and that the model of Fig. 9.11*b* reduces to the small-signal model of Fig. 7.10*a*. *Suggestion*: If $\Delta V_{EB} \ll (kT/q)$, the incremental behavior of the idealized diodes can be represented by an appropriately chosen conductance.

P9.6 Show that the small-signal behavior of the transistor in the saturation region can be represented by the model in Fig. 9.15 (ignore base-width modulation effects). Derive expressions for g_e, g_c, g_{mf}, g_{mr}, C_e, and C_e

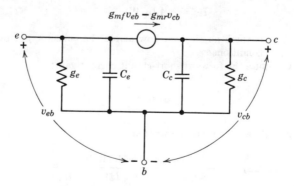

Fig. 9.15.

which show how these coefficients are related to the parameters of the idealized one-dimensional transistor and to the operating point, defined by (V_{EB}, V_{CB}). Note that v_{eb} and v_{cb} are instantaneous incremental voltages, whereas V_{EB} and V_{CB} are dc bias voltages.

P9.7 Consider a graded-base transistor having exponential grading (Eq. 9.16). Assume that the base is thin enough so that recombination in the base is negligible (i.e., assume that J_h is constant) and determine $p_b'(x)$. Consider normal region (active mode) operation with $V_{EB} > 0$, $V_{CB} \ll -kT/q$, and express $p_b'(x)$ and J_h in terms of V_{EB}. Sketch and dimension $p_b'(x)$ if $\mathcal{L} = W/4$.

P9.8 Derive an approximate small-signal model for the graded-base transistor discussed in P9.7. Assuming that base-width modulation effects are negligible, put your model in the form of Fig. 7.13a. Express the operating-point dependence of the coefficients of the model in terms of $|I_C|$. Compare the parameters of your model with the corresponding parameters derived for the homogeneous-base transistor.

Transistor Models for
Dynamic Switching

10.0 INTRODUCTION

In Chapter 9, the dc steady-state behavior of the transistor is
discussed in terms of the flow of minority-carrier currents in various parts of the device structure. The currents flow in response to
excess carrier concentrations established by the individual actions
of the emitter and collector junctions. Four operating regions—
cut-off, normal, inverse, and saturated—are defined (Sec. 9.3),
and a simple model (Fig. 9.4) is developed, which is adequate to
express the dc steady-state behavior of the device in each of these
regions.

The device characterization of Chapter 9 may be visualized in
terms of the minority-carrier charge density distributions for the
various operating regions (see Figs. 9.8, 9.10, 9.12). These charge
diagrams emphasize the one-to-one correspondence between the
operating state, defined in terms of terminal voltages and currents,
and the *internal charge distributions*—a given operating condition
can only be set up by supplying the appropriate charges (of minority *and* majority carriers) to the device from the external circuit.
Similarly, *changes* in the operating state during transient excitation

are directly related to corresponding *transient* changes in the minority-carrier charge distributions in the device. In this chapter we develop models which characterize dynamic behavior of the transistor in terms of internally stored charges.

Before proceeding further, we must emphasize that a complete characterization of the transistor under dynamic conditions would be far too complicated to be of practical use. Distributed processes govern the flow of current in all parts of the structure, and departures from steady-state conditions are therefore expressed by partial differential equations. Furthermore, the associated boundary conditions—the Boltzmann relations of the *pn* junctions—are nonlinear. As in Chapter 6, however, it is possible to simplify the situation considerably by representing the distributed carrier distributions in a device by a lumped model. More specifically, in this chapter we replace the distributed stored charge in the base region with two constituent lumped-charge components, corresponding to the individual effects of forward and reverse injection of minority carriers from the two junction boundaries. By this means, a satisfactory compromise between completeness and simplicity of description is achieved, and the resulting model of the transistor is sufficiently accurate for expressing dynamic behavior under most practical conditions of transient stimulus.

10.1 BASIC IDEAS: CHARGE DEFINITION OF DEVICE PROPERTIES AND CHARGE CONTROL

In order to concentrate on essentials, a number of simplifications will be made initially. Only the (uniform) base region of the idealized one-dimensional *pnp* transistor discussed in Chapter 9 will be considered. The emitter and collector regions are assumed to be of such high impurity concentration and short lifetime that minority-carrier storage in them is negligible (as is the case for a device with alloyed emitter and collector junctions). Recombination processes will, for simplicity, be taken to occur only in the base and to be defined by a uniformly constant lifetime τ_B.* Throughout the discussion it will be assumed that low-level injection conditions hold

---

* We have previously used τ_b to designate the base lifetime. The symbol τ_B is used in this chapter to be consistent with the other notation which is developed therein.

in the base. Properties of the space-charge layers are disregarded at this stage, but are treated later.

We begin by establishing certain basic properties of the transistor in terms of the excess stored charge in the neutral base region (between the space-charge layer boundaries); for this purpose, it is most convenient, first, to discuss the dc steady state. No matter what the values of the terminal currents of the transistor, in the dc steady state the stored excess minority-carrier charge $(+q_B)$ of holes and the corresponding equal majority-carrier charge $(-q_B)$ of electrons are maintained constant by a "sustaining" base current I_B, which replenishes the majority electrons at a rate equal to that of recombination with the injected holes. That is,[†]

$$\frac{d\,(-q_B)}{dt} = -\frac{(-q_B)}{\tau_B} + I_B = 0$$

or

$$I_B = (-q_B)/\tau_B \tag{10.1}$$

This simple relationship is important because it emphasizes the direct connection between *base current* and *base charge*. Evidently, in Eq. 10.1, the charge considered should be the excess majority-carrier charge $(-q_B)$, since base current is a flow of majority carriers—electrons—into the base region.

When conditions of operation of the transistor are changing with time, the charge of majority or minority carriers stored in the base region is changing. Such change is the result of deviation of the base current from the value which just maintains the stored charge in the dc steady state: a larger in-flow of electrons at the base terminal causes the stored charge to increase with time, while a smaller rate of supply results in a decline of stored charge. The base current is, in fact, a natural *control* quantity; not only does it sustain existing base charge, but any charge of majority carriers must previously have been supplied by flow of base current, this being the only source of supply. In general, during *changing* conditions, we can write quite explicitly,

$$i_B = -\left(\frac{q_B}{\tau_B} + \frac{dq_B}{dt}\right) \tag{10.2}$$

[†] Note that these equations may also be derived from the continuity equation for either electron or hole concentration in the base in the steady state.

that is, the instantaneous base current i_B has two components, a *charging* current $d(-q_B)/dt$ and a *maintaining* current $(-q_B)/\tau_B$. This simple relationship between q_B and i_B is at the heart of the concept of *charge control*, namely, that the stored base charge is at any time defined completely by the past history of the externally impressed base current up to the time concerned.

The connection between emitter or collector current and excess stored charge in the base is, in general, much less direct than for base current. Considering forward injection only, for example, injected holes (emitter current) not only charge the base region with q_B of minority carriers, but also traverse the base region and leave it as collector current.

Turning attention now to the currents flowing at the emitter and collector terminals, it is evident that these are quite unspecified if only the base charge q_B is known, since the total stored charge may be resolved in an infinity of ways into forward and reverse components. That is,

$$q_B = q_F + q_R \qquad (10.3)$$

where, in the dc steady state, q_F and q_R are the forward and reverse components of stored minority-carrier charge, defined by the emitter-base and collector-base junction voltages, respectively. Figure 10.1 illustrates the resolution of q_B into these two independent components in the situation where both junctions are forward-biased, for the ideal one-dimensional uniform base specified above. If, however, the components q_F, q_R of stored charge are known individually, it becomes possible to define the instantaneous values of i_E, i_C provided *that* the base charge is assumed to undergo only relatively *slow variation*. Without this assumption, the dynamic behavior of the transistor can only be characterized by partial differential equations, representing the truly distributed nature of diffusive carrier (or charge) flow in the base. The assumption of slow stored-charge variation allows the total base charge to be resolved into two lumped components q_F, q_R corresponding to forward and reverse injection, respectively, just as in the dc steady state, and the dynamic variation of these charge components will be seen to be characterized by simple first-order ordinary differential equations. Furthermore, it is found that the imposed restriction to the rate of variation of q_B is not the severe limitation

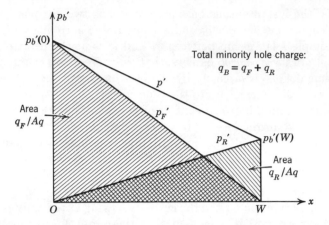

Fig. 10.1. Forward- and reverse-injected components of excess minority-carrier concentrations in the base. The case shown is a uniform base, of constant cross-sectional area A; both V_{EB} and V_{CB} are positive.

that might perhaps be expected, and models based on this assumption are able to give a sufficiently accurate representation of dynamic behavior of the device for most practical applications. The question of the accuracy of the device model developed below is taken up in some detail in Sec. 10.3.

It is now necessary to be specific about the way in which q_B is divided into its two components q_F, q_R. Let us initially consider the transistor to be operating with forward injection only, i.e., $v_{EB} \neq 0$ but $v_{CB} = 0$, so that $q_F \neq 0$ while $q_R = 0$. The important step is now taken of supposing that, in response to the control action of base current in setting up base charge q_F, there is established a collector current which is proportional to the instantaneous value of q_F and is defined by q_F exactly as in the dc steady state. In other words, it is supposed that the rate of variation of q_F is sufficiently slow for the relationship between q_F and i_C to be essentially the same as in the dc steady state. Thus, expressing this property in equation form, we have:

$$i_B = -\frac{q_F}{\tau_B} - \frac{dq_F}{dt}$$

$$i_C = -\frac{q_F}{\tau_F}$$

$$(10.4a,b)$$

and the emitter current is

$$i_E = q_F \left(\frac{1}{\tau_B} + \frac{1}{\tau_F} \right) + \frac{dq_F}{dt} \qquad (10.4c)$$

comprising three physically distinct components.

The new parameter τ_F relates the collector current to the base charge q_F, and is defined on the assumption that this relationship is negligibly different from that in the true dc steady state. To examine the significance of τ_F for the idealized form of device under consideration, we note that if the slight departure from constant minority-carrier concentration gradient in the base, due to recombination, is neglected, then for base cross-sectional area A,

$$q_F = q p_b'(0) \frac{WA}{2}$$

where $p_b'(0)$ is the injected excess hole concentration at the emitter space-charge layer boundary and W is the base width. Further,

$$I_C = \frac{-q p_b'(0) D_b A}{W}$$

Both expressions apply for the dc steady state. Accordingly,

$$\tau_F = \frac{-q_F}{I_C} = \frac{W^2}{2D_b} \qquad (10.5)$$

The dynamic behavior of the terminal currents of the transistor is thus expressed in a very simple manner in terms of the excess stored charge in the base region; for forward injection only, the two *charge control* parameters, τ_B, τ_F, are sufficient to specify this behavior. These parameters also define the dc current gains of the transistor for forward injection:

$$\beta_F = \frac{I_C}{I_B} = \frac{\tau_B}{\tau_F}$$

$$\alpha_F = -\frac{I_C}{I_E} = \frac{1}{1 + \tau_F/\tau_B} \qquad (10.6)$$

These relationships are evident from Eqs. 10.4. It is clear that $\tau_B \gg \tau_F$.

At this point it is worthwhile to summarize the concepts of charge control, as represented by the above relationships, Eqs. 10.4, for forward injection:

(a) The base charge q_F is defined uniquely by the past history of the base current.

(b) Collector current is proportional to base charge q_F, or is *controlled by* this charge.

If, in general, the total base charge q_B is considered, the first property still holds, as discussed earlier. A similar relationship to (b) also applies for reverse injection only, in this case the emitter current being proportional to the reverse charge component q_R. By superposition of the effects of both independent components of the total base charge q_B, all three terminal currents of the transistor may be defined explicitly in terms of q_F, q_R as follows:

$$i_B = -\left(\frac{q_F}{\tau_{BF}} + \frac{dq_F}{dt}\right) \qquad -\left(\frac{q_R}{\tau_{BR}} + \frac{dq_R}{dt}\right)$$

$$i_C = \qquad -\frac{q_F}{\tau_F} \qquad + q_R\left(\frac{1}{\tau_R} + \frac{1}{\tau_{BR}}\right) + \frac{dq_R}{dt} \qquad (10.7a,b,c)$$

$$i_E = q_F\left(\frac{1}{\tau_F} + \frac{1}{\tau_{BF}}\right) + \frac{dq_F}{dt} \qquad -\frac{q_R}{\tau_R}$$

The contributions of the various components of current due to change, recombination or flow (through the base region in one direction or the other) of q_F or q_R are quite evident in these expressions for the terminal currents. Care has been taken to use distinct symbols for the charge-control parameters associated with the forward and reverse charge components (τ_F, τ_{BF} for forward, τ_R, τ_{BR} for reverse). In the case of a perfectly symmetrical device, of course, $\tau_{BF} = \tau_{BR} = \tau_B$ and $\tau_F = \tau_R$. Actual devices do not possess such symmetry, however, and are often grossly asymmetrical, so that $\tau_{BF} \neq \tau_{BR}$, $\tau_F \neq \tau_R$. For example, in an asymmetrical alloy junction device in which the collector is of larger area than the emitter, $\tau_R > \tau_F$ since, in addition to the base charge set up between emitter and collector, there is for reverse injection a considerable amount of charge stored external to this region, far more than for forward injection. The difference between conditions for forward and reverse operation in such a device is illustrated

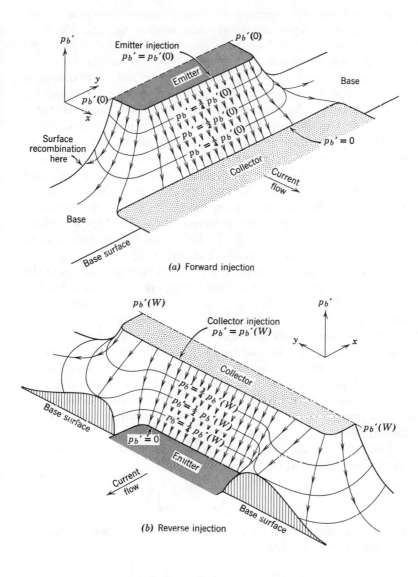

Fig. 10.2. Illustrating excess minority-carrier concentration distributions set up by forward and reverse injection in an asymmetrical alloy-junction transistor.

in Fig. 10.2, where the excess hole concentration is shown as a "surface" above a two-dimensional cross section through the base region. The "contours" of the surface are lines of constant hole concentration, and these are intersected orthogonally by flow lines of diffusion current. It is clear that the charge needed to sustain a given current traversing the base may be considerably larger for reverse than for forward operation. Even the "equivalent life time" τ_B takes different values for the two modes of injection in a real device, for surface recombination contributes to this parameter in a different way for forward and reverse operation; this is also clear from Fig. 10.2 since the surface distributions of excess hole concentration are quite different in the two cases. The use of the two "effective base lifetime" parameters τ_{BF}, τ_{BR} is thus necessary.

Evaluation of the transient behavior of the transistor in a given problem entails the solution of the charge-control relations of Eqs. 10.7 for the two independent charge components q_F, q_R. The charge components also define the junction voltages v_{EB}, v_{CB} if the assumption is made that the base-charge distribution during the transient behavior closely approximates the corresponding steady-state concentration distribution for the instantaneous values of q_F, q_R; this assumption was made, in fact, in the development of the charge-control relationships of Eqs. 10.7. It will be seen in Sec. 10.3 that the requirements for accurate representation of the relationships between *currents* and *charges* are much less stringent than the above comments suggest, but that for accurate definition of the junction voltages, near-steady-state conditions do have to be assumed.

Thus, considering the stored charge q_F, for forward injection alone, we would obtain in the dc steady state:

$$I_E = q_F \left(\frac{1}{\tau_F} + \frac{1}{\tau_{BF}} \right)$$

Hence, regardless of the value of q_R, the diode *V-I* relationship for the emitter junction gives:

$$v_{EB}(t) = \frac{kT}{q} \ln \left[\frac{p_b{}'(0,\, t)}{p_{bo}} + 1 \right]$$

where $p_b{}'(0,\, t)$ is the excess hole concentration at the emitter boundary of the base region, corresponding to $v_{EB}(t)$, and p_{bo} is the equilibrium value of hole concentration in the base. Realizing that the same constant of proportionality relates $p_b'(0,t)$ to I_E for forward operation only, and p_{bo} to the reverse saturation value I_{ES} of emitter current (forward operation only), the expression for the junction voltage may alternatively be written

$$v_{EB}(t) = \frac{kT}{q} \ln \left[\frac{q_F}{q_{FS}} + 1 \right] \qquad (10.8a)$$

where, utilizing again steady state dc conditions,

$$q_{FS} = \frac{I_{ES}}{1/\tau_F + 1/\tau_{BF}}$$

Similarly, from consideration of reverse injection alone,

$$v_{CB}(t) = \frac{kT}{q} \ln \left[\frac{q_R}{q_{RS}} + 1 \right] \qquad (10.8b)$$

where

$$q_{RS} = \frac{I_{CS}}{1/\tau_R + 1/\tau_{BR}}$$

It is readily checked that Eqs. 10.8 are simply an alternative statement of the familiar dc diode characteristic relationships with stored-charge variables used instead of boundary minority-carrier concentrations. The accuracy of the above expressions for the junction voltages under dynamic conditions of operation of the transistor is discussed in Sec. 10.3.

10.2 THE TWO-LUMP MODEL OF THE TRANSISTOR

The above charge-control relationships express the dynamic behavior of the transistor in terms of the two lumped components q_F, q_R of the total base charge q_B. Essentially, these relationships specify a two-lump model of the device. An alternative approach to the derivation of such a model is to employ the procedure of Chapter 6, in which the base region is divided into a number of volume lumps. If this is done, the model of Fig. 10.3 is obtained, in which as many lumps may be used as is necessary to achieve the desired accuracy of characterization of the device. The end lumps, it should be noted, are related to the junction voltages, in that the

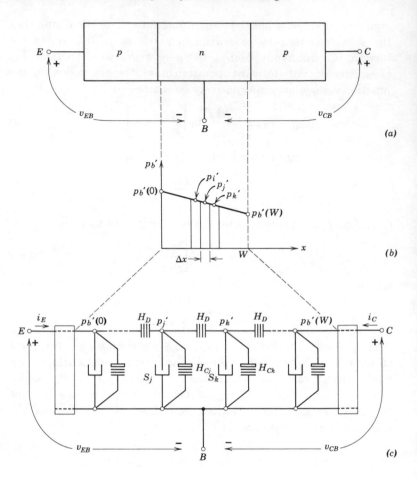

Fig. 10.3. Lumped model of the transistor.

injected excess hole concentration $p_b'(0)$ or $p_b'(W)$ acts as a boundary condition for the volume lump and governs the excess charge stored in it. The junction voltages themselves are developed across the "box" representations of the junction space-charge regions. In general, the storance S_j represents the charge stored in the jth lumped volume of the base, this stored charge (of minority carriers) being $S_j p_j'$ where p_j' is the average excess hole concentration in this lump. As discussed in Chapter 6, the rate of recombination of stored charge in the jth lump is defined by the combinance element H_{Cj}, this rate being $H_{Cj}p_j'$; furthermore, assuming a uniform base, the flow of minority carriers in the base is by diffusion alone and the diffusion current from the jth to the $(j + 1)$th volume lump is $H_D(p_j' - p_{j'+1})$, where H_D is the diffusance between these lumps.

For practical use, the model needs to be as simple as possible. The simplest possibility is evidently where only a two-lump subdivision of the base is made: the total excess charge stored in the base is then divided into two independent lumped components contained in these two volume lumps; i.e., into two lumped components, each defined by a boundary condition of junction voltage or injected excess minority-carrier concentration at one extreme or the other of the base region. Such a two-lump model of the base region is shown in Fig. 10.4. Clearly, the model is equally an expression of the charge-control relationships developed in Sec. 10.1 since, for the model to be representative of the charge-storage properties of the base for all combinations of junction voltages, it is necessary that the charge stored in the storance adjacent to the emitter-base junction should be q_F, and that the charge in that adjacent to the collector-base junction should be q_R. The two storances are accordingly designated S_F, S_R and their values must be such that they contain the charges q_F, q_R, respectively; i.e., if these storance values

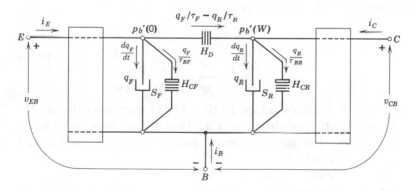

Fig. 10.4. Two-lump model of the transistor. In general,

$$S_F \neq S_R, \; H_{CF} \neq H_{CR}$$
$$\tau_F \neq \tau_R, \; \tau_{BF} \neq \tau_{BR}$$

are related to the boundary values of injected excess minority-carrier concentration, then

$$q_F = S_F p_b{}'(0)$$
$$q_R = S_R p_b{}'(W) \tag{10.9}$$

Expressed in terms of the lumped-model elements, the terminal currents of the transistor, for *forward injection* only, are:

$$i_B = -H_{CF} p_b{}'(0) - S_F \frac{dp_b{}'(0)}{dt}$$
$$i_C = -H_D p_b{}'(0) \tag{10.10a,b,c}$$
$$i_E = (H_D + H_{CF}) p_b{}'(0) + S_F \frac{dp_b{}'(0)}{dt}$$

Comparing these equations with Eqs. 10.4, in terms of the forward charge q_F, the following identities between the charge-control and lumped-model parameters are observed:

$$\tau_F = \frac{S_F}{H_D}$$
$$\tau_{BF} = \frac{S_F}{H_{CF}} \tag{10.11}$$

The steady-state dc current gains of the transistor are also seen to be as follows, for forward injection only:

$$\beta_F = \frac{\tau_{BF}}{\tau_F} = \frac{H_D}{H_{CF}}$$
$$\alpha_F = \frac{1}{1 + \tau_F/\tau_{BF}} = \frac{H_D}{H_D + H_{CF}} \tag{10.12}$$

Similar relationships to Eqs. 10.10 and 10.11 may be written for the reverse injection condition, relating the charge-control parameters τ_R, τ_{BR} and the lumped model parameter ratios S_R/H_D and S_R/H_{CR}, respectively.

For the uniform base transistor, the two-lump model may be regarded as an expression of the dynamic properties of the device *either* in terms of the boundary excess hole concentrations $p_b{}'(0)$, $p_b{}'(W)$, in the manner of Chapter 6, *or* in terms of the stored-charge components q_F, q_R.* As far as the latter alternative is concerned,

---

* The latter possibility is also true for a *graded* base; see Sec. 10.3.1.

the model of Fig. 10.4 is simply a graphical representation, or statement in diagram-form, of the charge-control relationships, all current components being as indicated in terms of q_F and q_R; the lumped-model symbols merely indicate the physical nature of these various current components. Later in this chapter *the charge-control interpretation of the two-lump model will be used*, with the advantage that attention is focussed on measurable quantities and parameters. The charge-control parameters may, in fact, be measured very simply for a given transistor—for example, the parameters τ_F, τ_{BF} can be determined as the ratios of q_F to I_C and I_B, respectively—and are thus particularly appropriate for characterizing the dynamic behavior of the device. A practical method of measurement for these parameters is discussed briefly at the end of Sec. 10.3. It should be noted that it is not possible to determine the values of the lumped-model parameters H_D, etc., by terminal measurements on an actual device—only ratios of these parameters can be measured, as expressed in Eqs. 10.11.

10.2.1 *Relationship of the Two-Lump Model to the dc Models of Chapter 9*

It is useful to relate the two-lump model of Fig. 10.4 to the dc model developed in Chapter 9 (Fig. 9.4); for the latter, the relationships between the terminal currents and voltages are expressed as:

$$I_E = \quad I_{ES}(e^{qV_{EB}/kT} - 1) - \alpha_R I_{CS}(e^{qV_{CB}/kT} - 1) \qquad (10.13a)$$
$$I_C = -\alpha_F I_{ES}(e^{qV_{EB}/kT} - 1) + \quad I_{CS}(e^{qV_{CB}/kT} - 1)$$

By inspection, the dc emitter and collector currents of the two-lump model of Fig. 10.4 are:

$$I_E = p_b'(0)(H_D + H_{CF}) - p_b'(W)H_D \qquad (10.13b)$$
$$I_C = -p_b'(0)H_D + p_b'(W)(H_D + H_{CR})$$

Substituting the relationships

$$p_b'(0) \ = p_{bo}(e^{qV_{EB}/kT} - 1)$$
$$p_b'(W) = p_{bo}(e^{qV_{CB}/kT} - 1) \qquad (10.14)$$

equations 10.13a and 10.13b are seen to be identical, with the identifications:

$$p_{bo}(H_D + H_{CF}) = I_{ES}$$
$$p_{bo}H_D = \alpha_R I_{CS} = \alpha_F I_{ES} \qquad (10.15)$$
$$p_{bo}(H_D + H_{CR}) = I_{CS}$$

Consistency between the two-lump and dc models is thus verified; the following comments are also appropriate:

1. Since α_F, α_R, I_{ES}, I_{CS} are measurable, so are the quantities $p_{bo}H_D$, $p_{bo}H_{CF}$, and $p_{bo}H_{CR}$. If p_{bo} is known, H_D, H_{CF}, and H_{CR} are measurable, although for terminal-response calculation purposes, only $p_{bo}H_D$, etc., need to be known.

2. As already noted, the two-lump model applies to device structures that are *not* one-dimensional, as do the results of Chapter 9. (But see the discussion of Sec. 10.3.1 for a *graded-base* device. The two-lump model is valid also for such a device if expressed in terms of stored charges, but not in terms of $p_b'(0)$, $p_b'(W)$.)

3. Since the model provides proper representation of dc behavior, transient response calculations must necessarily converge to correct end points.

10.3 CONDITIONS OF VALIDITY OF THE TWO-LUMP MODEL AND CHARGE-CONTROL EQUATIONS

It has been stressed from the outset that the basic two-lump model of the base region is an accurate representation of dynamic behavior if the stored charges are changing sufficiently slowly. For simplicity, let us consider only forward injection ($q_R = 0$). Now, although the relationship of Eq. 10.4a between base charge and base current is exact (provided that the base is of uniform lifetime), it is clear that the other two equations of the charge-control set of Eq. 10.4 are approximate and involve small errors only if the "equivalent steady-state" relationship

$$i_C = -\frac{q_F}{\tau_F} \tag{10.4b}$$

is reasonably representative of the true situation under dynamic conditions. By invoking the condition of "slow variation of state," a simple proportionality between i_C and q_F, equivalent to the steady state in this respect even though q_F is varying, may be justified conceptually. However, Eq. 10.4b can be a surprisingly accurate statement even though the base-charging current is comparable with the collector current, as may be appreciated from

Fig. 10.5. In the figure, the instantaneous excess hole concentration distribution corresponding to increasing base charge in a uniform base is shown: the injected hole current (and, therefore, also the magnitude of base current) is considerably larger than the steady-state value for the instantaneous base charge q_F, but only results in appreciable departure from the steady-state hole concentration near to the boundary of injection. The total excess charge q_F therefore differs negligibly from the steady-state value corresponding to the instantaneous collector current in the illustrated situation (compare the relevant areas in the diagram), and Eq. 10.4b is a good approximation. On the other hand, Fig. 10.5 illustrates that under transient conditions the injected excess hole concentration $p_b'(0)$ may depart appreciably from the equivalent steady-state value for the instantaneous charge stored in the base. Thus we conclude that while the relationships between the base-charge components q_F, q_R and the terminal *currents*, expressed by the two-lump model and the corresponding charge-control equations, may give accurate representation of true device behavior for quite rapid transients, the relationships of Eqs. 10.8 between the charge components and the junction voltages v_{EB}, v_{CB} are much less accurate.

It is worthwhile to illustrate these conclusions further by examining the dynamic response of the transistor in terms of the two-lump model for the practical situations of an applied step-change of base current or emitter current. Forward injection only is con-

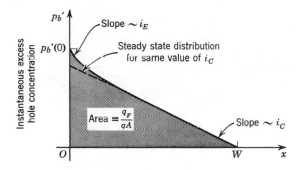

Fig. 10.5. Instantaneous excess hole concentration distribution in the base region under dynamic conditions for forward-injection conditions only: base charge increasing due to large injected charging current.

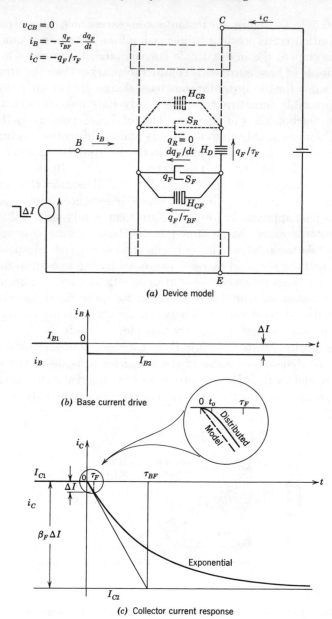

(a) Device model

(b) Base current drive

(c) Collector current response

Fig. 10.6. Response to a step-change of base current: forward injection only.

sidered ($v_{CB} = 0$), for which the model takes the common emitter form shown in Fig. 10.6a. The situation would be almost identical if the collector junction were reverse-biased, the reverse charge q_R being negligible compared with q_F under typical operating conditions. By inspection of either the model or the corresponding equations it is clear that the response of base charge q_F or collector current to a step-change of *base current* is exponential, with time constant τ_{BF}; the final current gain, as $t \rightarrow \infty$, is $\beta_F = \tau_{BF}/\tau_F$.

After a time τ_F the collector current has changed by an amount almost exactly equal to the step-change of base current; that is, unity current gain is realized after time τ_F has elapsed. Up to this time, the base current is actually greater than the collector current. However, the model gives very close prediction of the true collector-current waveform, the exponential response being almost indistinguishable from the waveform derived by distributed analysis of a "one-dimensional" uniform base region. As illustrated in Fig. 10.6c, the only noticeable discrepancy between the waveform derived by distributed analysis and that given by the model is a short delay, of order $t_o = 0.2\,\tau_F$, exhibited by the former before the response calculated from the lumped model develops.

Figure 10.7a shows the lumped model, for forward injection only, in common-base form. Again, comparing the expressions for emitter and collector current, it is evident that the collector-current response to a step-change of *emitter current* is exponential, as illustrated, with time constant

$$\frac{\tau_F}{1 + \tau_F/\tau_{BF}} = \alpha_F \tau_F$$

The rapidity of variation of collector current (or q_F) is relatively much greater than for the previous case of a step-change of base current, since $\alpha_F \tau_F \ll \tau_{BF}$. It is interesting to compare the predicted waveform of collector current with the result of distributed analysis of a uniform-base region, as illustrated in Fig. 10.8a. In the case shown, carrier recombination is neglected so that $\tau_{BF} = \infty$, $\alpha_F = 1$. Although the base-charging current is comparable in magnitude to i_C over the whole transient waveform shown, and for $t < 0.7\,\tau_F$ exceeds i_C, the lumped model is seen to give very good representation of the device. Again, the main discrepancy is that the response derived by distributed analysis shows no appreciable

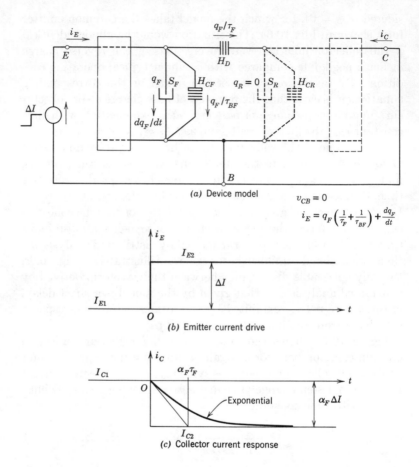

(a) Device model

$$v_{CB} = 0$$

$$i_E = q_F\left(\frac{1}{\tau_F} + \frac{1}{\tau_{BF}}\right) + \frac{dq_F}{dt}$$

(b) Emitter current drive

(c) Collector current response

Fig. 10.7. Response to a step-change of emitter current: forward injection only.

change in collector current until a time of about $t_o = 0.2\,\tau_F$ has elapsed, after which the current changes in approximately exponential manner.

Figure 10.8b also compares the response of junction voltage v_{EB} predicted by the lumped model with the response derived by distributed analysis of a uniform base, for a step-change of emitter current. Because of the nature of the relationship (Eq. 10.8a) between v_{EB} and the injected charge q_F for the model, it is convenient

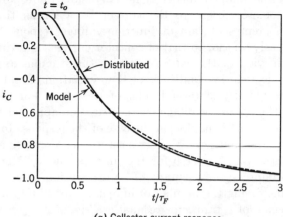

(a) Collector current response

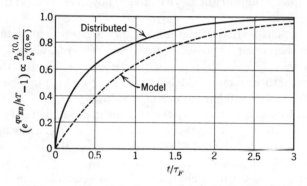

(b) Response of junction voltage or injected minority carrier concentration

Fig. 10.8. Responses of collector current and emitter junction voltage to a step-change of emitter current, assuming $\tau_{BF} = \infty$ so that $\alpha_F = 1$.

to plot the responses in the normalized form shown; the actual quantity plotted is proportional to the excess hole concentration $p_b'(0)$ injected by the emitter, or q_F, and therefore undergoes an exponential variation with time constant $\alpha_F \tau_F$. As expected on the basis of the typical instantaneous excess charge distribution of Fig. 10.5, during changing conditions in the base, the lumped model is unable to represent the rapidity of response of junction voltage to change of injected current. The waveform of v_{EB} calculated from the lumped model is initially slow in response, but approaches more closely to the correct behavior as time progresses. The representation of junction-voltage response by the model is clearly inferior to that of collector current, and this is not surprising in view of the extent to which the stimulus applied to the device violates the conditions of slow variation of state necessary for the validity of the relations of Eqs. 10.8. For less rapid transients, the junction-voltage characterization approaches much closer to the correct behavior; in the case of the response to a base-current step, the model gives a very accurate representation.

As discussed in Chapter 6 for the junction diode, it is always possible to improve the accuracy of representation of the lumped model by increasing the number of lumps. A three-lump model of the base region of a transistor results in a significantly closer approximation to the true response of v_{EB} shown in Fig. 10.8. In practical applications of the device model, however, two lumps are usually quite adequate.

A final demonstration of the remarkably accurate characterization of the relationship between charges and currents, given by the two-lump model, is of value. If a transistor is subjected to the base-drive conditions of Fig. 10.9, application of the input-voltage step results in the sudden supply of a charge $(-Q)$, of majority carriers, to the base followed by the establishment of a steady base current. Effectively, the transistor operates in the forward mode. According to the charge-control relations of Eqs. 10.4, or as visualized from the lumped model, if the time constant of the base-drive circuit is $RC = \tau_{BF}$, a base charge $q_F = Q$ is suddenly established and subsequently held constant. The collector current should therefore undergo a *step-change*, according to the model. In practice, the response of collector current (or collector voltage) is, in fact, observed to be almost a perfect step, as illustrated by the typical waveform shown in Fig. 10.9 (comparison should be made with the waveform, also shown, for $C = 0$). Yet the dynamic conditions in the base are made to undergo very rapid changes indeed, far more so than for the step-change of emitter current illustrated in Fig. 10.7. We conclude that a local "packet" of excess carrier charge, injected at the emitter boundary of the base as in the base-drive situation of Fig. 10.9, can settle down by diffusion to the steady-state distribution in an exceedingly short time; distributed analysis

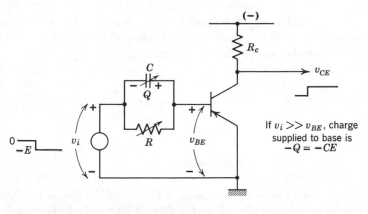

(a) Circuit arrangement.

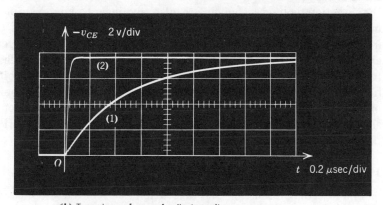

(b) Typical waveforms of collector voltage.
(1) Capacitor C absent, response as in Fig. 10.6
(2) With adjustment so that $RC = \tau_{BF}$

Fig. 10.9. Response of the transistor to a step-change of base charge: a charge $(-Q) = -EC$ is supplied to the base via C, while R supplies the corresponding maintaining current to hold this charge in the steady state.

of a uniform base shows that this settling process takes almost exactly the time $t_o = 0.2\,\tau_F$ referred to in the above discussions.

The circuit arrangement of Fig. 10.9 is used in practice for the measurement of charge-control parameters of the transistor. If charging processes associated with the space-charge layers were completely negligible (they have been disregarded throughout all preceding discussion), then with adjustment of RC for a step response of collector current (or voltage),

$$RC = \tau_{BF}$$

If, further, the collector voltage change is equal to the input voltage step,

$$R_cC = \tau_F$$

Similar considerations to the above apply for operation of the transistor in the reverse injection mode, or for simultaneous injection from both junctions. In practice, however, the charge supplied to the base region as a result of the flow of base current is not composed only of the forward and reverse. excess minority-carrier charges q_F, q_R. The charges supplied to the space-charge layers as the junction voltages change are also significant. For example, in the circuit of Fig. 10.9 the charge $(-Q)$ supplied to base via C includes a component that modifies the emitter space-charge layer charge. The representation of space-charge layer charges is added to the model in Sec. 10.5. Before dealing with this elaboration, however, Sec. 10.4 is devoted to an illustration of the application of the two-lump model and associated charge-control relationships in a practical problem, with space-charge layer charges still neglected.

10.3.1 *Model Representation of Graded-Base Transistors*

The foregoing discussion and derivation has referred specifically to a uniform-base device. All relationships in terms of forward and reverse stored-charge components q_F, q_R are, however, valid for a base of any grading of impurity concentration. The charge-control concepts are perfectly general, and for quantitative expression only require the specification of the parameters τ_F, τ_{BF}, τ_R, τ_{BR} for the device concerned. The two-lump model is also quite general if it is regarded as "charge defined." All currents in the model are expressed in terms of the charges of q_F, q_R in the storances S_F, S_R; in particular, the current flowing through the element H_D (that is, traversing the base) from emitter to collector is $q_F/\tau_F - q_R/\tau_R$. On the other hand, the two-lump model is *not* able to express device properties in terms of the boundary excess minority-carrier concentrations $p_b'(0)$, $p_b'(W)$ for a *nonuniform* base, because the current traversing the base is not simply proportional to the difference in these carrier concentrations (carrier transport being by a combination of diffusion and drift mechanisms).*

10.4 EXAMPLE OF USE OF THE LUMPED MODEL FOR TRANSIENT CALCULATIONS

In this section a simple example of the transient behavior of a transistor is studied in terms of the two-lump model. The example shows how the analysis centers on the determination of the stored charges q_F, q_R from the differential equations defined by the model, and also allows some conclusions of general significance to be drawn, in particular for transient behavior in the saturation region of operation. From the outset the device is idealized by the neglect of space-charge layer charging effects.

The circuit to be studied is shown in Fig. 10.10a in which the transistor is used as an electrically activated switch. With the base connected to ground, only a very small collector current I_{CS} flows in the load resistance R_L, which is thus effectively disconnected from the voltage supply V_L. At $t = 0$ the base is connected to the source V_S, R_S which supplies base current; assuming that $|v_{EB}| \ll V_S$, a step of base current is applied at $t = 0$. With V_S, R_S such that

$$-I_B = \frac{V_S}{R_S} > \frac{V_L}{R_L}\frac{1}{\beta_F}$$

the transistor must eventually enter the saturation region of operation after the switching transient has elapsed. The voltage between collector and emitter is then almost zero and the transistor acts as a closed switch in series with the load resistance.

We wish to calculate the behavior of the transistor as it proceeds from the initial cut-off condition to the final saturated state.

The calculation is in two stages. During the first stage, collector current increases from $I_{CS}(\cong 0)$ to a value of almost exactly

---

* The two-lump model may, however, be expressed in terms of the carrier-concentration variables if an added element is included to represent the drift process of carrier flow through the base. The interested reader should consult Ref. 10.4, Chapter 5.

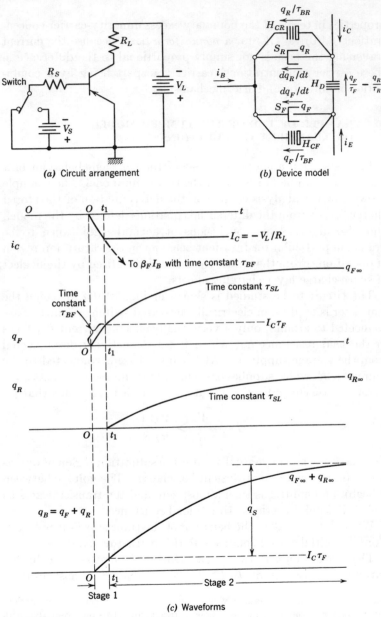

(a) Circuit arrangement

(b) Device model

(c) Waveforms

Fig. 10.10. Example of dynamic response of a transistor when switching from the cut-off to the saturation state.

$(-V_L/R_L)$, assuming that in the saturation state $|v_{CB}| \ll V_L$. During this time, the collector junction remains reverse-biased and base current is causing the build-up of forward stored charge q_F. The first stage of the transient is completed when v_{CB} becomes zero and $i_C \cong -V_L/R_L$.

The second stage of the transient begins when the transistor enters the saturation region, as the base-charging current continues to increase the base charge above the forward value $q_F = V_{LT_F}/R_L$ just necessary to sustain the collector current $(-V_L/R_L)$. The collector junction then becomes forward-biased and injects a steadily increasing reverse charge q_R. During this second stage the collector current remains almost constant at $(-V_L/R_L)$. Ultimately a steady state is reached with certain q_F, q_R values, and with total base charge q_B exceeding the amount V_{LT_F}/R_L at the end of the first stage by a saturation charge q_S. The charge q_S is of considerable importance, for if it were desired to switch the transistor back to the initial cut-off state (for example, by reducing I_B to zero) a certain delay would occur before the collector junction voltage could *start* to reverse bias, during which q_S was being removed from the base.

10.4.1 *Active Region Behavior, Involving Forward Injection Only*

Calculation of the transient behavior will be worked out in terms of charge variables, these being most directly connected with circuit performance of the transistor. The lumped model is shown in Fig. 10.10*b* with the various base-current components indicated. Throughout the first stage of the transient,

$$-i_B \cong \frac{q_F}{\tau_{BF}} + \frac{dq_F}{dt} + \frac{q_R}{\tau_{BR}} = \frac{V_S}{R_S} = |I_B| \qquad (10.16)$$

since, with the collector junction reverse-biased, the reverse charge $q_R = p_b'(W)S_R$ is almost exactly $(-p_{bo}S_R)$ and the associated charging current is negligibly small. Neglecting the very small current q_R/τ_{BR}, or assuming $|q_R| \ll q_F$ throughout the transient (so that $q_B \cong q_F$), with the initial condition $q_F = 0$, the solution of Eq. 10.16 is:

$$q_F = \frac{V_S}{R_S}\tau_{BF}(1 - e^{-t/\tau_{BF}}) \qquad (10.17a)$$

giving

$$i_C = -\beta_F \frac{V_S}{R_S} (1 - e^{-t/\tau_{BF}}) \qquad (10.17b)$$

As illustrated in Fig. 10.10c, the above solutions apply until the collector current becomes

$$i_C \cong -V_L/R_L = -|I_C|$$

and the time t_1 taken for the collector current to increase to this value is (from Eq. 10.17b):

$$t_1 = \tau_{BF} \ln \left(\frac{1}{1 - |I_C|/\beta_F|I_B|} \right) \qquad (10.18)$$

10.4.2 *Behavior in the Saturation Region*

Throughout the second stage of the transient, the transistor operates in the saturation region, and both q_F and q_R are positive and time dependent, while i_C is constant at $(-I_C)$. Referring to the model of Fig. 10.10b, the following equations may be written down for the base and collector currents, both of which have circuit-defined constant values:

$$-i_B = |I_B| = \frac{q_F}{\tau_{BF}} + \frac{dq_F}{dt} + \frac{q_R}{\tau_{BR}} + \frac{dq_R}{dt} \qquad (10.19a)$$

$$-i_C = |I_C| = \frac{q_F}{\tau_F} - \left(\frac{1}{\tau_{BR}} + \frac{1}{\tau_R} \right) q_R - \frac{dq_R}{dt} \qquad (10.19b)$$

where $|I_B| = V_S/R_S$, $|I_C| = V_L/R_L$.

These equations may be solved with the initial conditions $q_F = |I_C|\tau_F$, $q_R = 0$ at $t = t_1$. The solutions for q_F or q_R involve two decaying exponential modes, the time constants of which are found from the characteristic equation formed from Eqs. 10.19, namely,

$$s^2 + s \left\{ \frac{1}{\tau_F} + \frac{1}{\tau_R} + \frac{1}{\tau_{BF}} + \frac{1}{\tau_{BR}} \right\}$$
$$+ \left\{ \frac{1}{\tau_F \tau_{BR}} + \frac{1}{\tau_R \tau_{BF}} + \frac{1}{\tau_{BF} \tau_{BR}} \right\} = 0 \qquad (10.20)$$

where s is the complex frequency variable.

Substitution of typical values of the parameters shows that, for practical devices, the constant term in this equation should be very small compared with the square of the coefficient of s. On this assumption, Eq. 10.20 is readily solved to yield a large and small time constant corresponding to slow (SL) and fast (FA) modes, respectively:

$$\frac{1}{\tau_{FA}} = \frac{1}{\tau_F} + \frac{1}{\tau_R} + \frac{1}{\tau_{BF}} + \frac{1}{\tau_{BR}} \tag{10.21}$$

$$\frac{1}{\tau_{SL}} = \frac{1/\tau_F\tau_{BR} + 1/\tau_R\tau_{BF} + 1/\tau_{BF}\tau_{BR}}{1/\tau_F + 1/\tau_R + 1/\tau_{BF} + 1/\tau_{BR}} \tag{10.22}$$

where $\tau_{SL} \gg \tau_{FA}$.

A detailed analysis reveals that the fast mode represents a rapid redistribution of charge between q_F and q_R (that is, between the storances S_F, S_R); the forward and reverse charges have fast mode components of opposite sign. The slow mode, on the other hand, represents the growth (or, in other situations, the decay) of *both* q_F and q_R due to the influence of base-charging current in the presence of recombination. The slow-mode components of q_F and q_R are of the same sign.

On evaluating the two components of q_F or q_R, it is found that, if $\tau_{SL} \gg \tau_{FA}$, the fast mode is of *very much smaller magnitude* than slow mode, in addition to decaying away much more rapidly. Accordingly, the fast mode may be neglected entirely in the present example. Neglect of the fast mode is also permissible in most practical switching situations, except where the actual process of redistribution of charge between forward and reverse injected components is of significance. Thus, in terms of the slow mode above, we have effectively:

$$q_F = q_{F(SL)}e^{-t'/\tau_{SL}} + q_{F\infty} \tag{10.23a}$$

$$q_R = q_{R(SL)}e^{-t'/\tau_{SL}} + q_{R\infty} \tag{10.23b}$$

where $t' = t - t_1$. Initial conditions at $t' = 0$ give $q_{F(SL)} + q_{F\infty} = |I_C|\tau_F$ and $q_{R(SL)} + q_{R\infty} = 0$.

The transient behavior of q_F and q_R is shown in Fig. 10.10c. The final values $q_{F\infty}$, $q_{R\infty}$ are readily calculated in terms of the circuit-defined terminal currents and the charge-control parameters of the transistor. The behavior of the total base charge $q_B = q_F + q_R$ is also shown, and this is seen to increase by an amount q_S. the "saturation charge," during the second stage of the transient. The saturation charge is, as mentioned earlier, of practical significance, since its removal is necessary before i_C can change when switching the transistor back to the initial cut-off state. Utilizing the definition:

$$q_S = q_{F\infty} + q_{R\infty} - |I_C|\tau_F$$

and Eqs. 10.19 in the steady state, the saturation charge is evaluated as:

$$q_S = \tau_S|I_{BS}| \tag{10.24a}$$

where

$$I_{BS} = I_B - \frac{I_C}{\beta_F} \tag{10.24b}$$

and

$$\tau_S = \frac{1/\tau_F + 1/\tau_R + 1/\tau_{BR}}{1/\tau_F\tau_{BR} + 1/\tau_R\tau_{BF} + 1/\tau_{BF}\tau_{BR}} \tag{10.24c}$$

The base current I_{BS} is the excess beyond I_C/β_F that drives the transistor into the saturation region of operation, while q_S is the corresponding saturation base charge in excess of $|I_C|\tau_F$. Substitution of practical values shows that, if $|I_{BS}| \gg |I_C|/\beta_F$, q_S can be much greater than $|I_C|\tau_F$, as illustrated in Fig. 10.10c.

Comparison of Eqs. 10.24c and 10.22 shows that in fact τ_S, which is often referred to as a "saturation charge-control parameter," differs negligibly from the slow-mode time-constant τ_{SL}. This property is seen even more directly by manipulating the two parameters into the alternate forms

$$\tau_{SL} = \frac{\alpha_F\tau_F + \alpha_R\tau_R}{1 - \alpha_F\alpha_R} \tag{10.25a}$$

$$\tau_S = \frac{\alpha_F(\tau_F + \alpha_R\tau_R)}{1 - \alpha_F\alpha_R} \tag{10.25b}$$

Thus, during transients in the saturation region involving the growth or decay of stored charge, the dynamic process may simply be visualized as involving the recombination of the saturation charge q_S with the effective saturation region lifetime $\tau_S \cong \tau_{SL}$, the initial base charge $|I_C|\tau_F$, defined by the constant collector current, being maintained in the steady state. This simplified version of the dynamic behavior of base charge may be written in the form of a "saturation region charge-control equation" as follows:

$$-i_B = \frac{|I_C|\tau_F}{\tau_{BF}} + \frac{q_S}{\tau_S} + \frac{dq_S}{dt} \qquad (10.26)$$

For example, if the time to remove the saturation charge from the base were required, with an applied positive base drive current, it would be necessary to solve Eq. 10.26 for the time when $q_S = 0$.

However, if we wish to evaluate the behavior of the terminal voltages of the transistor in the saturation region, it is necessary to resolve q_S into its forward and reverse components. Equations 10.8 give the collector response v_{CE} as:

$$
\begin{aligned}
v_{CE} &= \frac{kT}{q} \ln \left[\frac{q_R + q_{RS}}{q_F + q_{FS}} \cdot \frac{q_{FS}}{q_{RS}} \right] \\
&\cong \frac{kT}{q} \ln \left[\frac{q_R}{q_F} \cdot \frac{\tau_F}{\tau_R} \right]
\end{aligned}
\qquad (10.27)
$$

after utilizing the property in Eqs. 9.9 that $\alpha_F I_{ES} = \alpha_R I_{CS}$ and assuming the charges associated with the reverse saturation currents I_{CS}, I_{ES} to be negligible compared with q_R, q_F, respectively. This voltage commonly lies between a few millivolts and a few tenths of a volt. Transients in the saturation region are usually sufficiently slow for Eq. 10.27 to give good accuracy.

In concluding the discussion of this example we must stress that effects associated with the charging of the space-charge layers have not been considered. These will certainly influence transient behavior during the process of switching between cut-off and the boundary of the saturation state. In the saturation region, however, junction voltages are small and undergo little variation, so that the space-charge layer charges are almost constant; charging of these may thus often be neglected and for the saturation region the device characterization developed so far, in terms of stored excess minority-carrier charges in the neutral base region, is then quite adequate. The addition to the device model of the characterization of space-charge layer charges is discussed in the next section.

10.5 REPRESENTATION OF CHARGE STORAGE
IN SPACE-CHARGE LAYERS

The device model so far developed gives a complete definition of the charges and currents in the neutral base region for specified terminal voltages v_{EB}, v_{CB} (provided that these voltages are varying sufficiently slowly). However, the charge stored in the base depends not only on the carrier concentration injected at the base boundaries, but also on the base width between the space-charge layers—and the base width is, in turn, dependent on the values of *both* junction voltages. Thus, considering *normal* conditions of operation with the collector reverse-biased, q_F and therefore τ_F are to some extent influenced by v_{CB}, by virtue of the base-width modulation effect. The model gives the correct end result of changing the junction voltages from the equilibrium (zero) values, and τ_F, τ_R relate the final currents to the final established stored charges. During a process of change from one operating condition to another, the charge control parameters vary somewhat due to change in base width, but fortunately these changes are usually so small that negligible error is incurred if the parameters corresponding to the total changes of charge involved are employed.

Far more significant is the property that changes in space-charge layer charges are caused by junction-voltage changes. The associated charging currents flow as components of base current, and these can be comparable with the charging currents supplied to the neutral base region if the junction voltages are varying rapidly. The charge requirements of the space-charge layers may be included in the expression for the base current as follows:

$$-i_B = \frac{q_F}{\tau_{BF}} + \frac{q_R}{\tau_{BR}} + \frac{d}{dt}\left(q_F + q_R + q_{VE} + q_{VC}\right) \qquad (10.28)$$

The four charge components are identified in Fig. 10.11. The components $(-q_{VE})$, $(-q_{VC})$ are the majority electron charges that have to be supplied by flow of base current in order to neutralize the space-charge layer charge when this layer is narrowed due to forward-biasing of the junction. These charges are measured with respect to the equilibrium situation v_{EB}, $v_{CB} = 0$. The effects of q_{VE}, q_{VC} are included in the device model by addition of the charge

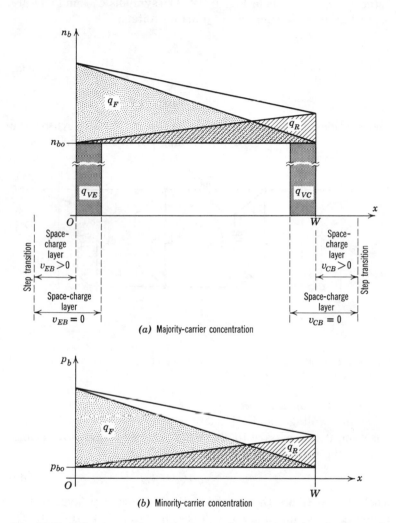

(a) Majority-carrier concentration

(b) Minority-carrier concentration

Fig. 10.11. Minority- and majority-carrier charges supplied to the base region when both v_{EB} and v_{CB} are made positive (saturation region). The indications q_F, q_R, q_{VE}, q_{VC} are intended to signify that the shaded areas involved are representative of these charges.

"stores" C_{VE}, C_{VC}, as in Fig. 10.12. The symbols C_{VE} and C_{VC} are defined as the ratio of charge to junction voltage:

$$C_{VE} = \frac{q_{VE}}{v_{EB}}$$

$$C_{VC} = \frac{q_{VC}}{v_{CB}}$$

(10.29)

The relationships of Eq. 10.29 are *nonlinear*; for this reason the symbol for a nonlinear capacitor is employed in the model.

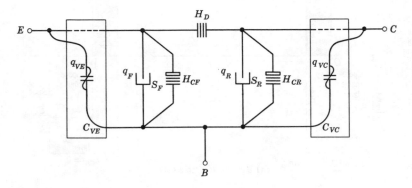

Fig. 10.12. Inclusion of space-charge layer charge storage in the model representation of the transistor.

The model now includes the basic feature that in order to change a junction voltage, and stimulate corresponding minority-carrier injection, it is necessary to change the charge in the space-charge layer of the junction. The charge involved is:

$$q_V = qN_DA\,(l_o - l_V)$$

(10.30)

where l_o and l_V are the widths of the space-charge layer in base region material for junction voltages of zero and V, respectively, N_D is the donor impurity concentration, and A is the junction area. For a *step junction*,

$$q_V = qN_DA\left[\sqrt{\frac{2\epsilon\psi_0}{qN_D}} - \sqrt{\frac{2\epsilon(\psi_0 - V)}{qN_D}}\right]$$
$$= A\,(2\epsilon qN_D)^{\frac{1}{2}}\,[\psi_0^{\frac{1}{2}} - (\psi_0 - V)^{\frac{1}{2}}]$$

(10.31)

where ψ_0 is the equilibrium potential barrier within the junction. This relationship is plotted in Fig. 10.13a for both positive and negative values of junction voltage (for a germanium device). It is seen that, if the voltage is taken from a forward to a reverse bias value, the charge required to change the junction voltage by a given incremental amount *diminishes* as the process progresses. Under forward-bias conditions it is perhaps more appropriate to express q_V in terms of the steady-state current injected into the base with the other junction voltage equal to zero; this may be done by writing the diode equation for the injecting junction in the form:

$$V = \frac{kT}{q} \ln \left(\frac{I}{I_S} + 1 \right)$$

so that

$$q_V = A (2\epsilon N_D q)^{\frac{1}{2}} \left\{ \psi_0^{\frac{1}{2}} - \left[\psi_0 - \frac{kT}{q} \ln \left(\frac{I}{I_S} + 1 \right) \right]^{\frac{1}{2}} \right\} \quad (10.32)$$

This relationship is plotted in Fig. 10.13b, and it is evident that, when forward-biasing the junction, the incremental charge demands of the space-charge layer *diminish* as the level of current injection is increased.

An alternative way of expressing Eq. 10.31 is in terms of the small-signal (incremental) capacitance C_j of the junction for junction voltage V; thus for a step junction:

$$q_V = \int_0^V C_j(V) dV = \int_0^V A \left\{ \frac{\epsilon q N_D}{2(\psi_0 - V)} \right\}^{\frac{1}{2}} dV \quad (10.33)$$

which leads to the result of Eq. 10.31. Taking a further step, the space-charge layer storage parameter C_V may be related to the space-charge layer capacitance C_j corresponding to the final state of the junction:

$$C_V = \frac{q_V}{V} = \frac{1}{V} \int_0^V C_j(V) \, dV$$

$$= 2C_j(V) \frac{\sqrt{(\psi_0 - V)\psi_0} - (\psi_0 - V)}{V} \quad (10.34)$$

$$= M_j C_j(V)$$

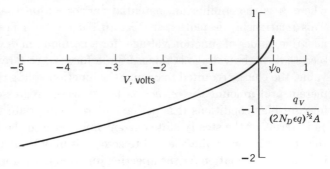

(a) Space-charge layer in terms of bias voltage

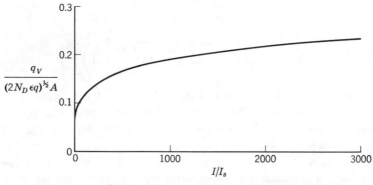

(b) Space-charge layer in terms of forward current

Fig. 10.13. Nonlinear charge storage in the transition region: example of a step junction (germanium device).

The quantity M_j depends on the junction voltage V, being less than unity for forward bias and between 1 and 2 for reverse bias.* For example, for a germanium device with $\psi_0 = 0.3v$, at $V = 0.2$ volt, $M_j = 0.73$; while at $V = -5$ volts, $M_j = 1.62$. In practice, sufficiently accurate results can usually be obtained by regarding the space-charge layer charge storage as represented by an equivalent constant capacitance $M_j C_j(V)$ when calculating the transient behavior involving a change of junction voltage from zero to V,

* These properties are for the assumed step junction. For less abrupt junctions, the possible range of M_j is reduced: in the case of a linearly graded junction, M_j lies between 1 and 1.5 under reverse-bias conditions.

or by using an appropriate capacitance value for voltage changes between two nonzero values.

The above process of "linearizing" the space-charge layer storage effects may be alternatively expressed in terms of a set of approximate charge-control equations. For forward injection alone, we can write:

$$-i_B \cong \frac{q_{FT}}{T_{BF}} + \frac{dq_{FT}}{dt}$$

$$-i_C \cong \frac{q_{FT}}{T_F} \qquad (10.35)$$

$$i_E \cong q_{FT}\left(\frac{1}{T_{BF}} + \frac{1}{T_F}\right) + \frac{dq_{FT}}{dt}$$

where $q_{FT} = q_F + q_{VE}$ and $(-q_{FT})$ is the total majority-carrier charge supplied to charge base *material* via the base terminal. The parameters T_{BF}, T_F are both larger than τ_{BF}, τ_F, respectively (though the ratios are both β_F), and would be measured in practice in terms of the charge supplied to the base to establish the final values of base and collector current involved in the transient behavior concerned. Normal active-region behavior may be analyzed in terms of Eqs. 10.35 in a manner similar to that illustrated in the example of Sec. 10.4.1 simply by substituting the *total* parameters for the charge-control parameters of the space-charge neutral base region.

Similar relationships to those of Eqs. 10.35 may be expressed for reverse injection. For either case, the linearizing procedure is applicable only if the charge component for the space-charge region *does not predominate.*

10.6 CHARGE STORAGE IN THE COLLECTOR AND REMOTE REGIONS OF BASE

10.6.1 *Collector Region Storage*

We have considered minority-carrier charge storage in only the base region in the foregoing discussion. The possibility of storage in the collector and emitter regions has been excluded from the outset for reasons of simplicity. Such storage is, in fact, negligibly small in an alloy-junction device in comparison with storage in the base, owing to the very large impurity concentration in the collector and emitter regions. For devices of graded-base type, however, collector storage can be important because the collector impurity concentration is here much less than for an alloy junction, so that the injected concentration of minority carriers in the collector, under forward-bias conditions of the junction, is correspondingly greater. On the other hand, because of the near-unity emitter efficiency of a practical device, minority-carrier injection into the emitter is quite negligible.

Figure 10.14a shows the steady-state distribution of excess minority-carrier concentration due to the injection into the collector and base regions of the transistor for v_{CB} positive and $v_{EB} = 0$ (reverse injection only into the base), assuming the collector to be of uniform impurity concentration, carrier lifetime, and cross section, and to be effectively semi-infinite in extent. In the case chosen for discussion, the diffusion length L_c of minority electrons in the collector is large compared with the base width. Under such conditions the charge stored in the collector is large compared with that in the base and has a major influence on the dynamic behavior of the device when the collector junction is forward-biased (as, for example, in the saturation region). In device fabrication, steps are usually taken to make the diffusion length L_c as small as possible to minimize the effects of charge storage in the collector; gold-doping of the collector material greatly reduces the minority-carrier lifetime and, therefore, L_c.

A lumped model of the collector-base junction diode may be developed, as discussed previously in Chapter 6; such a model is shown in Fig. 10.14b. The considerations treated in Chapter 6 apply here, the degree of lumping necessary for the representation of the collector region being dependent on the speed of the transient process involved. Reduction to a single-lump model is possible only if the variation of conditions is so slow that the shape of the excess electron concentration distribution in the collector is virtually independent of time—and therefore the same as in the steady state for the value of stored charge concerned. Under practical switching conditions, the rapidity of variation of state would be sufficiently great as to preclude the use of a single-lump model of the collector region, unless the diffusion length L_c were comparable with or less than the base width W.

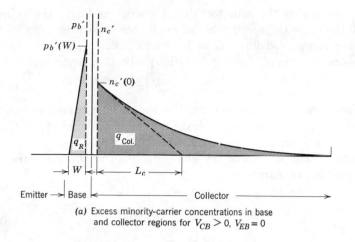

(a) Excess minority-carrier concentrations in base and collector regions for $V_{CB} > 0$, $V_{EB} = 0$

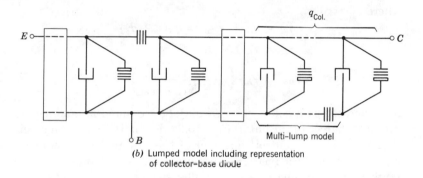

(b) Lumped model including representation of collector-base diode

Fig. 10.14. Lumped model representing minority-carrier charge storage in the collector and base regions, assuming an effectively semi-infinite collector region.

If a single-lump model of the collector is possible, then the base and emitter currents corresponding to forward bias of the collector junction only ($v_{EB} = 0$) may be written:

$$-i_B = \frac{q_R}{\tau_{BR}} + \frac{dq_R}{dt} + \frac{q_{\text{Col.}}}{\tau_{\text{Col.}}} + \frac{dq_{\text{Col.}}}{dt}$$

$$-i_E = \frac{q_R}{\tau_R}$$

(10.36)

where $q_{\text{Col.}}$ is the collector stored charge and $\tau_{\text{Col.}}$ the collector lifetime. On the assumption of negligible departure from steady-state charge distributions in base and collector, we can consider q_R and $q_{\text{Col.}}$ simply to vary in strict proportion, and write:

$$q_{\text{Col.}} = K q_R \qquad (10.37)$$

Note that this statement implies that the relationship between the charges and junction voltage v_{CB} differ negligibly from that of the steady state. Equations 10.36 can now be re-expressed in a form similar to that of the charge control relations for the base region above, namely,

$$-i_B = \frac{q_{R'}}{\tau_{BR'}} + \frac{dq_{R'}}{dt}$$

$$\qquad (10.38)$$

$$-i_E = \frac{q_{R'}}{\tau_{R'}}$$

where

$$q_{R'} = q_R + q_{\text{Col.}} = q_R(1 + K)$$

$$\tau_{R'} = \tau_R(1 + K) \qquad (10.39)$$

$$\tau_{BR'} = \tau_{BR}\left(\frac{1 + K}{1 + K\tau_{BR}/\tau_{\text{Col.}}}\right)$$

Although the parameters $\tau_{R'}$, $\tau_{BR'}$ may be measured in practice (as ratios of charges to currents), Eqs. 10.38 do not approach the precision of the charge-control equations of the base region (alone) as a representation of the relationships between stored charges and currents under dynamic conditions. The simple proportionality between $q_{R'}$ and i_E now holds only if the transient variation of v_{CB} is also accurately represented by the model (as required for Eq. 10.37 to be valid). The conclusions arrived at in Sec. 10.3, in regard to the accuracy of the charge control equations of the base region for rapidly varying transients, do not therefore apply to Eqs. 10.38, and it is misleading to regard these latter as an expression of charge control concepts.

10.6.2 *Charge Storage in Remote Regions of the Base*

In some situations a model of forward or reverse injection into the base involving *two* lumps (that is, four lumps in all) is necessary for the explanation or characterization of minority-carrier charge storage effects. This is because charging is not confined to the region of base material immediately between or near the emitter and collector boundaries, but also extends into distant regions located beyond the emitter periphery. Figure 10.2 illustrates clearly the possibility of such remote charge storage, particularly for reverse injection. In some practical applications transient limitations can arise because of the inherent slowness of response of remote charge stored in the base region. For example, in bringing the transistor out of the saturation region, charge stored immediately between emitter and collector can be removed quickly, but more remote charge then tends to diffuse slowly back to this region. The consequences of this effect are seen in the emitter voltage (v_{EC}) waveform of Fig. 10.15, which was obtained by operating the transistor in the circuit arrangement of Fig. 10.9, but with collector and emitter interchanged so that predominantly reverse charge storage in the base was involved. The opposite sense of input voltage-step (to that shown) was employed in order to remove from the base a stored charge corresponding to an initial forward-bias condition (not shown in the figure) of the collector-base junction. As seen from Fig. 10.15, after an initial rapid discharge of the region of the base close to the junctions, some recharging due to the diffusion into this region takes place, the final discharged state being attained some time later. This effect is commonly seen when switching the

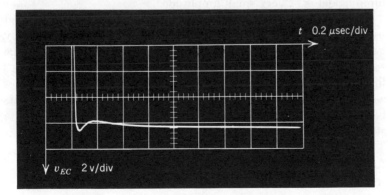

Fig. 10.15. Waveform of v_{EC} (or emitter current) in the circuit of Fig. 10.9 when removing stored charge from the base of an alloy-junction transistor, for reverse injection only. Deviation from a step response, after the initial fall of v_{EC}, is due to charge storage in remote regions of the base.

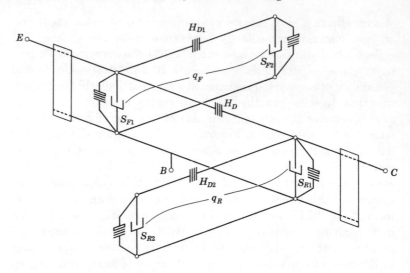

Fig. 10.16. Transistor lumped model with two-lump representation of either forward or reverse stored charge in the base. S_{F2}, S_{R2} represent charge storage in the more remote regions of the base.

transistor rapidly between different forward- or reverse-current states, using the circuit of Fig. 10.9, though usually the characteristic "wiggle" deviation from the step response predicted by the two-lump model is of very small amplitude.

The remote base storage effects just described can be represented by the model of Fig. 10.16. Here q_F and q_R are each modeled by two lumps; storances S_{F2} and S_{R2} correspond to remote charge storage that can flow to and from the junction sources at rates limited by the diffusances H_{D1}, H_{D2}, respectively. The combinances associated with S_{F2}, S_{R2} are of little importance, the main effects being caused by the charging currents due to change of remote stored charge components.

REFERENCES

On Charge Control

10.1 Beaufoy, R., and J. J. Sparkes, "The Junction Transistor as a Charge-controlled Device," *A.T.E. Journal*, Vol. 13, pp. 310–327, October 1957.

10.2 Sparkes, J. J., "Study of the Charge Control Parameters of Transistors," *Proc. I.R.E.*, pp. 1696–1705, October 1960.

10.3 Sparkes, J. J., "The Measurement of Transistor Transient Switching Parameters," *Proc. I.E.E.*, pt B, Vol. 106 Suppl. 15, pp. 562–567, May 1959.

On Lumped Models

10.4 Linvill, J. G., *Models of Transistors and Diodes*, McGraw-Hill, New York, 1963.

10.5 Linvill, J. G., and J. F. Gibbons, *Transistors and Active Circuits*, McGraw-Hill, New York, 1961.

PROBLEMS

The following problems all refer to a *pnp* transistor with uniform base-region material.

P10.1 For the purposes of the problem, a transistor is supposed to have an idealized "one-dimensional" base region (that is, to be of uniform cross-sectional area). The width of the space-charge neutral base is 0.001 cm and the area of cross section is 0.02 cm². The base material is *n*-type germanium of uniformly constant conductivity. The lifetime of minority carriers in the base is 1 μsec and surface recombination effects are taken to be negligible.

Determine the values of the parameters of the two-lump model (storances S, diffusance H_D, and combinances H_C) that characterize the behavior of excess minority carriers in the base region.

Evaluate also the charge-control parameters τ_F, τ_{BF}, τ_R, τ_{BR} of the transistor. Hence, calculate the forward and reverse current gains β_F, β_R in the dc steady state.

(*Given*: $D_b = 49.3$ cm² sec^{-1}, $q = 1.6 \times 10^{-19}$ coulombs)

P10.2 By considering the lumped model of the transistor, show that for incremental sinusoidal signals the common-emitter current gain i_c/i_b, corresponding to forward injection only, becomes of unit magnitude at the high frequency $f_\tau = 1/(2\pi\tau_F)$.

Evaluate this frequency for the device of Problem P10.1.

The frequency where the magnitude of the common-emitter short-circuit current gain is unity is quoted in performance specifications as an indication of transistor capability at high frequencies. As defined here, for the base region alone, f_τ is seen to be a statement of the sensitivity of the charge control action of the device, namely, control of i_c by q_F.

P10.3 The purpose of this problem is to verify the direct connection that exists between the lumped model of the transistor and the type of small-signal model developed in Chapter 7. By expressing $p_b'(0)$ in the lumped model as

$$p_b'(0) = p_{bo}(e^{qv_{EB}/kT} - 1)$$

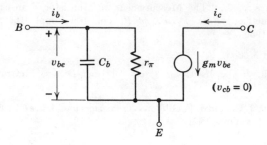

Fig. 10.17.

and considering that, in response to a small sinusoidally varying incremental emitter-junction voltage, the injected excess minority-carrier concentration $p_b'(0)$ also varies sinusoidally, show that in Fig. 10.17 the small-signal model applies for forward-injection conditions where:

$$g_m = \frac{q}{kT} |I_C|$$

$$r_\pi = \frac{kT}{q|I_C|} \beta_F = \frac{kT}{q|I_C|} \frac{H_D}{H_{CF}}$$

$$C_b = \frac{q}{kT} |I_C| \tau_F = \frac{q}{kT} |I_C| \frac{S_F}{H_D}$$

(*Note*: Assume that the forward mean dc bias condition is such that $e^{qV_{EB}/kT} \gg 1$, as would be usual in practice.)

P10.4 Starting from the two-lump model of the transistor, develop the *complete* set of charge-control equations for i_B, i_C, i_E in terms of the forward and reverse components of stored minority-carrier charge q_F, q_R.

Solve these equations for the two stored-charge components in the dc steady state when the transistor is operating in the saturation region with circuit-defined values of the terminal currents I_C, I_E. Show that the charge values are:

$$q_F = \frac{\alpha_F(I_C\alpha_R + I_E)}{1 - \alpha_F\alpha_R} \tau_F$$

$$q_R = \frac{\alpha_R(I_E\alpha_F + I_C)}{1 - \alpha_F\alpha_R} \tau_R$$

P10.5 A transistor has the following charge control parameter values (assumed to be independent of bias currents):

$$\tau_F = 12 \times 10^{-9} \text{ sec}$$
$$\beta_F = 100$$
$$\tau_R = 36 \times 10^{-9} \text{ sec}$$
$$\beta_R = 10$$

(a) Evaluate the forward stored charge q_F if the collector current $I_C = -2$ milliamperes and the transistor operates just on the boundary of the saturation region with $v_{CB} = 0$.

(b) Determine the base charge components q_F, q_R if the base current is now made $I_B = -0.5$ milliampere with still $I_C = -2$ milliamperes. Compare the total charge stored in the base in situations (a) and (b).

P10.6 In this problem the transistor is considered to be operating in the normal region ($v_{EB} > 0$, $v_{CB} < 0$) with $|v_{CB}| \gg kT/q$.

(a) Assuming the ratios I_{CS}/I_{ES} and τ_R/τ_F to be of the order of unity, establish that for the usual values of emitter current involved in practical operation of a transistor the reverse-charge component q_R is a negligible fraction of the whole excess minority-carrier charge stored in the base.

(b) Hence, by considering the lumped-model representation for forward injection only, evaluate the short-circuit current gain for "normal" operation of the transistor in (1) the common-emitter configuration and (2) the common-base configuration, for incremental sinusoidal variation of input current. Show that in both cases the plot of current gain magnitude against frequency exhibits a 3-db cut-off frequency f_o, where

$$f_o = 1/(2\pi \alpha_F \tau_F) \qquad \text{common-base}$$
$$f_o = 1/(2\pi \tau_{BF}) \qquad \text{common-emitter}$$

P10.7 A transistor is initially operating in the saturation region with circuit-defined constant values of I_C and $I_B = I_{B1}$ (as, for example, in the circuit arrangement of Fig. 10.10a). The base current is suddenly changed to a value I_{B2} of opposite sign to I_{B1} (positive for a *pnp* transistor), to switch the transistor to the cut-off region of operation. A "storage-delay time" t_s elapses, while I_C remains constant at the initial value, before the transistor leaves the saturation region; collector current then falls to zero, as the active region is traversed, in fall-time t_f.

By solving the charge-control differential equations of the device, and assuming that the fast transient mode is of negligible amplitude as discussed in Sec. 10.4, show that the storage delay-time is

$$t_s = \tau_{SL} \ln \left[\frac{I_{B2} - I_{B1}}{I_{B2} - I_C/\beta_F} \right]$$

where τ_{SL} is the time constant of the slow transient mode, given by Eq. 10.22 or Eq. 10.25a.

Show also that the same result is obtained, but with τ_S (as given by Eq. 10.25b) replacing τ_{SL}, if t_S is found by solving the saturation-region charge-control equation (Eq. 10.26).

The fall-time t_f may be determined by assuming that in the active region $|q_R| \ll q_F$, and solving the charge-control equation for forward injection only, to give $q_F = 0$. Hence, show that:

$$t_f = \tau_{BF}\ln(1 - I_C/I_{B2}\beta_F)$$

(Note that the influence of charges stored in the space-charge layers is neglected throughout this problem. A "linearized" calculation of fall-time, taking into account such charge storage, would yield the above result but with the effective parameter T_{BF} replacing τ_{BF}; T_{BF} is defined in terms of the *total* charge removed from base material in traversing the active region, including the effects of the space-charge layers.)

P10.8 The transistor of Problem P10.5 is operated in the simple switching circuit of Fig. 10.10a. Initially the device is in the cut-off state. Switching to the saturation region is effected in *rise-time* t_r by applying a constant input base-current drive I_{B1} (negative for *pnp* device). While in the saturation region, the collector current is constant at the circuit-defined value I_C. Switching back to the original cut-off state follows when base current is changed to the value I_{B2} (positive for *pnp* device).

If $I_{B1} = -0.5$ ma

$I_C = -2$ ma

$I_{B2} = +0.5$ ma

Calculate the rise-time t_r, storage delay-time t_s, and fall-time t_f of the resulting collector-current response. (See note at the end of P10.7.)

P10.9 When in the saturation state, the terminal voltage v_{CE} of a transistor is related directly to the forward and reverse components of minority-carrier charge stored in the base (see Eq. 10.27). Calculate v_{CE} for the transistor of Problem P10.5, if $I_C = -2$ ma, $I_B = -0.5$ ma.

Show that if the transistor is operated in the common-emitter configuration with very heavy base drive current ($|I_B| \gg |I_C|$), then

$$v_{CE} \cong \frac{-kT}{q} \ln \frac{1}{\alpha_R}$$

Evaluate for the P10.5 device.

A Closer Look at the pn-Junction Space-Charge Layer

A.0 INTRODUCTION

The depletion approximation introduced in Sec. 2.3.2 is of limited accuracy in describing the properties of the junction space-charge layer because it neglects the regions which are neither fully depleted nor approximately neutral. In this section we examine somewhat more carefully the potential and charge distributions in the space-charge layer for the dual purpose of evaluating the depletion assumption and of illustrating several important analytical methods and concepts. We consider the junction first in equilibrium and then with a bias.

A.1 THE SPACE-CHARGE LAYER IN EQUILIBRIUM

The fundamental relationship between the electric field and the charge in the space-charge layer is Gauss's law, discussed in Sec. 2.3.1.

$$\frac{d\mathcal{E}}{dx} = \frac{q}{\epsilon} \left[(p - n) + (N_d - N_a) \right] \tag{A.1}$$

245

In equilibrium the carrier concentrations are related to the electrostatic potential by the Boltzmann factors:

$$p = n_i e^{-q\psi/kT}$$
$$n = n_i e^{+q\psi/kT}$$

(A.2a,b)

where we have defined the potential reference so that $\psi = 0$ in intrinsic material ($n = p = n_i$). If these expressions for p and n are substituted into Gauss's law, and if the electric field ϵ is expressed in terms of the electrostatic potential ψ as $-d\psi/dx$, the result can be written as:

$$\frac{d^2\psi}{dx^2} = \frac{2qn_i}{\epsilon}\left(\sinh\frac{q\psi}{kT} + \frac{N_a - N_d}{2n_i}\right)$$

(A.3)

Inasmuch as $(N_a - N_d)$ is a specified function of position for any pn junction, this differential equation, together with the requirement that the space charge be a dipole layer, determines the electrostatic potential $\psi(x)$. Consequently, $n(x)$, $p(x)$, and the space charge $\rho(x)$ are determined as well.

This differential equation cannot be solved exactly in closed form in any simple way, although various approximate solutions can be obtained. The depletion approximation leads to one such approximate solution. Numerical solutions can be obtained readily if specific values are assigned to the net impurity concentration $(N_a - N_d)$. We illustrate the important features of the results by referring to the solutions of two specific problems which have been obtained by straightforward numerical techniques.

Figure A.1 shows the dependence of space charge, field, and potential on position for an abrupt junction that is symmetrically doped with $N_A = N_D = 4 \times 10^4 n_i$. This impurity concentration corresponds at $300°K$ to donor and acceptor concentrations of about 10^{18} cm^{-3} in germanium and about 6×10^{14} cm^{-3} in silicon. Consequently, the results apply to a rather heavily doped germanium pn junction, or to a rather lightly doped silicon pn junction. The results are displayed in a normalized form in which distance is measured in units of L_i, the *intrinsic Debye length*, defined by:

$$L_i = \left(\frac{\epsilon kT}{2q^2 n_i}\right)^{1/2}$$

(A.4)

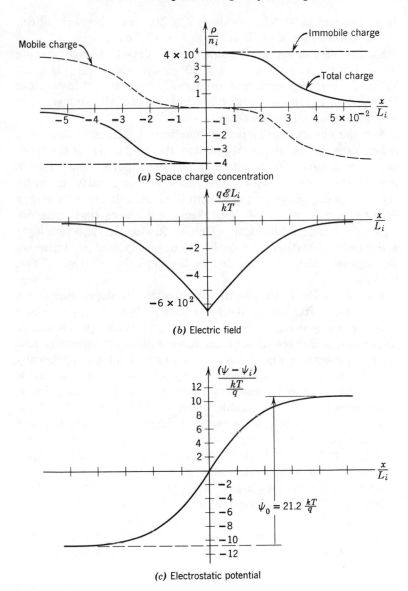

(a) Space charge concentration

(b) Electric field

(c) Electrostatic potential

Fig. A1. Electrical behavior in the space-charge layer, abrupt symmetric junction.

In germanium at $300°$K, L_i is about 7×10^{-5} cm, whereas in silicon at the same temperature it is about 2×10^{-3} cm.

Similar results for an asymmetrically doped junction having $N_A = 4 \times 10^1 n_i$ and $N_D = 4 \times 10^2 n_i$ are shown in Fig. A.2. These doping concentrations could easily be obtained in a rather lightly doped germanium junction, but are probably too small to be realized in a silicon junction.

For the symmetrically doped junction of Fig. A.1, there is a region near the metallurgical junction at $x = 0$ in which the space charge is entirely the result of immobile impurity ions. This is the *depleted region* in which the mobile charge density, given by $q(p - n)$ is negligible compared with the immobile impurity charge density, given by $q(N_d - N_a)$. Figure A.1 shows that there are regions of considerable width which lie outside the depletion layer and which are neither fully depleted nor nearly neutral. These are the regions which are neglected in the depletion analysis of Sec. 2.3.2.

Figure A.2 shows that in the asymmetrically doped junction a much smaller fraction of the space charge layer is depleted and that the depleted region does not span the metallurgical junction. This result is characteristic of the smaller impurity concentrations used in generating Fig. A.2 and is *not* true of all asymmetrically doped junctions. In fact, if the impurity concentrations on each side of the junction were increased by two or three orders of magnitude, a depletion layer of appreciable width would appear.

These examples both show that the charge density and the electric field become vanishingly small at points far away from the junction. This occurs because the space-charge region is a *dipole layer* in that the total positive charge to the right of the junction is exactly equal to the total negative charge to the left of the junction.

Because the space charge is zero far enough away from the junction, these remote portions are called the *neutral regions*. In these regions the mobile charge density is approximately equal to the immobile charge density, so that Eq. A.3 reduces to:

$$\sinh \frac{q\psi}{kT} = \frac{N_d - N_a}{2n_i} \tag{A.5}$$

which can be used to compute the height of the equilibrium potential barrier ψ_0.

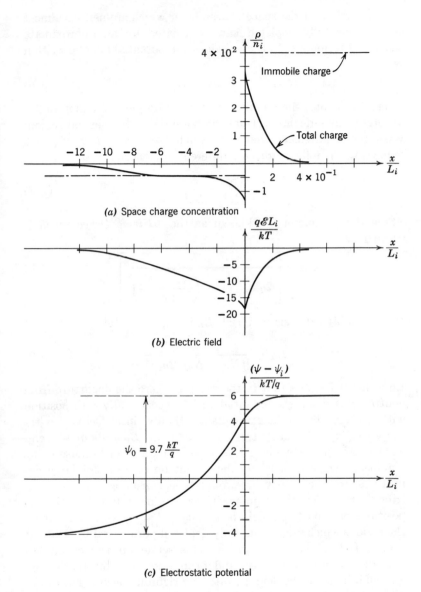

(a) Space charge concentration

(b) Electric field

(c) Electrostatic potential

Fig. A2. Electrical behavior in the space-charge layer, abrupt junction with 10:1 asymmetry in impurity concentration.

The portions of the space-charge layer which are neither almost neutral nor fully depleted can be treated by an approximate analytical technique. In these regions the potential may be written as:

$$\psi = \psi_N + \phi \tag{A.6}$$

where ψ_N denotes the potential in the nearly neutral region and ϕ denotes a small deviation from the potential of the neutral region. With the requirement that ϕ is much less than kT/q, Eq. A.3 reduces to the following *linear* differential equation in ϕ:

$$\frac{d^2\phi}{dx^2} = \frac{\phi}{L_D{}^2} \tag{A.7}$$

where the parameter L_D, known as the *extrinsic Debye length* is defined by:

$$L_D = \left[\frac{\epsilon kT}{2q^2 n_i \sqrt{1 + \left(\dfrac{N_d - N_a}{2n_i}\right)^2}} \right]^{\frac{1}{2}} \tag{A.8}$$

In reasonably extrinsic material, L_D is approximately

$$L_D = \frac{L_i}{[(N_d - N_a)/2n_i]^{\frac{1}{2}}} \tag{A.9}$$

Equation A.7 shows that in the regions where the departure from neutrality is small, the potential varies *exponentially* with position with a characteristic length equal to the extrinsic Debye length. For a net impurity concentration of 10^{16} cm^{-3}, L_D is about 10^{-6} cm.

The intrinsic Debye length is a useful parameter because if the potential were exponentially dependent on position for large departures from neutrality, we would expect distances of 5 or 6 extrinsic Debye lengths from positions of almost full depletion to positions of almost complete neutrality. That is, we would expect the regions which are neither fully depleted nor neutral to be about 5 or 6 Debye lengths in width. This semi-empirical conclusion appears to be approximately valid for junctions of arbitrary doping, although it cannot be demonstrated by rigorous means. For example, it is easy to show that all of the regions of transition from depletion to neutrality shown in Figs. A.1 and A.2 are of the order of 6 extrinsic Debye lengths in width.

A.2 CHANGES PRODUCED BY A BIAS VOLTAGE

There is no simple way of calculating the precise distributions of potential and charge in the space-charge layer when a bias is applied. However, we can estimate the errors introduced by the depletion assumption by noting that as the height of the potential barrier changes, the *shape* of the smeared out regions does not change significantly. Consequently, about the same potential change is required before the charge density can change from full depletion to full neutrality, so that these regions are still spread out over 5 or 6 extrinsic Debye lengths.

Therefore, the entire space-charge region can be visualized as a depleted region, which is given with fair accuracy by the depletion analysis of Sec. 2.3.2, sandwiched between two regions of transition, which are of fixed shape. It follows, then, that the depletion approximation gives relatively good results at large reverse bias when the depleted region is much greater in width than the regions of transition. It is less valid for small reverse and forward bias where the regions of transition may comprise most of the space-charge layer. However, very heavily doped junctions which have very small values of L_D may be treated with the depletion assumption even at small forward bias.

We may well ask at this point whether the errors that accompany the depletion assumption justify its use in making space-charge layer calculations on real junctions. Clearly, the depletion assumption predicts space-charge layers which, except at modest reverse bias, are too narrow by significant amounts. Furthermore, not all of the potential barrier at the junction is developed across the fully depleted region, as shown in Figs. A.1 and A.2, which increases the inaccuracy of the calculations made with the depletion assumption.

Nevertheless, these calculations are of value in important practical situations where we are interested not so much in the complete electrical behavior of the space-charge region as we are in the *changes* produced by changes in the bias voltage. We have seen in Chapters 5 and 8 that the development of diode and transistor circuit models depends on a calculation of the change in the space charge region produced by a bias-voltage change. Figure A.3 illustrates schematically the changes which occur in the space-charge region of an abrupt *pn* junction when the bias voltage is increased

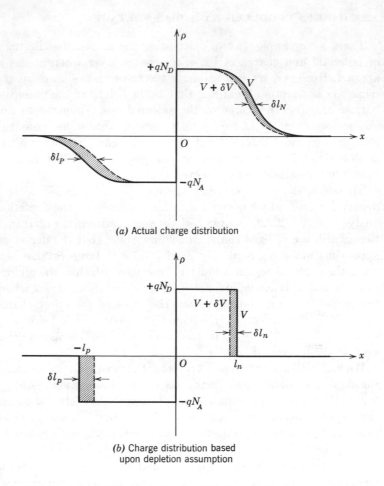

(a) Actual charge distribution

(b) Charge distribution based
upon depletion assumption

Fig. A3. Illustrating the effects of a small charge in bias voltage on the space charge distribution.

by a small amount δV. Since the height of the potential barrier decreases by δV, the width of the region must decrease slightly. Because the *shape* of the regions in which the space charge changes rapidly does not depend appreciably on the bias voltage, the change in actual distribution shown in Fig. A.3a can be described as a simple translation toward the junction of the two curves with the decrease in over-all width being taken up at $x = 0$. In the approxi-

mate calculation shown in Fig. A.3b the change can also be visualized as a translation of the rectangular distributions inward.
Since the planes defined by $+l_n$ and $-l_p$, which bound the depletion
region in the approximate treatment, fall near the center of the
regions of the actual distributions in which the charge is changing
rapidly, the translations of the actual and approximate distributions are approximately equal; that is:

$$\delta l_N \cong \delta l_n$$

$$\delta l_P \cong \delta l_p$$

and the shaded areas which correspond to the charge *changes* are
all approximately equal. To this extent, the depletion assumption
gives results which correspond rather well to the actual situation.

Our interest in the electrical behavior within the space-charge
region is limited principally to consideration of the *changes in width
and charge* illustrated in Fig. A.3, and for these purposes the approximate calculation gives reasonably accurate results, particularly
with reverse bias in excess of a few volts. However, we should not
expect accurate results of the calculation of *over-all width* of the
space-charge region based on the assumption that the region is
fully depleted.

The Electric Field in the
Neutral Regions of a pn Junction

B.1 THE ELECTRIC FIELD

As we have shown in Figs. 3.2 and 3.4, majority-carrier currents exist in the *pn*-junction diode and constitute the entire current except near the junction. We now examine the electric field associated with these flows of majority carriers. This investigation permits us to check the assumption that the *minority*-carrier drift current is negligible compared with the minority-carrier diffusion current. It also makes possible an investigation of the accuracy of our assumption that the regions outside the space-charge layer are neutral. This check is possible because the space rate of change of the electric field is related to the net space charge through Gauss's law.

The following discussion is phrased in terms of the majority-carrier (electron) phenomena in the *n*-type region of the diode, although similar results obtain on the *p*-type side.

The excess majority-carrier distribution is the same as the excess minority-carrier distribution because the regions outside the space-charge layer are assumed to be essentially neutral. Consequently, the majority-carrier diffusion current has the same distribution as the minority-carrier diffusion current, except that it is oppositely directed (because the majority carrier in the n-type region is charged negative, whereas the minority carrier is charged positive), and it differs in magnitude by the ratio of the diffusion constants. Thus the diffusion component of the *electron* current density in the n-type region is, from Eq. 3.15:

$$(J_e)_{\text{diffusion}} = -p_{no}q \frac{D_e}{L_h} (e^{qV/kT} - 1)e^{-x/L_h} \tag{B.1}$$

Since we know the *total* electron current from consideration of the continuity of the total (hole plus electron) current, the electron drift current must be such that when added to the electron diffusion current the required total majority-carrier current is obtained. This resolution of the majority-carrier current into drift and diffusion components is shown in Fig. 3.11. These curves show that, near the junction, the majority-carrier current has both drift and diffusion components, whereas far from the junction the majority-carrier current is all drift current.

The electric field can now be determined because the electron drift current is specified. If we designate the *total* current density (which is, of course, the same at every plane in the diode) as J_o, the *total* (drift plus diffusion) electron current density is:

$$\begin{aligned} J_e &= J_o - J_h \\ &= J_o - qp_{no} \frac{D_h}{L_h} (e^{qV/kT} - 1)e^{-x/L_h} \end{aligned} \tag{B.2}$$

The drift component of electron current is (using Eq. B.1):

$$\begin{aligned} (J_e)_{\text{drift}} &= J_e - (J_e)_{\text{diffusion}} \\ &= J_o + qp_{no}\left(\frac{D_e}{D_h} - 1\right)\frac{D_h}{L_h}(e^{qV/kT} - 1)e^{-x/L_h} \end{aligned} \tag{B.3}$$

Consequently, the electric field, which has the same distribution as $(J_e)_{\text{drift}}$, shown in Fig. 3.11, is:

$$\begin{aligned} \mathcal{E} &= \frac{(J_e)_{\text{drift}}}{qn_n\mu_e} = \frac{J_o}{qn_n\mu_e} \\ &+ \left(\frac{p_{no}}{n_n}\right)\left(\frac{D_e - D_h}{D_e}\right)\left(\frac{kT/q}{L_h}\right)(e^{qV/kT} - 1)e^{-x/L_h} \end{aligned} \tag{B.4}$$

We can now consider the effect of the electric field on the minority carriers, an effect which has been neglected so far. The electric field approaches the value $J_o/(qn_n\mu_e)$ far from the junction, whereas the minority-carrier diffusion current decays exponentially with distance from the junction. Thus it is obviously incorrect to neglect the minority-carrier drift current in comparison with the diffusion current in these distant regions. However, the minority-carrier concentration has decayed to its equilibrium value in this distant region, so that we need not have been concerned about the inadequacy of our assumption of field-free diffusion, *at least* in the far regions. Near the junction, the effect of the field depends on the relative magnitudes of hole and electron currents crossing the space-charge region. If we designate the ratio of the hole current at the space-charge layer to the total current as γ, the ratio of the minority-carrier drift current to the minority-carrier diffusion current at the edge of the space charge region is:

$$\frac{(J_h)_{\text{drift}}}{(J_h)_{\text{diffusion}}} = \frac{p_n}{n_n}\left[\frac{1-\gamma}{\gamma} + \left(\frac{D_e}{D_h} - 1\right)\right]\frac{D_h}{D_e} \qquad (\text{B.5})$$

The ratio D_h/D_e is of the order of $1/3$ to $1/2$ for silicon and germanium. Consequently, if the injection ratio γ approaches unity (most of the current at the junction is caused by the flow of holes), Eq. B.5 shows that $(J_h)_{\text{drift}}$ is negligible compared with $(J_h)_{\text{diffusion}}$ as long as the minority-carrier concentration p_n is small compared with the majority-carrier concentration n_n; that is, if the injection level is low. If, on the other hand, γ is small,* the drift component of minority-carrier current may become comparable to the diffusion component at relatively low injection levels. However, if this happens, the resulting breakdown of the field-free diffusion assumption does not invalidate our result for the total diode current because a small value of γ implies that the hole current is negligible anyway.

We see, therefore, that our previous statement about the field-free diffusion equation, made in Sec. 3.2, is in fact borne out by analysis of the *pn*-junction diode. That is, in a *homogeneous extrinsic semiconductor*, the effect of an electric field on the flow of minority carriers is negligible whenever the minority-carrier current is a significant component of the total current, *if* the injection level is low.

---

* γ can be controlled by adjusting the relative doping of the *p*-type and *n*-type regions.

B.2 THE SPACE CHARGE

We also wish to investigate the validity of our assumption that the regions outside the space-charge layer are electrically neutral. This can be done readily because we now know the form of the electric field (Eq. B.4) and can therefore use Gauss's law to find the net space-charge concentration. The result of this calculation for $x = 0$ (neglecting the dependence of n_n on x) is:

$$\rho = q(p_n' - n_n') = \epsilon \frac{d\mathcal{E}}{dx} = -\frac{\epsilon kT}{qL_h^2}\left(1 - \frac{D_h}{D_e}\right)\left(\frac{p_n'}{n_n}\right) \quad (B.6)$$

This result is difficult to interpret in this form, but can be simplified by remembering that $\epsilon kT/q^2 n_n$ is approximately equal to the square of the extrinsic Debye length L_D in the n-type material.* Thus the net deviation from neutrality is:

$$(p_n' - n_n') = -p_n'\left(\frac{L_D}{L_h}\right)^2\left(1 - \frac{D_h}{D_e}\right) \quad (B.7)$$

The extrinsic Debye length L_D in either silicon or germanium, with typical impurity concentrations of 10^{16} cm^{-3}, is of the order of 10^{-6} cm. The diffusion length L_h is of the order of 10^{-2} cm. Therefore, the *difference* between the excess hole and electron concentrations is certainly negligible compared to p_n' (and thus to n_n'). Thus we have shown that the assumption of electrical neutrality outside the space-charge region is valid as long as the diffusion length is much greater than the Debye length.

The two calculations presented in this section are good examples of the use of a self-consistent approach to the analysis of complicated physical situations. That is, we started out by *assuming* that the regions outside the space charge layer were electrically neutral and that the effect of the electric field on the minority carriers was negligible in these regions. Although we could not present rigorous *a prioré* justifications of these assumptions, and could only try to make them plausible, it was absolutely essential that the assumptions be made in order to obtain a manageable problem. We have now completed the analysis by showing that these two assumptions are consistent with the results that their use predicts, in the sense that another iteration of the solution would not produce a significant change in the minority-carrier distribution or current.

* Appendix A, Eq. A.8.

Index

Abrupt junction, 8, 32, 94, 123, 246
ac diffusion length, 91, 144
Active base region, 4, 155, 177
Active mode, 7, 125, 174, 188
Admittance model, 140, 154
Alloy junction, 4, 8, 72, 122, 201, 235
Avalanche breakdown, 64, 66
Avalanche multiplication, 65

Base charge, 206, 215, 238
Base current, 5, 129, 142, 155, 202, 206, 230
Base impedance, 164
Base region, 3, 121, 155, 177, 192, 201
Base resistance, dc large signal, 156
   extrinsic, 155, 161
   intrinsic, 156, 160
   small signal, 162
Base width modulation, 129, 136, 141, 148, 185, 187, 230
Base width modulation factor, 152, 171
Boltzmann distribution, 2
Boltzmann factor, 19, 246

Boltzmann relations, 25, 41
Breakdown, 57, 63, 86
Built-in field, 13, 52, 170, 194
Built-in potential barrier, 13, 19, 70, 246

Carrier storage, 77, 80, 92, 103, 138, 195, 200, 238
Charge control, 203
Charge control parameters, 206, 228, 235
Collector doping, 131, 236
Collector region, 4, 121, 235
Combinance, 103, 211
Common-base configuration, 183, 217
Common-base current gain, 138, 183
Common-emitter configuration, 7, 140, 187, 217
Common-emitter current gain, 138, 165
Complex diffusion length, 91, 144
Conductance, small signal, 45, 92
Conductivity modulation, 59, 85, 156, 161

Contact, metal, 14, 57, 59, 69, 113, 123
Contact potential, 13, 19, 29, 70, 246
Continuity equation, distributed, 39, 81, 89, 99, 176, 195
  lumped, 81, 89, 101
Current, majority-carrier, 36, 38, 50, 108, 129, 148, 155, 254
  minority-carrier, 33, 39
  total, 35, 42, 50, 108, 255
  transverse base, 124, 131, 148
Current crowding in the base, 132, 159, 160, 162, 168
Current gain, 135, 137, 138, 165, 168, 183, 205, 212
Cut-off region, 187

Debye length, 246, 257
Defect, recombination, 135, 137, 153, 198
Depletion approximation, 20, 94, 172, 245
Depletion layer, 20, 67, 70, 94, 248
Depletion layer capacitance, 94, 248
Differential operator, 140
Diffusance, 107, 211
Diffused junction, 2, 122, 192
Diffusion constant, 27, 29, 40, 105
Diffusion equation, 39, 42, 78, 91, 176
Diffusion length, 41, 92, 114, 143, 236
Diode, abrupt, 8, 32, 94, 123, 246
  asymmetric, 30, 66, 100, 248
  backward, 69
  diffused, 2
  diffusion limited, 54
  idealized, 33, 65, 100
  pn junction, 1, 32, 77
  reverse current, 3, 38, 43, 61
  saturation current, 43, 61
  small-signal conductance, 45, 92
  storage time, 88, 117
  symbol, 81
  temperature dependence, 47, 60, 62
  thin region or thin base, 73
  transient response, 81
  tunnel, 69
  voltage regulator, 65

Diode (*cont.*)
  volt-ampere characteristics, 3, 45, 47, 57
  zener, 64
Dipole layer, 11, 93, 245
Displacement current, 94, 113

Ebers-Moll equations, 180, 213
Electrical neutrality, 18, 26, 29, 39, 50, 108, 142, 248, 257
Electric field, neutral region, 52, 57, 58, 194, 255
  space-charge layer, 11, 66, 246
  transverse, 131
Emitter crowding, 132, 159, 160, 162, 168
Emitter doping, 130, 236
Emitter efficiency, 198, 236
Emitter region, 4, 121, 198, 236
Energy gap, 48
Equilibrium, 9
Equilibrium concentrations, 10, 180
Excess concentration, 26, 40, 50, 128
Extraction, minority carrier, 37, 129
Extrinsic base resistance, 155, 161

Forward bias, 2, 15, 33, 42, 60
Forward injection, 183, 203

Gain, power, 5, 135
Gauss's law, 18, 29, 52, 245
Graded base, 170, 180, 214, 222, 236
Graded junction, 27, 30

Homogeneous semiconductor, 39, 123, 256
Hybrid-pi model, 169

Idealized diode, 33, 65, 100
Idealized transistor, 123, 175, 201
Impact ionization, 64
Incremental model, 132, 174
Inhomogeneous semiconductor, 29, 52
Injection, minority carrier, 2, 33, 121
Injection efficiency, 55, 191, 198, 236

Injection into the emitter, 129, 135, 198, 236
Input admittance, 140
Intrinsic base resistance, 156, 160
Inverse region, 189, 192

Junction, abrupt, 8, 32, 94, 123, 246
    graded, 27, 30
Junction breakdown, 57, 63, 86
Junction capacitance, 94, 112, 139, 142, 168, 233, 253
Junction diode, 1, 33, 77
Junction transistor, 3, 121

Leakage currents, 57, 61
Lifetime, 40, 72, 130, 201, 208
Lifetime measurement, 88
Linear excess carrier distribution, 126, 131, 141, 177, 205
Linearity between current and excess charge, 42, 113, 195, 202
Low-level injection, 25, 39, 78, 84, 175, 201
Lumped models, 100, 201

Majority-carrier current, 36, 38, 50, 108, 129, 148, 155, 254
Metallurgical junction, 8
Metal-semiconductor contact, 14, 57, 59, 69, 113, 123
Minority-carrier current, 33, 39
Minority-carrier diffusion equation, 39, 42, 78, 91, 176
Minority-carrier extraction, 37, 129
Minority-carrier injection, 2, 33, 121
Mobility, 27, 29

Neutral region, 13, 15, 254
Neutral region voltage drops, 14, 58, 254
Neutrality, space-charge, 18, 26, 29, 39, 50, 108, 142, 248, 257
Normal mode, 7, 125, 174, 188
Normal region, 188, 192

Offset voltage, 45, 59

Ohmic contact, 14, 59, 69, 113, 123
One-dimensional approximation, 8, 14, 32, 123, 201
Open-circuit saturation current, 189
Output admittance, 140
Overlap diode, 168

Parameter measurement, 171, 183, 213
pn junction diode, 1, 33, 77
Potential barrier, 13, 19, 29, 70, 246
Power gain of a transistor, 5, 135
Punch-through voltage, 172

Quasi-neutrality, 29, 257
Quasi-static approximation, 89, 141, 145, 203

Reciprocity, 180, 195
Recombination, 33, 40, 72, 103
    base region, 124, 126, 129, 162, 177, 201
    bulk, 40, 72, 103
    defect, 135, 137, 153, 198
    space-charge layer, 36, 57, 59, 110, 128, 138, 178
    surface, 72
Regions of operation, 187, 200
Reverse bias, 3, 15, 37, 43, 61, 252
Reverse breakdown, 57, 63, 86
Reverse current, 3, 38, 43, 61
Reverse injection, 183, 203

Saturation charge, 225, 227
Saturation current, 43, 61, 180
    open-circuit, 189
    short-circuit, 183, 209
    temperature dependence of, 47, 62, 180
Saturation region, 191, 223, 229, 236
Series resistance, 58, 60, 84
Short-circuit current gain, 183, 197
Short-circuit saturation current, 183
Slow variation of excess concentrations, 89, 141, 145, 203
Small-signal admittance, 92
Small-signal conductance, 45, 92
Small-signal model, 132, 174

Space-charge capacitance, 94, 112, 139, 142, 168, 233, 253

Space-charge layer, 11, 13, 62, 77, 93, 110, 136, 139, 149, 193, 222, 245

Space-charge layer recombination, 36, 57, 59, 110, 128, 138, 178

Storage delay time, 88, 117

Storance, 103, 211

Stores of excess carriers, 77, 80, 92, 103, 138, 195, 200, 238

Surface leakage, 57, 61

Surface recombination, 72

Symbol, diode, 81
    lumped model, 102, 107
    transistor, 7, 124

Thermal generation, 38, 44, 48, 61

Total current, 35, 42, 50, 108, 225

Transconductance, 135

Transfer admittance, 140

Transistor, graded base, 170, 180, 214, 222, 236
    junction, 3, 121
    power gain of, 5, 135
    symbol for, 7, 124
    terminal variables, 124, 140, 183

Transport factor, 198

Transverse base current, 124, 131, 148

Transverse voltage drops in the base, 131, 148, 156

Two-diode model, 181

Varistor, 46, 55

Voltage drops in neutral regions, 14, 58, 60

Voltage gain, 135

Voltage threshold, 45, 59

Volt-ampere characteristics, diode, 3, 45, 47, 57

Zener breakdown, 64, 68